THE
BEATLES
FROM
A TO ZED

THE
BEATLES
FROM
A TO ZED

An Alphabetical Mystery Tour

PETER ASHER

HENRY HOLT AND COMPANY   NEW YORK

Henry Holt and Company
Publishers since 1866
120 Broadway
New York, New York 10271
www.henryholt.com

Henry Holt® and ® are registered trademarks of Macmillan Publishing
Group, LLC.

Illustration credits appear on page 248.

Library of Congress Control Number: 2019948929

ISBN: 9781250209597

Our books may be purchased in bulk for promotional, educational, or
business use. Please contact your local bookseller or the Macmillan
Corporate and Premium Sales Department at (800) 221-7945, extension
5442, or by e-mail at MacmillanSpecialMarkets@macmillan.com.

First Edition 2019

Designed by Meryl Sussman Levavi

Printed in the United States of America

1   3   5   7   9   10   8   6   4   2

To Wendy and Victoria,
my two favourite Beatles fans

THE
BEATLES
FROM
A TO ZED

Introduction

Paul (singing): Please lock me away . . .

John: Yes, okay. End of song.

—The conversation that changed my life

I grew up in a musical household, so in some ways it is not surprising that I gravitated to the world of music and recordings. My father was an amateur pianist and a committed lover of Gilbert & Sullivan as well as a distinguished physician, and my mother was oboe professor at the Royal Academy of Music; she had played in various major orchestras and gave oboe lessons at home as well. So as my sisters and I were growing up, there was always music in our house at 57 Wimpole Street on the corner of New Cavendish Street in Central London.

By the time I was fourteen or fifteen, I had had not only piano lessons but some instruction on the oboe and the double bass as well, but my appalling laziness about practising prevented me from achieving any real competence despite my great love of the music itself. I loved the music of my parents—I am still very happy to listen to a Corelli oboe concerto or a Gilbert & Sullivan operetta— but my passion became all the non-classical music I was hearing from American sources. I loved the bebop of Charlie Parker and

Our family home at 57 Wimpole Street, London.

1

his contemporaries and modern jazz of all kinds and ended up with an extensive record collection in that field. I loved the folk music of Woody Guthrie, Cisco Houston, Lead Belly, Sonny Terry & Brownie McGhee, and so on—and went to Dobell's Record Shop in the Charing Cross Road to buy what I now realize must have been bootleg acetates of all that wonderful music. And I loved R&B and blues. My curiosity about America itself (a miraculous land of plenty from our point of view, both materially and artistically) was matched only by my love for its music. So I got my first guitar and learned a few chords.

I met my friend Gordon Waller at Westminster School in London—and he loved much of the same music and knew a couple more chords than I did. We started singing together, playing pubs and clubs and coffeehouses, calling ourselves (it sounds odd now) "Gordon & Peter." Eventually, we got a fancier gig late at night in this eating and drinking club called the Pickwick. And while we were playing there one night, a man in a very shiny suit came up to us and introduced himself as Norman Newell, an A&R (artists and repertoire) manager for EMI Records, and asked us if we would come and do an audition at EMI Studios in Abbey Road in the St. John's Wood section of London. We were thrilled to death, as one might imagine. We went there several days later, recorded a few songs, and awaited the results. Fortunately and joyfully, the result was that they offered us a contract. We signed it, of course.

Norman told us he had booked some studio musicians and had reserved Studio Two at EMI for a date about a month in the future, and he started to talk about which songs we should record. He had picked some songs from our Pickwick Club set and was talking to a couple of songwriters. But he also said, "Look, if you know of any other good songs that might be right for you to arrange and record, please let me know. We're interested in some new songs as well as the ones you're already doing. Oh, and by the way, we are changing your name to 'Peter & Gordon' because we think it sounds better." Who was I to complain?

Now this is where coincidence plays a role in our story. I

had at the time (and still have, I'm happy to say) two very beautiful sisters, Jane and Clare. And my sister Jane, two years younger than me, two years older than Clare, was already a very successful actress in Britain, well known and much admired to this day. And it was in that context, as a music-loving celebrity, that she had been asked to

My sister Jane and me.

go see this new band all the girls were screaming over. A band that had just come down from Liverpool and had their first hit. *Radio Times* magazine had asked Jane if she would attend their London performance and write a review and see if she could figure out what all the fuss was about. She was delighted to do so; she had never seen the Beatles but had read a lot about them, as we all had.

Jane was most impressed—she thought the music was fantastic, and when she met them all afterwards, she found them charming, witty, and cool, and she liked them very much. They liked her, too; one of them liked her in particular and asked her out. That's how she ended up going out with Paul McCartney for a few years. And one of the side effects was that Paul was hanging around our house all the time.

In the end, our parents kind of took pity on him and offered him the guest room at the top of the house, next to my bedroom. So Paul ended up moving in, and he and I shared the top floor of that house for a couple of years. During that time, I was fortunate enough to hear some songs he was writing, and one of those songs was called "A World Without Love." I had heard it as a fragment, and I told Paul I thought it sounded really good. He explained to me that the Beatles were not going to record it. It didn't seem to be quite right for them. (I found out later that John did not like

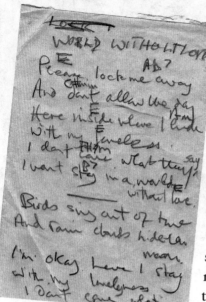

Paul McCartney's handwritten lyrics to the verses of "A World Without Love."

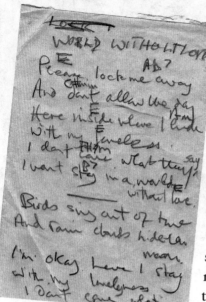

The bridge.

the opening line, "Please lock me away.")

And so it was almost in the reject pile, or at least in the pending pile, and it was also unfinished. He had written a couple of verses but no bridge. So when Norman Newell asked if I knew of any other songs that might be good to record, I thought, *Maybe I do.*

I went back to Paul that night and said, "Look, we've got a record deal now and we're looking for songs. Is that song 'A World Without Love' still kind of an orphan song?"

And he said, "Yes, we're not going to record it."

And I said, "Can we record it if we work out a version that sounds okay? Because we've got a day in the studio coming up, and we're all excited."

And Paul said, "Yes, you may."

So he very graciously wrote out the chords and the lyrics for me, and he also recorded a little demo so that we wouldn't screw it up when we made our record. (I still have that demo.) Paul made it on a reel-to-reel tape machine in my bedroom that day in late 1963. Gordon and I worked out our version of this new song, which we loved—but it was still incomplete. As the date of the session drew near, I did have to nag Paul gently about the missing bridge. Eventually, he went into his bedroom with a guitar for an infuriatingly short eight minutes or so and emerged with a whole new section which was utterly perfect.

We went ahead and recorded that song on January 21, 1964, along with four or five others, and by the end of the session, there was no question in anyone's mind but that "A World Without Love" was going to be our first single. It came out a month later, which is very fast, went to No. 1 in the UK, No. 1 all over Europe, finally to our utmost incredulity and infinite joy No. 1 in America, which meant so much to us. Gordon and I and all of our friends idolized American music; we idolized America. So the day we got the phone call saying, "You are number one in *Billboard* magazine in America," is a day I'll remember forever and one that changed my life. I began my career in the music business.

In time I moved away from performing and became a producer, and I was asked to be the first head of A&R for Apple Records, where I worked with all four Beatles in identifying new talent and getting their music recorded. It was during that time that I met a young singer-songwriter named James Taylor and signed him to his first record contract, and when Apple (and the Beatles as a band) began falling apart in the late '60s, James and I decided to leave Apple. James returned home and I moved to California, where I became his manager and producer, and over the course of my career I worked with many other recording artists, including Linda Ronstadt, Cher, Diana Ross, Neil Diamond, Joni Mitchell, Robin Williams, and Steve Martin.

In 2017 I began broadcasting a radio program on SiriusXM's The Beatles Channel called *From Me to You*, spinning records and telling stories about my experiences in the music business, all with some connection to the Beatles, of course. Listeners send me emails, and I get a lot of interesting questions and comments, along with detailed Beatles questions, like "What did John mean by this lyric?" or "Who played this instrument on this track?" or "What's the order of the guitar solos?" and I don't know the answers! There are people who are serious Beatles experts and scholars and write giant books with giant indexes, and I am not one of those people. I just offer my personal insights into the music and recollections of the time when I was lucky enough to be around and to be part of so many interesting events and to spend time with such remarkable people.

After a few months of bouncing from topic to topic, I had an idea as to how to organize my show. I decided to embark on a new project, a new path, a new protocol—something different, something I thought might be cool. It sounds very mundane when one first explains it, but I think maybe you'll agree with me that it can lead in some interesting directions.

I decided to use the alphabet as a way for me to take a personal and at times idiosyncratic look at the Beatles—their music, their history, their influences, their legacy. I took a leaf out of *Sesame Street*'s book, as it were, starting with the letter A and going all the way through to Zed.

(I hope you don't mind that I'm using the English pronunciation of that particular letter. It seems appropriate under the circumstances. I'm bilingual myself, but this is a Beatles book, so we shall stick to English.)

I'm going to use letters as a guide not only to songs (Beatles songs, Wings songs, Traveling Wilburys songs, individual Beatle solo songs, cover versions, all that good stuff) but also to topics, instruments, people, and places. So we won't just use song titles. For example, when we get to the letter D, I shall be talking about drum fills along with everything else. The letter G will find us on a trip to Germany. T for time signatures. Things like that. And the more I thought about it, the more other people, other projects, and other ideas associated with particular letters occurred to me that might be interesting to explore.

Many of you may wonder at the end of a particular chapter why I left out certain obvious songs that begin with that letter. For example, in the chapter on the letter A you won't find "A Day in the Life" or "A Hard Day's Night" or "All You Need Is Love." Not to worry—they are all here, just in different parts of the alphabet, where they make new connections and show different sides of themselves. I hope you will find it worth the wait.

This project was never intended to be an encyclopaedia or a comprehensive account of everything having to do with the Beatles. It is more of a journey whose destination becomes clear only as it unfolds, an alphabetical mystery tour, if you will, drawing on my own impressions and observations of these four remarkable individuals and the timeless music they have given us.

That plan seemed to work on the radio, so now the idea has metamorphosed into a book. I hope you enjoy the journey.

We begin our alphabetical journey, with drastic unoriginality, with the letter A. There are so many Beatles songs that begin with A, but there are few better than the classic tune "All My Loving." It was primarily a Paul McCartney composition and certainly one of Paul's major early works. Recorded in July 1963, the song was written a couple of months earlier, while the Beatles were on tour with one of their American heroes, the great Roy Orbison. Even though it was never released as an actual single, "All My Loving" was certainly a big hit with pop music fans across the world and remains a favourite of mine as well. A great song, a great singer, and some imaginative harmonies on the third verse that Paul sang with himself.

In fact, this early song contains multiple examples of the originality, creativity, and brilliance of each individual Beatle and his

John Lennon, George Harrison, George Martin, and me in Studio Two at EMI Studios.

9

contribution to the arrangement. In the verse, Paul plays a walking bass part that moves effortlessly through the chord changes. Ringo rides the hi-hat in his splashy yet precise style, creating a joyfully unique shuffle feel; he also plays a syncopated snare part which switches to straight quarter notes in the bridge. John's giant contribution was a perfect electric rhythm guitar part composed of driving triplets (at a snappy tempo) throughout the verses and then syncopated backbeats in the bridge—not an easy part to play at all, let alone with the rocking precision that John delivers. And finally we have George's wonderful Chet Atkins–flavoured, Country Gentlemen–style guitar solo.

Paul's lead vocal sounds effortless, as does the high harmony he overdubbed on the last verse. I believe that when they sang this song live, Paul would go up to the harmony for the last verse, and George would take over the melody—the harmony goes up to a high G-sharp which Paul could (and still can!) hit easily, and then he saves a perfect falsetto high C-sharp for the licks at the end.

Another significant A song comes from the other end of the Beatles' time together as a band, and that is "Across the Universe," composed mainly by John Lennon, and about which a lot has been written. Some have speculated about whether it was competing with "Lady Madonna" to be released as a single in 1968. There are various different versions of the song, and I honestly am not sure how many. I'm also not sure which version is the best. I confess that I am no expert on that stuff. The original version was recorded for a benefit album for the World Wildlife Fund, and it was already a fine song. It seems John was not completely happy with the way it came out, whether in this version or any of the subsequent variations. Phil Spector had a go at the song as well at one point, but I am told that John did not like that, either. My guess is that John was so happy with the lyrics when they first made themselves known to him (for that is how he felt, apparently) that he never quite believed that he had found a musical bed for them of equal quality and brilliance—despite many different overdubs, an orchestra, a choir, exotic instruments, and so on.

Given the poetic nature of the lyrics themselves, that makes sense to me. I especially love how the lyrics actually (and perhaps transcendentally) describe the process of their own creation: "Words are flowing out like endless rain into a paper cup / They slither while they pass, they slip away across the universe."

This remarkable song also gave rise to a movie called *Across the Universe*. It was written by some brilliantly witty and creative writers who are friends of mine, Ian La Frenais and Dick Clement, who wrote many great British TV comedies and some excellent screenplays. They wrote *The Commitments* movie, and for TV they wrote the classic *Porridge*, which is brilliantly funny, if you ever have the chance to see it, and *Lovejoy*, and so on. *Across the Universe* was directed by the astonishing Julie Taymor, who is famous for being the director of *The Lion King*, the unbelievably successful stage musical in New York using Elton John's music. She also did so much extraordinarily creative work in the theatre before that. But we are talking about Beatles music, and *Across the Universe*, the movie, had some creative cover versions of Beatles songs in it. The most radical was performed by someone I very much admire, the brilliant actor and comedian Eddie Izzard. If you don't know his work, look him up and watch everything. He's a genius. Check out Darth Vader in the canteen on the Death Star—it's amazing. But in *Across the Universe*, Eddie Izzard takes on "Being for the Benefit of Mr. Kite!" and turns it into a surreal and eccentric recitation over an arrangement that, to my mind, owes more to the Bonzo Dog Doo-Dah Band than to the Beatles. Remarkable.

There were also quite a few excellent Beatles covers done for *I Am Sam*, a Sean Penn movie which used only Beatles songs, each sung by a different artist. One of those, strikingly enough, was "Across the Universe," sung on this occasion by Rufus Wainwright. He is a singer I really admire. He comes from an amazing family. His father, Loudon Wainwright III, is a fantastic songwriter; his mother was Kate McGarrigle of the wonderful McGarrigle sisters; and his sister is Martha Wainwright, so it's no wonder he's a very good singer himself. What I like about his version of "Across the Universe" is that it may actually bring out the sublime beauty of the melody almost more effectively than do the various Beatles recordings, some of which get quite heavy-handed in the complexity of the arrangement. And Rufus has a gorgeous tenor voice.

So listen to John Lennon's version for his creative genius, to Eddie Izzard's for the eccentricity of the song itself, and to Rufus Wainwright's for its elegant and movingly definitive beauty.

Now it's Ringo's turn to join us under the heading of the letter A. The song that comes immediately to mind is an obvious choice but a great one. Two things Ringo is really good at: playing the drums and acting naturally. And we have him doing both in "Act Naturally," a song he found for himself, listening to a Buck Owens record. Ringo is a country music fan, and the "Bakersfield sound" and style of Buck Owens suited him perfectly. Written by Johnny Russell and Voni Morrison, the undemanding vocal range of the melody and the self-deprecating humour of the lyric might as well have been designed for Ringo—and once his performance was released on record it became an in-concert favourite as well.

We move on to George Harrison, still under the letter A. Another obvious choice, and such a great record, is "All Things Must Pass," the title track from George's excellent first solo album. With an astonishing cast of star musicians, an elegant string arrangement, and a heartfelt George vocal, this could be one of the finest and wisest solo Beatles records ever made. Though George may have originally hoped that the song would end up on a Beatles album, I believe it was best served by coming out the way it did and establishing the genius of George as a solo composer, producer (working in tandem with the unpredictable Phil Spector), and artist.

That album, *All Things Must Pass*, was made after the sessions for the final album the Beatles recorded, *Abbey Road*. And indeed, some of those songs might have made it onto *Abbey Road* and inexplicably did not, but their omission helped create the masterpiece that the album *All Things Must Pass* became.

Abbey Road itself is still a work of extraordinary genius from all the Beatles collectively, so we are going to go backwards in time from *All Things Must Pass* to the *Abbey Road* sessions that preceded it. They were, by all accounts, surprisingly congenial sessions, despite the rancour that was tearing the band apart. The recording came out so well that one would never know.

Abbey Road is a very big subject in its own right under the letter A. It is of course a street in the north of London in the area known as St. John's Wood. The nearest tube station is indeed St. John's Wood Station—originally on the Bakerloo Line but now on the Jubilee Line. (Probably more information than you need, but you never know; you might be heading there one day.) That's the tube you take if you want to get by public transport to Abbey Road Studios. It was originally called EMI Recording Studios. The house it is in was built in 1829, a beautiful Georgian town house. In 1931 it was turned into EMI Studios and opened by the brilliant composer Sir Edward Elgar.

You may think you do not know or are not sure who Edward Elgar is. But you do actually know because you are undoubtedly familiar with one of his biggest hits. I guarantee it. His big hit, which is still played today—talk about a golden oldie—is "Pomp and Circumstance March No. 1." I am told it is played at the majority of graduation ceremonies in the United States, whether college or high school. Apparently, this very tune is the most frequent accompaniment to that glorious moment. That was Edward Elgar's monster hit, still a hit today—and it has words, too. The words are all about a "Land of Hope and Glory," a reference (it goes without saying) to Great Britain. What I did not know until I looked it up is that Elgar didn't originally have words to it at all. King Edward VII told Elgar to put words to it. So because Edward was the king, Elgar did exactly what he was told to do. And it became another hit which everyone sings. Drunken and patriotic aging Englishmen sing it at any opportunity—though with a considerable degree of irony. Speaking on behalf of that specific community, we love it. It is also sung every year at the conclusion of the famous Proms concerts at the Royal Albert Hall. The BBC actually tried to exclude it (along with "Rule Britannia") at one point, in deference to "European viewers," but I am happy to say that public outrage won the day and it was reinstated.

EMI Studios was initially used for classical recording. But in 1958 something happened. The very first rock and roll record ever produced at EMI Studios was recorded in Studio Two. And that record ("Move It") was by a man called Cliff Richard, a major influence on all of us in British rock and roll. John Lennon said, "Before Cliff and the Shadows, there had been nothing worth listening to in British music." It was a huge hit in England. We all fell in love with Cliff, and he is still a big star today.

Though Cliff Richard's backup band is famously known as the Shadows, in 1958 they were called the Drifters. It eventually dawned on everyone that there was a very successful band in America already called the Drifters, and Cliff's backup band became the Shadows. But "Move It," their first record and a British song written by Ian Samwell, was actually credited to Cliff Richard and the Drifters and released on August 29, 1958—and that date can be said to mark the beginning of the history of British rock and roll, our ongoing tribute to a great American art form.

In that same studio, Studio Two at EMI Studios, the Beatles made nearly all of their records for the next several years, including the album they decided to call *Abbey Road*, which they recorded and released in 1969. They named the album after the street the studio was in, of course, not after the studio itself. But then in 1970, somebody at EMI had the bright idea of changing the studio name to Abbey Road Studios, and that is what they did. It remains one of the most significant and important studios in London. Well worth a visit. They have just built a whole new Dolby Atmos mixing room. Giles Martin, George Martin's son, who is also a brilliant record producer, has a room there. It's a really cool studio, and I use it whenever I am in London and have the opportunity to do so. Even to someone like me who has used Studio Two very often over many decades, there is still something magical about being in the "Beatles' studio," and to newcomers it must be intense. Running up and down those stairs between the live room and the control room (the only studio I have ever used with such an idiosyncrasy) remains both exciting and nostalgic.

While we're still on the subject of Abbey Road the studio, I'd like to turn our attention to one of my favourite tracks off *Abbey Road* the album, George Harrison's "Something." Now, as many of you know, James Taylor had a song called "Something in the Way She Moves" which he and I recorded for the album we made for Apple Records. A little while after that, George Harrison wrote a song that contained the same lyrical phrase, "something in the way she moves," and somebody said, "Aha! Maybe he borrowed that from James," in response to which James explained that actually, in his song "Something in the Way She Moves," he had borrowed the lyric "I feel fine," from the Beatles song of that title, and he used it twice because he loved the song. He sang, "She's been with me now quite a long, long time, and I feel fine." So lots of lyric borrowing goes on in every direction all the time, and it has given rise to so many great songs, and no one is complaining about it.

Another obvious A related to the Beatles is Apple, a topic so big that it could be a book of its own. My relationship with Apple Records began even before I made that record with James. Paul McCartney and I had talked about the Apple idea from the day of its conception, and I shared his vision of what it could be—a new kind of label with a much more generous and respectful attitude towards artists than was current at the time. Paul, in turn, was closely aware of my enthusiasm for producing records (he had actually played drums for me on my first-ever production!), and he offered me the position of head of A&R for Apple Records, which I happily accepted. Shortly thereafter, James Taylor came my way through a series of coincidences. On an early Peter & Gordon tour I had become close friends with the brilliant guitarist in the band backing us up, Danny Kortchmar, who had been best friends with James Taylor from childhood. When James was planning a trip to London, Danny gave him my information, and James showed up at my flat one evening, played a tape he had made along with a couple of songs performed live on my guitar, and blew me away with his genius. I introduced him to the Beatles and signed him to Apple as quickly as I could—they shared my admiration for James's music. Indeed, in the song "Carolina in My Mind" the "holy host of others standing around me" which James mentions in the lyrics is a reference to the Beatles themselves.

There is also a very curious A character who played a key role in the Apple story. Soon after the Beatles created the company, there was a man on staff for a while called Magic Alex. His full name was Alexis Mardas, and his is an interesting story. I believe he was a friend of John's initially, and George liked him as well. He was

Paul and me around the time Apple was being planned.

a scientist, and he was, to some degree, a real scientist as far as I could tell. He had some great ideas and was very up to date on a lot of cool new research. But in the end, he got a bit beyond himself and was talking about things that *might* happen as if they really existed already. Some of them eventually did exist. I remember him talking about voice recognition technology and face recognition technology. He was telling the Beatles he could create speakers that were made like wallpaper that you'd just stick on the wall. Such things are starting to happen now. So I don't think Alex was a complete fraud, but I do think he was substantially over-optimistic about what he could actually build and when he could build it.

I remember him talking about a problem in the studio that has always existed—the sound from one instrument leaking into other microphones in the room beyond the one specifically intended for that instrument. For example, the drums would leak into the vocal mics and things like that, and we would put up big wooden barriers called baffles to try to prevent this. Alex was telling us, "Oh, you won't need those—we can create invisible barriers that will prevent the sound waves from leaving that area and entering another area." Again, something that may happen in the future, but it doesn't work yet, and it certainly did not work then. Anyway, in the end everyone lost confidence in Alex. He was kind of a half scientist with a considerable hint of con man perhaps in there as well. I liked him personally. He was a cool guy. He was charming and eloquent, and I was sad to read recently that he died. Alex Mardas was a significant part of the Apple team—as Magic Alex, he was a close friend of the Beatles and certainly a relevant part of our letter A, but *not* (I am sorry to say) actually magic!

As I recall, Paul might have been the least credulous when it came to Alex's extravagant pseudoscientific claims—and I'll take this opportunity to mention a Paul solo track. While there are lots of A songs from which to choose, I'm going to show how far back the letter A goes in Paul's musical life. I especially like Paul's version of a song that is not a Beatles song at all but rather one of my very favourite Elvis Presley records, "All Shook Up," written by Otis Blackwell, a legendary songwriter from that era. Elvis himself actually took credit for the title—he apparently woke up one morning feeling "all shook up," liked the phrase that had come to mind, and suggested it to Blackwell as the subject for a song. It is always hard to figure out how to sing an Elvis song without lapsing into a lame Elvis impersonation. Gordon and I used to sing this song as well and did a slow and slinky duet arrangement in order to avoid imitating the Elvis groove, but Paul took the opposite approach, taking the tempo up a bit and turning "All Shook Up" into a hard-driving, full-on rock song. He recorded it on his excellent 1999 album *Run Devil Run*, and it really works well.

John has a long history with the letter A, too. I particularly admire his cover version of a song he and Paul did not write but one they recorded, written by the great Arthur Alexander (A. A.!), and the song is called "Anna (Go to Him)." Perhaps more A's than we can handle, but there you go. Arthur Alexander is one of the largely unsung heroes of rock and roll. To give you just a hint, he is the only songwriter to have had songs recorded by the Beatles, the Rolling Stones, and Bob Dylan. Even more widely recorded than "Anna (Go to Him)" was his country-soul masterpiece "You Better Move On"—a key part of the Stones' repertoire from the day I first saw them; it was recorded by many other significant British artists as well. Despite his brilliant work, like so many other writers of that era, Alexander had trouble getting the recognition (and income) he was due and spent several years back at his original job—as a bus driver. I never met him or had the chance to tell him how much I admired his writing, but I have no doubt it must have been a great joy to him when the Beatles burst onto the scene, and John Lennon delivered Alexander's song to a whole new and wildly appreciative audience—and with such a fine and viscerally powerful vocal. I have to admit that I think that on the bridge John even beats Alexander's original version for emotional intensity.

I shall conclude with one more A song that brings us back to where we began this chapter. Our opening number was a Paul song, "All My Loving," from 1963, and less than a year later Paul wrote another A love song that might even be better than the first: "And I Love Her." A beautiful song and a perfect record. Paul and I both remember him singing this song in our family home to the various Ashers who happened to be on the premises at the time, on the grand piano in the main upstairs sitting room. As I recall, the song did not have a bridge yet and that part (we might have called it a middle eight back then) was added in the studio following a gentle nudge from George Martin. I love that there are no drums—just congas and clave—and only acoustic guitars. The delicious modulation (up a semitone) into George's beautifully elegant classical-style guitar solo is a charming surprise, and the whole production is perfect in its restraint and its clarity. Not a rock and roll record at all, and yet another demonstration of the versatility and overall musicality of the Beatles—and thus why we are all still such devoted fans!

Having taken our journey through the letter A, we naturally move on to B.

To start us off, I have picked one of my favourite Beatles recordings that begins with B, "Baby It's You," partly because it was written by Burt Bacharach—a lot of B's there. It was originally recorded by the brilliant girl group the Shirelles, and the Beatles did a great cover version. As with so many other songs they recorded or performed, I suspect that by creating such a convincing version of the song they brought it to the attention of many people on both sides of the Atlantic who had not even heard the original. This is a common phenomenon. There are still people who think, for example, that "Twist and Shout" is an original Beatles song.

Gordon and I had the pleasure of sharing the bill with the Shirelles back in the '60s—and they were terrific every night.

Badfinger (from left to right): Pete Ham, Tom Evans, Joey Molland, and Mike Gibbins.

Three remarkable singers, sometimes switching who was singing lead and who was singing harmonies and responses—but remaining perfectly balanced and unequivocally soulful throughout. They had many excellent hits, including the first No. 1 record ever by an African American girl group, "Will You Love Me Tomorrow"—before the Supremes or anybody else. They were inducted, deservedly, into the Rock and Roll Hall of Fame in 1996. I went to that ceremony and got to say hello to them again after a gap of several decades. My favourite Shirelle was Doris Coley because I got to know her well during the tour, and it was exciting to see her again. We used to sit next to each other on the bus and talk, and it was Doris who had to explain to an overconfident and self-righteous white English boy that the two of us should *not* necessarily sit together when we stopped to eat at diners in certain parts of the South, even in the '60s.

That tour with the Shirelles was the Dick Clark's Caravan of Stars, and it lasted for a couple of months in 1965. One of the fun things about this tour was that there was such a variety of acts on the bill. In this case, there were the Shirelles, the Drifters, Brian Hyland (if you remember "Itsy Bitsy Teenie Weenie Yellow Polkadot Bikini"), and Tom Jones—and, of course, Peter & Gordon. We were all on a regular Greyhound bus, sleeping in hotels only every other night but having the time of our lives despite the considerable discomfort. It was really fun.

The Beatles were big Shirelles fans, of course, and "Baby It's You" is not the only Shirelles song they recorded—or even the only B song from the Shirelles. There is also "Boys," one of Ringo's great vocal performances, and he still does it from time to time when he is out with his All-Starr Band, and it's always a pleasure. Maybe it makes more traditional sense sung by a woman, but Ringo sings with such declaratory ebullience and joyful confidence that it totally works. I saw him perform it recently at Joe Walsh's birthday party, and the way he plays and sings simultaneously with such an intense groove and his uniquely splashy hi-hat style has never rocked more than it does now!

On to another B song, a couple of B's right there, "Baby's in Black." Three B's to be exact—a veritable swarm of B's. Listening to this song, one can tell that among the Beatles' greatest influences were the great Everly Brothers (who were also a major influence over my early career). The Beatles were huge fans.

All of us listened to the Everlys and tried to emulate their beautiful singing, the kind of close-harmony major thirds that they executed so perfectly. And one of the classic records which was a huge hit in the UK and which we all learned to play and sing (and I guarantee you, even though I don't think there are any recordings of it, that John and Paul must have sung this song as well) was "Bye Bye Love." George Harrison loved this song so much that he did kind of a rewrite. It is notable that the version George Harrison recorded of "Bye Bye Love" has him credited as an additional writer, and indeed it is a pretty radical rethink of the song and a very cool one. He totally changes what used to be the very simple rhythm and structure of the song, introducing all kinds of syncopation and rhythmic movement along with a lot of contrapuntal instrumental parts. George's own twelve-string acoustic rhythm part holds it together, but the fretless bass and the slide electric guitar noodle around all over the place in an interesting way—and the song itself is no longer a straightforward duet but less predictable all round. It is always worthwhile approaching a good song in an entirely new way, and I would rate this as a largely successful experiment.

Most of us Everly fans took a more conventional approach in creating our versions of their songs. Certainly, we duos tried to match the brilliance of their arrangements as closely as we could. But the originals were always the best.

Now, when I say that none of us were as good as the Everly Brothers, a duo that certainly came very close was John Lennon and Paul McCartney. A fine example of John and Paul singing together in the Everly style is "Baby's in Black," which is sung with rock and roll strength. It's got a bit of John's intensity in there that really makes it rock. Though of course the Everlys could rock like crazy as well when they had a mind to. Check out "The Price of Love," for example.

Staying with early influences in the letter B, let's move on to a song that was a great favourite of John Lennon's. Everyone—the

Beatles, Peter & Gordon, and all the British Invasion bands—were major Gene Vincent fans. Gene Vincent and His Blue Caps were a bigger deal in the UK than they were in America. And one thing we all had in common was great affection for their first and biggest hit, of which John Lennon did a great cover for his *Rock 'n' Roll* album, a definite B song called "Be-Bop-a-Lula."

I think my favourite version of that song is Gene Vincent and His Blue Caps doing it in the great movie *The Girl Can't Help It*. If you get a chance, jump on YouTube and watch it. Everyone is in that movie. Fats Domino is in it, Gene Vincent is in it, Little Richard is in it—and Jayne Mansfield is in it, which is a whole other thing, of course! It is well worth watching. One of the great rock and roll movies, and the Beatles were big fans of it, too. In fact, in 1968 the Beatles interrupted the recording session for "Birthday" when they realized that they were about to miss the premiere of *The Girl Can't Help It* on British television. They all walked to Paul's house in Cavendish Avenue to watch it.

Now on to a couple of very important B composers, Chuck Berry and Ludwig van Beethoven—two more B's who are certainly on the A list—and in one of his most famous songs (one that the Beatles covered brilliantly), Chuck is urging Ludwig to roll over! Every guitar player learned from Chuck Berry, who virtually invented a simple and highly effective style of rock and roll guitar playing all his own, incorporating a straightforward rhythm under the singing with wildly imaginative solos. These included some signature licks which occurred often in his work, but we never tired of them. Indeed, we tried to play every one. George Harrison was no exception, and you can hear a lot of Chuck Berry's influence in much of his work.

The Beatles didn't just listen to Chuck Berry's records, of course; they also covered some of his songs. In the Beatles' cover of "Roll Over Beethoven" (a bit slower than Chuck's original), George begins with a straight Chuck lick, virtually unaltered, but from then on they make a number of interesting arrangement changes—adding handclaps on every quarter note, which propels the track along very effectively—and then they change the pattern for the "feel like it" verse, giving that section an almost bridge-like quality. Thus are some imaginative production ideas applied to a classic song in a way at which the Beatles excelled. But one thing Chuck still has over them is the excellent piano work of Johnnie Johnson, Chuck's brilliant accompanist—and there is a whole story there for anyone interested. Many musicologists believe that Johnnie deserved co-writing credit on many of Chuck's songs— yet when Keith Richards searched for Johnnie in order to ask him to play in the band for the *Hail! Hail! Rock 'n' Roll* Chuck Berry documentary in the 1980s (for which Keith was the bandleader), he found him driving a bus for a living.

One final note on "Roll Over Beethoven" (and its witty lyrical concept) which I cannot resist is that even if Beethoven had got the message from Chuck about the invention of rock and roll, he could not have actually told Tchaikovsky the news—at least not on this earth. Beethoven died in 1827 and Tchaikovsky was born in 1840—I suppose Ludwig could have left a note!

The Beatles didn't just learn from other musicians, of course; they also reciprocated in so many ways. They were by far the most influential band of all time, and they went to great lengths to help other musicians—indeed, that was the original concept behind Apple Records. When I was head of A&R for Apple (which was an extremely fun job, I assure you), we signed quite a number of bands including one called the Iveys. The Iveys were brought into Apple by Mal Evans, the Beatles' old friend, confidant, and roadie. It is worth remembering that when the Beatles began, Neil Aspinall and Mal Evans were the whole team, and Mal was a solid and reliable presence in whom everyone had great confidence. I liked him very much, and we were all delighted when he brought a tape of this excellent band he had found into one of my weekly A&R meetings. We signed them. We made an album. It had one small hit in the UK, "Maybe Tomorrow," but it didn't do much in America. And then we had an idea. First, we changed the Iveys' name to Badfinger; I think the name change suggestion originated with Capitol Records in the U.S., who were not happy with "The Iveys" as a name. Neil recalled that the original working title for "With a Little Help from My Friends" was "The Badfinger Boogie," and he suggested Badfinger as a new name for the Iveys. Then Paul gave them a song which he had written for the purpose, and it was a huge hit—"Come and Get It," with its catchy opening line, "If you want it, here it is, come and get it."

Paul recorded a demo of the song and then produced it with the band and apparently pretty much insisted that the produced version be exactly the same as his demo. I've heard both, and they are extremely similar, it must be said. Paul produced another cool song for Badfinger called "Carry on Till Tomorrow" which has a really excellent and imaginative string arrangement from George Martin.

Both "Come and Get It" and "Carry on Till Tomorrow" were part of the soundtrack for a movie called *The Magic Christian*, the stars of which were Peter Sellers and Ringo Starr. So let us move on to Ringo for a minute and explore a couple of his B songs. Ringo is more than just a brilliant, amazing, inventive drummer; he is also a reliably good and enthusiastic singer. And he is at his jolliest and most enthusiastic on his solo record "Back Off Boogaloo," a song that he wrote himself. Ringo was inspired, apparently, by Marc Bolan of the band T-Rex, who encouraged him to write those lyrics and begin the song. George Harrison helped him finish the song and then produced the record for him. And the two of them came up with a really catchy song which was a major hit.

Another irresistible Ringo record is a quadruple B, "Bye Bye Blackbird," an old and classic tune that Ringo included on his *Sentimental Journey* album. It also features the banjo, another B and an instrument I love.

Since we are talking about songs that start with the letter B and I just mentioned blackbirds, we cannot of course fail to give every possible consideration to one of Paul's finest songs, "Blackbird." I remember hearing it shortly after it was written. I seem to recall that Paul had already moved out of my family's home by that time, and I was visiting him in his house at Cavendish Avenue. The song impressed me then, and it impresses the hell out of me now, I must say. It is a remarkable composition and a beautiful piece of guitar playing.

What I didn't know at the time was that "Blackbird" was influenced heavily, and Paul has explained this, by the Bourrée in E Minor by another very fine composer beginning with B, Johann Sebastian Bach. (A *bourrée* is a lively French dance.) To the casual listener, the two pieces do not appear to have that much in common—when great composers are influenced by each other's work, the connection is not always obvious—but when Paul explains how he had worked up a simplified and somewhat rearranged version of the Bourrée to play on guitar (and which became something of a party piece), it all starts to make sense. I imagine that Paul had heard a version by Segovia or someone like that (there were many Segovia albums lying around in our house, and I was already a fan) and that he had then skipped the bits he could not quite figure out and created an edited version which led him eventually to the creation of "Blackbird." So the story ended very well indeed!

George had a lot of cool B songs, too, but I think my favourite is probably "Beware of Darkness" from the *All Things Must Pass* album. Brilliant song, brilliant record. A remarkable composition which includes some very surprising and emotionally spooky chord changes. No sooner has the introduction got us sitting comfortably in the key of B than it takes a disconcerting chromatic slide down to G major followed by an even more unexpected half step up to G-sharp minor and C-sharp minor. Not necessarily comfortable but certainly beautiful in its own way, as if the spiritual darkness and temptation we are being advised to avoid (I take this song to have a kind of "Get thee behind me, Satan" theme) were following just behind through these jagged changes. And cool lyrics as well. I especially like "Beware of soft shoe shufflers, dancing down the sidewalks"—certainly plenty of those in the music business!

Another very cool storytelling song that starts with B comes from John: "The Ballad of John and Yoko." A Beatles record officially, but as far as I know it's just John and Paul on the record, with Paul doing those great harmony parts. It's also the ballad of Mr. B in the sense that Peter Brown is referred to in the lyrics. Peter Brown was the Beatles' right-hand man and organized everything in their lives, including evidently the John and Yoko wedding and various travel details while also fending off the press and so on. Peter is a good friend of mine and now lives in New York. I see him from time to time when I am there, and dinner is always a pleasure, and that song made him famous.

Another lyric I found interesting is "you can get married in Gibraltar near Spain," and looking at it again, I wondered whether it had been an issue at the time. The status of the tiny peninsula of Gibraltar has long been a big issue between Britain and Spain. Gibraltar is, currently and in fact, part of Britain. It's just about all that's left, I think, of the British Empire at this stage! But Spain (with, it must be said, a certain geographically irrefutable logic) thinks it should be part of Spain. So "Gibraltar near Spain" is, politically, hugely incorrect from a Spanish perspective. I looked it up and the Spanish did actually lodge an official protest at the time against Gibraltar being described in the song as "near Spain" when they regard it as part *of* Spain!

But in fact it is still British. God Save the Queen! Let's move on.

Our final song, our final Beatles B song for this chapter, one of my very favourites influenced by both Chuck Berry and the Beach Boys, a couple of B's right there, is "Back in the U.S.S.R." It's kind of a tribute to Chuck Berry's "Back in the U.S.A." and probably is even better known now than the original song. (I say that even though Chuck's original was a great favourite of mine to the point where I enjoyed a giant hit when I produced a new version of it with Linda Ronstadt in 1978.) The Beach Boys–style harmonies on "Back in the U.S.S.R.," of course, are unmistakable.

Yet again we see the Beatles (and Paul as a composer) break totally new ground with this song. Combining the influences of two very different and equally legendary schools of American rock, they use that blend as the basis for a witty, international, and surprising twist on the traditional home-sweet-home song format—and thus provide a fitting ending for this chapter and for our exploration of the very important letter B, which, as we can never forget, is for Beatles.

C

We are now well embarked
on our journey exploring,
excavating, and sometimes
explaining the Beatles from A to Zed.
And so we find ourselves at the letter C.

Rather than kick things off with something bouncy and jolly, for some reason I feel inclined to talk about a song that is painful. When I was thinking about Beatles songs that start with the letter C, this one came to mind. It's actually a John Lennon song,

A meeting with three Capitol Records executives (in suits, with their backs to the camera) during the Apple days.

not a Beatles song—a very intense and moving song called "Cold Turkey." John Lennon was accompanied on this track by the truly excellent band of Eric Clapton, Klaus Voormann, and Ringo Starr.

So much has been written about the relationship between society and drugs, between music and drugs—and especially between music on the jazz/R&B/rock and roll spectrum and drugs, in particular. Yet even those of us who believe that blanket condemnation of psychoactive substances of all kinds is silly, that "just say no" is an impractical prescription, and that the legal "war on drugs" is absurd have to admit that the evidence is very clear that taking heroin is never a productive plan and that any imagined benefit is vastly outweighed by the giant disadvantages. In particular, by the dual problems of how dangerous it is—and how extremely difficult and painful it is to stop. The Beatles (and other artists) may have, on occasion, credited some other drugs with some possible creative boosts or inspirational moments, but I do not think heroin has ever been thanked for anything!

"Cold Turkey" is a grim song about the hell that quitting heroin cold turkey can apparently be. I guess both John and Yoko at one point were experimenting with heroin, and that never has a happy ending, and it did not in their case.

But of course the important thing is that they survived. They came out the other end sadder and wiser but no longer strung out.

So now we move on to another, more famous John Lennon composition—one of the Beatles' very best songs, best arrangements, and best productions, "Come Together."

"Come Together" was written for Timothy Leary's campaign against Ronald Reagan in the election for governor of California. Leary and his wife Rosemary had traveled to Montreal for John and Yoko's bed-in for peace, in June 1969. The Learys asked for a campaign song based on the phrase "Come Together," but John could not come up with one. In the process, though, he came up with the song we know from *Abbey Road*, which clearly was unsuitable for the original purpose. "You wouldn't have a campaign song like *that*, right?" John said. For his part, Leary was not pleased at having been passed over, though he recognized that the new song was better than any campaign song could be. He sent a note to John, who replied (Leary said) "with typical Lennon charm and wit that he was a tailor and I was a customer who had ordered a suit and never returned. So he sold it to someone else."

After the bed-in and the release of John and Yoko's "Give Peace a Chance," I noticed that the song made a reference to Timothy Leary and his wife Rosemary. I knew Timothy quite well; he was a very interesting (if confusing) man. But when I knew him, his wife was called Barbara, and I realized that they must be consecutive wives. Indeed they were, so I looked him up, and Timothy Leary actually achieved something most of us havn't come close to. He had five wives, which is quite impressive, and Rosemary was number four and Barbara (the one I knew) was number five. Rosemary is the wife referenced in "Give Peace a Chance." There's that bit, "Everybody's talking about John and Yoko, Timmy Leary, Rosemary, Tommy Smothers, Bobby Dylan, Tommy Cooper, Derek Taylor, Norman Mailer, Allen Ginsberg, Hare Krishna."

I bet you know who everyone is on that list with the possible exception of Tommy Cooper, who was a legendary British magician and comedian; you must see him if you get a chance. Look on YouTube and check out some Tommy Cooper clips. He's great. The Beatles loved him. We loved him. He was a star. And thus Tommy Cooper well deserved his shout-out on "Give Peace a Chance."

The song that Timothy Leary requested/commissioned and John Lennon turned into a Beatles masterpiece, "Come Together," is brilliant, with an amazing arrangement. Great drum part. Great bass part. Great weird sounds on it. Simply one of the best things they ever did. It is such a great song that it has been covered quite often but (like so many Beatles covers) is not easy at all. To my mind, the best cover of "Come Together" was recorded by Aerosmith. I confess that I usually prefer cover versions which take a radically different approach, but this one pretty much sticks to the Beatles' arrangement—same key, a little bit faster. That said, Steven Tyler spits out the lyrics with supreme conviction, as only he can, and Joe Perry adds some fascinating new guitar lines—I think the song just suits that band in particular. I am even more certain that the weirdest cover of "Come Together" was recorded by Robin Williams and Bobby McFerrin and produced by George

Martin. It is fascinating in its sheer oddness and unpredictability. It starts with Bobby McFerrin singing the instrumental intro alone but in multiple overdubs, adding a rock rhythm section, then a big orchestra, allowing Robin to sing/recite the lyrics in various accents, Bobby to do some scat vocals, and so on. All very curious and well worth a listen. And a joy to see George Martin return to some degree to the comedy production he did so well at the beginning of his career (and for which we all admired him so much), when he worked with performers like Peter Sellers and Spike Milligan.

Now, C, of course, is also for Chuck Berry, whom I discussed properly under the letter B, but he plays an important role regarding this song in particular. John Lennon wrote some of "Come Together" inspired by, or as a homage to, a great Chuck Berry song, "You Can't Catch Me." Both songs contain the lyric, "Here come old flat top." And that shared lyric led to a lawsuit from Morris Levy, who was a notorious crook, legendary music business hustler, mob guy, whatever, who owned Chuck Berry's publishing rights at the time. Levy sued for that "stolen" lyric (as he saw it), and after various suits and countersuits, John agreed to record several songs to which Morris Levy held the rights. The songs appeared on John's *Rock 'n' Roll* album. There's a lot written about Morris Levy; he was a fascinating character but evidently not someone you particularly wanted to know back then. He was a dangerous man.

Artists often borrow from one another and are certainly inspired by one another, and when there is a dispute, it usually ends up later on that the publishers all sue each other and sort it out. I'm sure John copied bits of the Chuck Berry song just because he loved it. And I'm sure that Chuck Berry, even though he may have profited from the lawsuit, was also very flattered by John's attention and the fact that John obviously was a big fan, which all of us and all of the Beatles certainly were.

Moving on from the masterful Mr. Lennon to the still sometimes underrated brilliance of George Harrison and a favourite track of mine, "Crackerbox Palace." Recorded with a top flight all-American rhythm section (including legends like pianist Richard Tee, whose work many of you may know from all the great Paul

Simon records he played on and many others), it is only George's distinctive and memorable guitar work that gives the arrangement of the track a Beatles connection at all. Alvin Taylor's drums and Willie Weeks's bass parts are excellent in their own way and very different from what Paul and Ringo would have come up with. George sounds as if he is enjoying his artistic freedom, and the track has a joyous air to it.

Crackerbox Palace was George's nickname for his very remarkable new home, Friar Park, a huge (120-room) mansion in Henley-on-Thames. When George bought it, the house was in a state of almost total disrepair and heading towards inevitable demolition. George saved the house, wrote an excellent song about it, and even the video he made for "Crackerbox Palace" has that same sense of fun and excitement that seems to have pervaded the whole project. Directed by the brilliant Eric Idle and filmed on the grounds of Friar Park, it featured (among many other people) George's future wife Olivia, who is the current mistress of Friar Park and under whose care and painstaking commitment the house and grounds—and lake and grotto and underground passages!—have grown more stunningly beautiful than ever. On a recent visit, I was overwhelmed all over again by the attention to detail and impeccable love and determination that have suffused and inspired such a great house, from the day George acquired it to its present-day perfection.

The actual name Crackerbox Palace, however, was *not* George's invention. It was the name of the house of a certain Lord Buckley, of whom we all (and George in particular) were big fans. That might be someone worth looking up if you have a spare minute. Lord Buckley was an American comedian, stage performer, and monologist, who was very widely admired. He was described by the *New York Times* as possessing an unlikely persona, part English royalty, part Dizzy Gillespie. If you do look him up online, look for the recording "God's Own Drunk." That was his most successful routine and one that we all admired back in the day. George wasn't his only fan, by the way. Bob Dylan, in his book *Chronicles*, described Buckley as the hipster bebop preacher who defied all labels. So check it out if you get a minute.

George got to visit the original "Crackerbox Palace" in Los Angeles when he met Buckley's former manager George Greif—and passing references to all of this can be found in the song.

Let's move on to our next Beatle under the letter C, where we find Paul McCartney. One of Paul's catchiest songs from his solo career was "Coming Up," from 1980. It was a No. 1 record. In some ways this track could be said to summarize Paul's genius and the breadth of his achievements. It was part of an album (*McCartney II*) which was a totally solo effort—Paul in one or more of his home studios experimenting sonically and musically, looking for interesting sounds and new arrangements, playing every instrument and doing so with great skill and inventiveness—and at the very same time, it is an example of Paul's stunning ability to (with seemingly little effort) come up with incredibly catchy pop songs that are such a pleasure to hear, to learn, and to sing along with. "Coming Up" could be said to be the best of both worlds. Some odd pitch changing, an experimental vocal sound, a cool stereo guitar riff all combine to create the kind of "earworm" hit record that makes every other producer and songwriter jealous. Paul the sonic explorer and Paul the hit maker combined their efforts to create a track that has become a frequent part of his live repertoire.

Now we have one Beatle left to introduce. When I was thinking about Ringo and the letter C, I landed on a slightly obscure song that Ringo wrote as well as recorded—"Cryin'," from the cool *Ringo's Rotogravure* album. It was produced by my dearly missed friend Arif Mardin, who was a brilliant producer, and also, by the way, an amazing arranger. He wrote the horns and strings on many of the great Aretha Franklin records that we love so much and even arranged the strings on the James Taylor version of "Up on the Roof," which I produced. He was a legend in the music business and a highly skilled musician. I know Arif had a great time making that record. I have had the pleasure of working with Ringo myself in the studio, and it is an exciting and rewarding experience. Sometimes it can be dangerous or disappointing to meet and work with one's musical heroes, but Ringo's extraordinary and profoundly creative playing (and his personal charm and wit) exceed expectations.

"Cryin'" is an interesting track, an odd track. And if you have a musical bent, you'll notice that it's got some odd bars in it. It's got some 2/4 bars. It's got some extra beats making 5/4 bars, but it all works, and Ringo plays through it all on the drums brilliantly. It also, by the way, has some great pedal steel work. Ringo is a country fan, and you can definitely hear his country influence on this song.

Now enough talk of all these solo Beatles tracks. Time to turn our attention to some old good-time Beatles music. One C song that was recorded while Paul was still living at my house back in the old days remains a classic: the great "Can't Buy Me Love." The youth and energy and enthusiasm and commitment in that song is what pop music is all about. It's just brilliant.

"Can't Buy Me Love" was on the soundtrack of the classic movie *A Hard Day's Night*. It is always a pleasure to see that movie; it stands up to repeated viewings, and it is an extraordinary achievement for a first film. It was directed by a man called Dick Lester, as you probably know. To the best of my knowledge, the Beatles discovered Dick Lester's work the same way I did, from watching a short film called *The Running Jumping & Standing Still Film*, starring Peter Sellers. It's a film in which all that happens is that the actors run around, jump, and stand still, hence its charmingly accurate title! It's only about nine minutes long, and it's very funny. If you get a chance to watch it, and I am sure it is on YouTube or somewhere these days, you will see that a lot of the nifty stuff that the Beatles do at Dick Lester's direction in *A Hard Day's Night* was presaged by what happens in *The Running Jumping & Standing Still Film*. So, interestingly, it means that it is through Peter Sellers, in a way, that the Beatles not only became aware of (and then met) the director of their first film, but the same could be said of the producer of their records, George Martin. As you may know, the moment the Beatles realized how much they already admired George Martin was when they found out that he had produced Peter Sellers's records. We were all Peter Sellers fans, big fans of *The Goon Show* and stuff, so a Peter Sellers connection for us was golden. It meant somebody was incredibly cool, and George Martin certainly was incredibly cool. So was Dick Lester.

There is another C song that occurred to me, but the funny part is that I remember it as a B song, not the C song it actually is. I know that sounds weird, but you will understand what I mean as soon as I tell you the title. It is "The Continuing Story of Bungalow Bill." Written by John Lennon in Rishikesh, in India, to make fun of an American visitor who had headed out into the jungle to shoot tigers, it is John at his most sardonic and satirical and yet with his ability to write a catchy chorus clearly intact. A surprisingly but very effectively sloppy track with lots of little overdubs and interjections—mellotron samples, Yoko, other guests, and so on. John would, at other times, occasionally be critical of Paul's music hall approach, but this song of John's actually comes pretty close to that idiom itself.

Let us turn in a different direction, towards a very significant C in the Beatles lives, and that was Capitol Records.

Capitol Records was and is one of the biggest record companies in America. It had Frank Sinatra, the Beach Boys, and so many other major artists. It was owned by EMI Records, a British company, which gave Capitol the option to release in the U.S. anything that EMI had released in the UK. And most of you probably know that Capitol initially turned down the early Beatles records like "Please Please Me," "From Me to You," and "Love Me Do." They essentially said, "No, thank you, we're not sure if that's going to make it in the American market." The songs were released, but on smaller labels and achieved no success. Finally, and it was a roundabout process and story, but Capitol Records decided yes, they would release a Beatles record. The first one they agreed to release, the one that eventually led America into a giant fit of Beatlemania, was "I Want to Hold Your Hand." And it turned out then that the song went to No. 1 in pretty much every country that existed at the time, including America, and changed the world forever.

Capitol Records was not only important in the Beatles' lives; it was important in mine, too. Peter & Gordon were signed to EMI Records in London and that, of course, gave Capitol Records the right to put out our first record, "A World Without Love," in America if they so chose. And I'm delighted to say they did choose to do so, and it, too, went to No. 1. Yet another debt I owe to the

Beatles, of course—without their prior success, Capitol would not have been nearly as welcoming, I have no doubt!

In fact, Capitol Records' huge success in the 1960s largely depended upon its involvement with the British Invasion and, most particularly and significantly, its involvement with the best and biggest rock and roll band of all time, the Beatles. Capitol's business relationship with the Beatles continues to this very day and will probably continue forever. You are probably thinking, *But what about Apple Records? Didn't the Beatles start their own independent record company? Wasn't Peter Asher the head of A&R there?* Yes, but there's a catch.

It is well known that the first Beatles record ever with an Apple label on it was "Hey Jude." But in a business sense it wasn't really an Apple record, to be quite honest. The Beatles had a record deal with EMI in the UK and thus with their subsidiaries in the rest of the world (including Capitol in America). Clearly, EMI had no interest in ending this relationship or giving the Beatles any kind of total release from the deal in any territory. Indeed, subject to numerous amendments and adjustments the relationship exists to this day. But what they did do as a courtesy was to stick Apple Records labels on the Beatles singles and albums, so that visibly, physically, and conceptually the Beatles were on their own label, Apple, but in the business realities of the hard, cold, tough music business, deep down they were really still signed to EMI (and thus to Capitol). The acts we signed up for Apple, like James Taylor, Mary Hopkin, and Badfinger, were signed directly to Apple, an independent company which made their records—though Apple did then have a promotion and distribution deal with EMI and Capitol.

Capitol Records itself has endured numerous and various changes of ownership, rights, and financial structure since those days, but in terms of public perception what makes Capitol Records legendarily famous will forever be the iconic tower and its studios, and the musical legacy of the Beach Boys, Frank Sinatra—and, of course, the Beatles.

Having wet our feet with A, B, and C, we are now ready to plunge into the rest of the alphabet. Next up is the letter D.

The first D song that I'd like to explore is a real favourite of mine. A great guitar riff, a great song: "Day Tripper." Starting off the song and repeated throughout is an R&B-flavoured lick that the Beatles invented. To my ear, it owes a bit to the riff in the Temptations' song "My Girl" (written by Smokey Robinson and Ronald White) that we all love so much (and many of us learn to play pretty early in our guitar-playing journey), but the "Day Tripper" motif has an extra sting in its tail as it ends with a very cool extra couple of notes. I love the way they both have the same kind of effect, though I don't know if that was what the Beatles were consciously doing. Probably not, but I love those

Ringo Starr and me at an Apple event, with (from left to right), Ken Mansfield of Capitol Records, Carol Padden, and Barbara Bennet.

kinds of riffs, and they played it really well. That song, by the way, was half of a single, the other side of which was "We Can Work It Out." I am not even sure which was the A-side or which was the bigger hit. Two great songs for the price of one.

Of course, the lyrics to "Day Tripper" were very much discussed. In England, *day tripper* has a fairly specific meaning: somebody who goes on a one-day vacation. One takes a day trip (often to the seaside) and comes back the same night. The term is not as common in the U.S., but the meaning would be the same. So she is just a day tripper, only here for the day. Now since that time, of course, all kinds of drug connotations have been attributed to the song, but I simply do not know for sure whether such attribution is correct—I strongly suspect not, because it was a bit early for the term *tripping* to mean anything other than a physical trip down to the seaside.

What I *do* know is that Paul was delighted by another aspect of the lyrics, which was the phrase "She's a big teaser." He very specifically took pleasure in the fact that, phonetically and at a quick listen, this line could be mistaken for another phrase, one that describes more specifically a woman who may appear to be promising physical delights—a promise on which she eventually decides not to deliver. A big teaser indeed!

Now, of course, to make your day tripping much easier, it would really help if you didn't have to drive yourself there, and that's why you need a driver.

But while I believe "Day Tripper" to be a mostly Lennon song that McCartney helped finish, "Drive My Car" was the opposite; it was mostly a Paul song that John helped him finish. "Drive My Car," oddly enough, has also apparently been said to contain subtle sexual references—that whole "You can do something in between" and "I can show you a better time" and maybe even *driving your car* is a metaphor as well, who can say? Paul has talked in print about some of those references being sexual in nature. But what isn't? This is rock and roll, after all, and "Rock Around the Clock" was not really about dancing.

A fantastic cover version of "Drive My Car" recently came to my attention. I had not heard it before, I must confess, and I found it on the *Late Show with David Letterman*. It is by Sting, with a woman called Ivy Levan, with whom I was not familiar, but she is an amazing singer, as well as looking quite remarkable. I was very impressed by this version. What also caught my eye is that a friend of mine, Mike Einziger, a terrific guitar player who is in the band Incubus, is the guitarist in the band on this occasion and plays a killer solo. The video is well worth finding online.

George Harrison had a lot to do with the arrangement and some of the cool guitar licks that are in the original "Drive My Car," and he wrote some great D songs himself. One of my favourites is George's first songwriting credit for the Beatles, "Don't Bother Me." That was George in a kind of "I want to be alone" mood, telling us, "Don't come around, leave me alone, don't bother me." Don't talk to me, in effect. Seriously, though, we only wish we still could talk to him. Of course, we all miss George so much as a musician, as a friend, as a composer, and as an entirely remarkable and brilliant man.

That was the first three Beatles, and last but by no means least, let us take a look at Ringo and the world of D. It so happens that Ringo, like George, wrote a song that began with D as his very first songwriting credit for the Beatles. A song called "Don't Pass Me By," featuring Ringo in a kind of country mood as he often was, with fiddle played by Jack Fallon—and Mr. Fallon has an interesting and remarkable story to tell. He was born in Canada in 1915 and began playing classical violin at a very young age—but switched to double bass when he was twenty years old, played in a dance band in the Royal Canadian Air Force during the war, and settled in Britain after his discharge. He played bass with all the greats of the British jazz scene (Ronnie Scott, Ted Heath, and others) and even with visiting international legends like Duke Ellington, Count Basie, and Django Reinhardt. He also became a master of the bass guitar, an instrument rejected by many old-school double bass players. His Beatles connection was unrelated to what he had in common with Paul McCartney instrumentally but rather relates to the fact that he was also an entrepreneur, booking gigs for various bands, including the Beatles and the Rolling Stones. So somehow Jack Fallon ended up back on violin (stylistically, it would be more accurate to say "fiddle," I guess) while Paul McCartney played bass guitar as well as piano, and Ringo played drums, sang, and added a whole bunch of percussion on a Beatles recording session in 1968. Fallon was clearly one of those rare and valuable musicians without musical prejudices and possessed of genuine versatility—his fiddle part has a charmingly loose old-timey flavour and wobbly intonation which works perfectly with the strange piano sound (they fed the piano through a Leslie speaker) and fits in with the overall quirky oddness of the track. I like it.

So, having examined D songs written by John and Paul and George and Ringo, let's turn to a D song that none of them wrote but which they clearly all admired. It is a great rock and roll song, heavily influenced by the blues, as is so often the case, which the Beatles often performed live: "Dizzy Miss Lizzy." It was written and first recorded by Larry Williams, and the Beatles did an excellent cover in one of their BBC sessions that is worth tracking down.

Let us put song titles aside for a minute and look at other things that the letter D can stand for. And among the most important D things in the world of rock and roll are drums and drum fills and drummers.

So we are going to focus on Ringo for a bit. My admiration for his drumming is profound and well known. I talk about it a lot. His drumming was creative and brilliant and changed music and specifically changed the nature of rock and roll drumming forever.

When people hear a great drum sound (or any great instrumental sound) on a record, they often ask detailed questions. *What kind of drums did he use? What kind of sticks? How did they mic the snare? How did they record it?* I shall tell you that in most cases, with great musicians on any instrument, none of that is as relevant as who is playing in the first place.

Once, when I had the pleasure of working with Eric Clapton on a track, I was greatly concerned about providing whatever kind of amp or setup would make him happiest. His answers to my specific questions on the topic were very vague—and it turned out he was right. It really didn't matter what kind of amp it was. It probably didn't even matter what kind of guitar it was. He plugged in;

he sounded like Eric Clapton. And I can tell you from experience that when Ringo sits down at a drum kit, it is the way he plays—the way he hits the hi-hat, the way he does his weird backhanded fills, because he is a left-handed drummer on a right-handed kit—that makes the sound and the groove immediately unique and remarkable.

I'd like to take some time here to call attention to some of Ringo's classic and most legendary drum fills. I have decided to start with one of the great Beatles records of all time, which features some of Ringo's best fills. It's the classic song from the *Sgt. Pepper* album, "A Day in the Life," itself a bit of a D song with Ringo's great drumming on it and those amazing fills which are so cool and thumpy and weird. While some drummers tend to fill every tiny moment in the bar when given a space for a fill (a tradition Keith Moon maintained brilliantly), Ringo developed a style in which the fills were quite specific (as if written), with each beat beautifully placed in just the right spot. In "A Day in the Life," if you listen carefully to the drum fills that start after the line "He blew his mind out in a car" and continue to fill the second bar of each two-bar phrase after the vocal line ends—after "the lights had changed" and after "stood and stared"—you will hear what I mean. The drums then play around the vocal itself for a moment before resuming their responses after each line of the lyric. Brilliant stuff and extraordinarily innovative. Ringo starts each fill on the snare (itself unusual—most drummers would head for a tom-tom first), but each one is different and perfect for the space it occupies.

In early rock and roll, the drum fills were often a little less carefully crafted and a little more frantic but also kind of cool anyway. And indeed, Ringo himself on some of the early Beatles records did some really interesting, if less "composed," fills. Among my favourites of the early examples of a Ringo fill is "Thank You Girl." I particularly love the ones near the end after the "oh, oh, oh" bits. It kind of goes "oh, oh" rum diddly um bum bum, and then repeats pretty much the same fill, but with a further slight variation. So when you next listen to "Thank You Girl," you can also thank Ringo.

One can find great drumming throughout the entire Beatles

catalogue. It is very hard to choose. But one particular drum fill that should be included on any list of great drumming moments throughout the Beatles world is on "With a Little Help from My Friends"—a song Ringo also sings, of course. The fill between the first two verses is irreplaceably perfect—we have heard it so many times that we take it for granted, but give it another listen. It is deceptively simple yet exactly right. No one else plays anything during that two-bar gap, and Ringo, using only toms this time, keeps the groove going, makes a musical statement, and builds our anticipation of the next verse all at the same time. Also worth noting is that for the rest of the song he plays only straight time, leaving the syncopation between vocal lines to Paul's brilliant (Beach Boys–influenced?) bass part, with that great skippy rhythm to it.

The Beatles were not only incredibly successful, they were and remain wildly influential as well. Just as fans tried to emulate the clothes or the hair, musicians listened to every note that each of the Beatles played and studied every musical detail.

Ringo's drum fills, where each note is precisely in the right place, not simply a random acceleration of drum craziness but an actual part, changed the way drums got used on rock and roll records. And the records I made were no exception. An album I produced, James Taylor's *Sweet Baby James*, included the song "Fire and Rain," which became a big hit. If you listen to that song, you may notice a certain similarity between the fills that the amazing (and now legendary) drummer, my dear friend Russ Kunkel, plays on "Fire and Rain" to the fill Ringo plays on "With a Little Help from My Friends." And that is no coincidence. Russ was influenced by the Beatles and so was I. Proudly so. We were not aiming to copy Ringo, but there is no doubt that his style affected our thinking. Russ came up with a perfect variation, and we decided to use brushes instead of sticks—but Ringo's influence is still audible.

When it comes to Ringo's great drumming and his brilliant drum fills, another favourite of mine is "She Said She Said," from *Revolver*. I had almost forgotten about it until I heard it again recently; it has such amazing drumming throughout. It is suffused with little fills through the whole song. Ringo plays swung sixteenth notes throughout, which gives the song a great deal of the amazing groove that drives it along so well.

"She Said She Said" is also a Beatles song that has an acid-related connotation. Apparently, Peter Fonda was the one who came up with the line "I know what it's like to be dead." He shot himself in the stomach accidentally and thought he might be dying, but fortunately he was not. He lived to tell the tale—and included the phrase "I know what it's like to be dead" in the telling of it during a communal LSD trip, much to John's annoyance. John said later, "We didn't want to hear about that! We were on an acid trip and the sun was shining and the girls were dancing and the whole thing was beautiful and sixties, and this guy—who I really didn't know; he hadn't made *Easy Rider* or anything—kept coming over, wearing shades, saying, 'I know what it's like to be dead,' and we kept leaving him because he was so boring! . . . It was scary. You know . . . when you're flying high and [*whispers*] 'I know what it's like to be dead, man.'" It was John who came up with the line, "And she's making me feel like I've never been born."

We shall end our Ringo drum festival by considering one more song, a brilliant song with an astonishingly inventive bass part and an extraordinary drum part. It shows Ringo at his most creative, his musical collaboration with Paul perfectly executed—and that song is "Rain." The way Ringo uses his hi-hat as part of the fills is just extraordinary. And the drum sound is remarkable on that track, too. I understand the whole song was recorded at a faster tempo, and then they brought the pitch and the tempo down. That is one reason those drums sound so deliciously big and thumpy.

Turning back to song titles, we find another excellent Beatles song that begins with the letter D, the legendary "Doctor Robert"— about one of those doctors who overprescribe and give you just about anything that you think you want rather than what he thinks you need. Such doctors still exist today, of course. Indeed, the opioid epidemic from which America is currently suffering is no doubt due to a large number of Doctor Roberts all over the place prescribing fentanyl and other creepy stuff to people who don't need it but want it nonetheless.

There's also a trio of D songs that are all about asking a woman to do something or to get closer—or both. The first is "Dear Prudence," for which we have been told the story behind it. Prudence was the sister of the actress Mia Farrow, and they were all in Maharishi world in Rishikesh. Prudence would not come out of her room or something like that, and John wrote the song to tempt her into the outside world. I was not there, but that is the story. The song is also a homage to Buddy Holly's "Raining in My Heart," which contains the lyric, "The sun is out, the sky is blue," which John changed to "The sun is up, the sky is blue." His admiration for Buddy Holly and his lyric writing comes through, and there is certainly no higher compliment than when John Lennon borrows your words!

The second of this trio of D songs is one of two records officially credited to "The Beatles with Billy Preston," the B-side of "Get Back," "Don't Let Me Down." It was recorded at Trident Studios, not at Abbey Road, and I understand that Mal Evans and Jackie Lomax are on background vocals, which is pretty cool. In this song, John is imploring Yoko not to let him down, and of course she did not and she has not.

And the third of the trio is less imploring and more of an enticement, "Do You Want to Know a Secret" An excellent early Beatles record—written by John, sung by George, and later covered by Billy J. Kramer. Apparently, John was inspired by the memory of his mother singing to him the Disney song "I'm Wishing," which itself opens with the lyric "Want to know a secret? Promise not to tell?"

I don't think I know any really good secrets these days, but perhaps you do. And on that mysterious note, we depart the letter D.

If we are going to start off with a really great Beatles E song, there is one that cannot be beat—even though I suppose in a way it's slightly cheating, because it is not only an E song; it is also a number. And that song is "Eight Days a Week."

"Eight Days a Week" was a genuine co-write, to which both John and Paul contributed. Once they had the title, the song apparently fell into place quite quickly. John has gone on record as not thinking much of it, actually describing it as "lousy" in one interview. But if the Beatles are even capable of writing a lousy song, this is not it. And not only is it an excellent song but (as always) the arrangement and production are highly imaginative. The startlingly original novelty of the fade-in at the beginning of the

Elvis.

record—and fading in on that lovely guitar figure George played on his Rickenbacker twelve-string, which we do not hear again until the very end of the record. Paul's walking bass part sets off the shuffle groove of the whole track (Ringo's shuffle feel is unique as always), and the handclaps, mixed very loud against the band and which include the great double handclaps after "Hold me" and "Love me" which almost compel the listener to clap along. A lot of brilliant ideas.

I love it, I must say.

There are a couple of different stories as to where the title came from. I had always heard that it was Ringo's invention. But then I also read that it might have come through an overworked chauffeur to whom John was talking who said that he had been working too hard. He had been working eight days a week. Who knows? It is also of course the title of Ron Howard's brilliant documentary about the Beatles' touring years, and if you haven't seen it, I urge you to do so. It is excellent. I had the pleasure of speaking to Ron quite a lot during the research phase of his project, and he did an extraordinary job. The movie conveys accurately how incredibly different the touring world was back in those days—slapdash and amateurish. Not only was the technology primitive but so was the organization. The only sound systems used were whatever was already built into the arena or stadium—better suited for making an announcement than trying to get music across to thousands of people. And as for monitors (speakers which enable the performers to hear themselves), they had not been invented! Whole categories of staff did not exist. No stage designer, no lighting designer, no front of house mixer, no monitor mixer, no stage manager, no production manager, and so on and so on. It was another world.

One of the oddest scenes to watch in the movie, from a modern perspective, is when we see Ringo walk onstage in front of a giant audience only to discover that some rickety circular drum riser (with his kit on it) is facing in the wrong direction and wobbling like crazy—and we get to watch him single-handedly try to tug it into position before climbing aboard!

When Gordon and I toured back in that era, we took one

all-purpose tour manager with us—and when we got to tour with the Beatles, I was very impressed that they had *two* people on staff, Mal Evans and Neil Aspinall. If the Beatles were touring today, they would have a team of hundreds and multiple trucks and busses carrying sets and equipment, and each department would be fully staffed. They would be able to hear each other, and we would all hear them perfectly. One can but dream! The miracle is that when one *does* hear a live recording of the Beatles back then (as one can in Ron's movie—they have worked wonders with the audio), they are playing so stupendously well under such conditions.

The Beatles' E catalogue also features a song that none of them wrote. It was one of the covers they did so well: "Everybody's Trying to Be My Baby." We should all have such problems. This is an excellent Carl Perkins song from 1957 that the Beatles apparently recorded in only one take because they did it live so often. George Harrison, who sang the lead vocal, was a huge Carl Perkins fan, and in fact all four Beatles had the greatest respect for him. Ringo recorded "Matchbox" during his time with the Beatles, and Paul invited Carl to sing with him on the song "Get It" from the *Tug of War* album. It's a really cool duet. Carl has such an excellent voice, and he and Paul sound good together.

I would guess that Carl Perkins's most famous song is "Blue Suede Shoes." It's such an offbeat sentiment and instruction, such a great lyric, such a brilliant concept, and no one has ever worn blue suede shoes without loving the song and making reference to it. It was his friend Johnny Cash who pointed out to Carl that blue suede shoes were becoming *the* cool footwear in the South. And then a few days later, Carl looked out from the stage during a show and saw a very beautiful woman being fiercely berated by her dancing partner about the importance of her not stepping on those very shoes. Carl apparently thought the guy was being an idiot but nonetheless woke up at 3 a.m. with the words to the song in his head and wrote them down on a potato sack, which was all he could find. The creative process never fails to amaze. Of course, "Blue Suede Shoes" brings me to another huge E influence on the Beatles that we cannot ignore. I'm talking about the king of influences, the great Elvis Presley.

Elvis's importance cannot be overstated. The Beatles were huge Elvis fans. John Lennon actually said that without Elvis there would have been no Beatles. When they finally met him on August 27, 1965, they were extremely nervous and very excited. Elvis was the king. We all loved his records. We all admired him very much. Now to clarify that, let me explain something. The first time all of us in England heard Elvis, at least the first time I did, and I think the same is true of the Beatles (George Harrison has spoken about this) was when we heard "Heartbreak Hotel." It wasn't Elvis's first record, but it was the first record that was released in the UK or indeed anywhere overseas because it was his first record for a major label. He had been on a small U.S.-only label, Sun Records. Then he was on RCA, and they went for a worldwide promotional push.

We all went crazy when we heard "Heartbreak Hotel." We loved the sound of it. We loved the reverb. We loved the way Elvis sang. We loved everything about it. I remember hearing it on the radio and just thinking, *Oh my God, what an incredibly great record.* And then, of course, we all became aware of Elvis, and the furor he was creating in America, and "Elvis the Pelvis" and all that stuff they used to call him, and the outrageous influence he was going to have on young people, and how rock and roll was going to destroy our youth—which of course it did, and I'm happy to be a victim of that destruction. And then we went back and discovered all the great records he'd made before. We went back and listened to the Sun records. I especially loved "Mystery Train," which remains my favourite Elvis track of all time.

You may notice an interesting parallel between the discovery of Elvis in the UK and the subsequent discovery of the Beatles in the U.S. We heard "Heartbreak Hotel" courtesy of the efforts of a big international label, fell in love with Elvis, and then went back to his earlier recordings to discover "That's All Right (Mama)," "Blue Moon of Kentucky," "Mystery Train," and many more. America fell in love with "I Want to Hold Your Hand" in a similar fashion and then discovered "Love Me Do," "From Me to You," and "Please Please Me."

The Beatles made all the same Elvis discoveries, and they used to do a number of those songs in their live performances and in the BBC sessions, including "That's All Right (Mama)," the Arthur Crudup song covered by Elvis, which is how the Beatles heard it, and then they covered it themselves. They never made a record of it, though, and that's too bad.

Ringo was also an Elvis fan, and he covered one of Elvis's songs himself in his solo career, recording a very creditable version of "Don't Be Cruel"—a song the Beatles apparently sang live from time to time in their early days, but of which no recordings exist. I don't think anyone can top Elvis, to be honest, but Ringo's version is very good, sticking close to the original arrangement, with all the Jordanaires-style background vocals added in as well for good measure.

"Don't Be Cruel" was written by Otis Blackwell, who wrote a lot of great songs, for a lot of singers. He wrote "Return to Sender" and "All Shook Up" (Elvis), "Great Balls of Fire" (Jerry Lee Lewis), "Fever" (Peggy Lee), and many others. He played a role in my life as well. One day when I was working on the *JT* album with James Taylor, during a break, Danny Kortchmar and James were fooling around with the guitar lick from an Otis Blackwell song called "Handy Man." They started playing it much slower than the Jimmy Jones original record, just for the fun of it. And I said, "Hang on, gentlemen, that sounds really cool. Let me record a bit of that, just so we have it. You know, as an idea." I put up a couple of mics by the two acoustic guitars. We had Russ Kunkel, the genius drummer, playing a pair of conga drums, and that was about it. We did a couple of takes, maybe four or five at the most. I ended up adding some drums, some strings, some background vocals, and that became our record of "Handy Man," which turned out to be a big hit for James. So I owe a debt of gratitude to Otis Blackwell.

Now, on to a song written not by Otis Blackwell but by a major fan of his, Paul McCartney. And in fact it's a Paul McCartney track that is also a duet, as well as an E song and one of Paul's biggest hits. It was a huge No. 1 record: "Ebony and Ivory."

I have heard that the title is actually a quote from Spike Milligan. You may or may not be familiar with him. He was a brilliant British comedian, who created and wrote *The Goon Show*, of which the Beatles (and I) were all great fans. And apparently, Spike Milligan had said something to Paul about the black notes and the white notes on the piano and the fact that you needed both of them to make harmony. And Paul took that point and ran with it and wrote the song. I hope that's true because I am a great admirer of Spike Milligan.

And for the duet Paul invited Stevie Wonder—a supreme talent in his own right, of course, and a marvelous performer—to join him on the recording. Supposedly, Stevie showed up three or four days late for the video shoot, which is why a lot of this record and a lot of the video was constructed without Paul and Stevie in the same room at the same time. But they put it all together and came up with a very big hit record.

Now, if we were to take a vote as to the most loved E song that the Beatles ever wrote, my guess is that "Eleanor Rigby" would win. It is my favourite E song and could well be yours, too.

Incredibly, "Eleanor Rigby" was the B-side of "Yellow Submarine" and also appeared on the *Revolver* album. But it was much more than just a B-side. It was one of the Beatles' finest and most interesting, radical, and remarkable records, and one of Paul's most perfect songs. A beautiful melody, a brilliant lyric, an extraordinarily good arrangement by George Martin, and a wonderful sound and mix.

It is a revolutionary song in several respects. Quite a brilliant piece of songwriting on its own, and you must understand that it is not a song with strings added to it, as is very common in pop music. The strings are the entire band. There are no other Beatles playing on that song, no other instruments on that record. It is Paul McCartney and a double string quartet, which would mean four violins, two violas, and two cellos. George Martin and Geoffrey Emerick, the engineer, miked them in a particular way, close and with a careful choice of microphone, to get extra grit and rosin out of the strings. George Martin wanted the arrangement to have the toughness and emphasis that, for example, a Bartók string quartet does when the musicians really attack the instruments. And that is certainly what he achieved. The song has almost a rock and roll intensity to its rhythm but derives that strength only from a brilliant string arrangement—and from the strings being played with no vibrato. George Martin, of course, was great at all of that. He was a wonderful arranger as well as a great producer, capable of working with Paul to bring Paul's ideas to life and adding his own expertise on top.

I know for a fact that that song was written in our basement at 57 Wimpole Street because both John and Paul have mentioned that fact. Sadly, I was not there that day. I wish I could tell you an "Eleanor Rigby" story, but I cannot. What I can tell you is that Paul has said that Ray Charles's version of "Eleanor Rigby" is one of his favourite versions of any Beatles song. A radical departure from the original, it starts (almost deceptively) with the same four string section quarter notes as does George Martin's arrangement, but then it changes drastically—the strings doing all kinds of glissandos and slurs and other dramatic moves, an oboe playing some countermelodies, a horn section playing, too—and the glorious Raelettes adding responses. A whole new approach accompanying Ray's soulful reinterpretation of the timing and attitude of the original vocal melody.

And if "Eleanor Rigby" did turn out to win everyone's vote for favourite E song written by the Beatles, I guarantee you that a close runner-up would be "Every Little Thing." It is a great song, recorded at EMI Studios with Ringo playing timpani in addition to drums. I remember that in Studio Two there would often be a set of timpani covered up in one of those kinds of padded eiderdownlooking things they put on top of them, sitting unattended in the corner of the studio.

So my guess is that it just occurred to someone to roll out the timpani, take the cover off, find the right notes, and overdub them. I think it is the first and could even be the only time Ringo played timpani on record.

Let's travel next from a very early song to a very new song, from Paul McCartney's album actually entitled *New*. And to complete the circle, the song is called "Early Days." A touchingly nostalgic song with a kind of unassuming and unshowy but wholly convincing vocal performance from Paul. The executive producer of the album was Sir George Martin's immensely talented son Giles. The track "Early Days" itself was produced by Ethan Johns, a brilliant engineer and producer and the son of Glyn Johns, who produced so many classic Rolling Stones records and other great stuff, including his work with the Beatles. Ethan has done excellent work with Ryan Adams, Tift Merritt, and many others, and for "Early Days" he created a beautiful sea of acoustic instruments, starting with just an acoustic guitar and skillfully adding other stringed instruments and some kind of drone to provide a vaguely Celtic and emotionally gripping backdrop for Paul's reminiscences.

I'd like to turn next to another Beatles E song which one does not hear that often. With the weird title "Everybody's Got Something to Hide Except Me and My Monkey," it may not be some people's favourite, but it's really cool. It features a great George lead guitar lick repeated almost as if it were a loop (though he clearly played it live), insistent Ringo drums, and a lot of driving percussion. I think all four Beatles may have played some of the percussion—the cowbell part is particularly fine and alternates with a shaker to keep the excitement going. As for the unusual title, I know that everyone has a theory. My own guess is that "Everybody's Got Something to Hide Except Me and My Monkey" is not a drug reference. Just a John kind of weird comedic reference and a song he wrote for Yoko.

From John we move to George and an excellent song from his E album, *Extra Texture*. I'm not quite sure why he chose that album title, but it has a lot of good music on it. One song in particular has really grown on me after listening to it a couple of times: "This Guitar (Can't Keep from Crying)." I don't know what George's problem is with his lachrymose guitar. If it is not gently weeping, it is crying. But this song itself is underrated. Perhaps upset by some criticism he received during or after his 1974 tour, he successfully handed off some of his discomfort to his guitar in a well-crafted song with elegant chord changes, great slide guitar from George, and a fine additional lead from Jesse Ed Davis. What holds it all together and gives a real feeling of size and scope is the excellent orchestral arrangement from David Foster, a friend of mine and a truly brilliant arranger and producer—of Whitney Houston's "I Will Always Love You," just for a start.

Ringo also gave us a good E song on his 2017 album *Give*

More Love—"Electricity," which he wrote with Glen Ballard. Ringo recorded this album in his home studio, and he produced it, too. Of course, many of the players on the sessions (like Dave Stewart, Glen Ballard, and Don Was) are terrific producers themselves, so there would have been a lot of great ideas floating about. Ringo's brother-in-law, Joe Walsh, played guitar on "Electricity" as well, joined by the great keyboard player Benmont Tench, from Tom Petty and the Heartbreakers.

I suggest we allow Ringo to bring us to the end of this examination of the letter E by remembering and admiring his only drum solo on a Beatles record: his indispensable contribution to "The End," from *Abbey Road*, followed by Paul's words of wisdom, "And in the end, the love you take is equal to the love you make."

In dealing with Beatles songs and Beatles facts that concern the letter F, the first thing that comes to my mind, unsurprisingly, is the name of my radio show, which provided a home for *The Beatles from A to Zed* in the first place. So let us stop for a while to consider a great Beatles F song, the title I chose for my very own show, "From Me to You."

It turns out that I was not the first person to think that this title made good sense in connection with a radio show. Early on, the Beatles had a radio show of their own on the BBC, playing various pop records, including their own. They recorded a jingle for that show using "From Me to You" as a theme, changing the lyrics to "From Us to You." It is very short and can be found online.

"From Me to You" was one of several songs John and Paul wrote while they were on the road in 1963 on the Helen Shapiro tour. The Beatles were not headlining; this was very early in their career, and Helen Shapiro was already a very big deal at the age

The Beatles on the bill with Helen Shapiro in 1963.

of only sixteen. She had several huge hits, like "Walkin' Back to Happiness" (her best record, in my view) and "You Don't Know," and she was the main attraction—the Beatles were billed fourth out of eleven acts! Apparently, the Beatles played some of their new songs for Helen and asked her which one she thought should be their next single, and she chose "From Me to You." So to some extent I guess we have Helen to thank for the fact that "From Me to You" became such a huge hit, as indeed it did.

Let's move forward to a time after the Beatles had become the headliners themselves—indeed, a time when they got so big they did not even need to tour anymore. There are two brilliant F tracks that they created to be part of their movie *Magical Mystery Tour*. I remember Paul telling me all his ideas for the expedition, the movie, and the accompanying music. The first F song was an instrumental called "Flying," written specifically to accompany an aerial shot of the landscape of Iceland. Paul wrote the main melody; the structure is a simple twelve-bar blues and (as an instrumental with wordless vocals) the writing credit was divided equally among all four Beatles. Cool tremolo-effected guitar opens the track, and the main melody is played on a mellotron. I think it is on the trombone setting—even though to me it sounds more like a cor anglais. Yes, this track is an instrumental, but it is more accurately a piece of movie score. It is not as if the Beatles were trying to make an instrumental hit to rival, say, Cliff Richard's backup band the Shadows, who had a string of big instrumental hits, all of which the Beatles knew well, but rather that they wanted to create an evocative moody piece to match the cinematic moment. In that I think they were very successful.

"Flying" is a good track from *Magical Mystery Tour*. "The Fool on the Hill" is a great track. It shows Paul McCartney at his most creative, imaginative, and brilliant. I distinctly remember when Paul wrote that song, because he then played it to the whole of our family. We were in the sitting room on what we would call the first floor, and Americans would call the second floor, where there was a big grand piano in the drawing room, which also served as my father's office and consulting room. We stood around the piano as he played "The Fool on the Hill" just after he had written it. He explained to us (and sang) some of the flute parts and recorder parts that he already had in mind, and he had the whole arrangement already bubbling around in his head, as genius musicians do. We were all very impressed. A truly lovely song.

George Harrison was responsible for another great Beatles F song: "For You Blue," featuring John Lennon on the slide guitar. The song is a traditional twelve-bar blues in format, and you might notice that in the middle of the song, John is playing a cool slide solo, and George says, "Elmore James got nothing on this baby." I wonder how many of you know who Elmore James was. I hope you do. He was a classic blues slide guitar player whom we all admired very much. Again, there was this whole movement in England; everyone wanted to play the blues. We learned from the blues records we could get hold of in jazz record shops and from swapping records among ourselves. There was this collective desire to learn all that we could about the blues and its inventors, proponents, and disciples. Everyone was an Elmore James fan, and everyone who picked up a slide tried to play like Elmore James. And that is still the case. Bonnie Raitt (such a great singer who is sometimes overlooked as a remarkable guitarist) and all the great slide players of today began by admiring Elmore James and his seemingly effortless playing.

Does Elmore James really have nothing on John Lennon? Not so sure about that but it was a valiant effort on his part, and he was certainly an Elmore James fan. Paul was also playing, by the way, "prepared piano" on that track. Prepared piano is what they call it when you mess with the sound of the piano physically by putting things in it or on the strings or whatever. The technique is widely used in avant-garde music. John Cage used prepared pianos. So did John Cale in the Velvet Underground. And Paul was interested in and listened to a lot of that stuff. So maybe that had something to do with it. But he fiddled about with the piano, adding something to the strings until it had just the sound he wanted for that particular track.

Now, I have a confession to make. When I was poking around looking for interesting songs that began with the letter F, I found one that I had never heard before. This is a Ringo song called

"Free Drinks." I listened to it and I really liked it. It's got twangy Ennio Morricone–style guitars on it. It was written by Ringo, Mark Hudson, Steve Dudas, Dean Grakal, and another friend of mine, Gary Burr, who is a great Nashville songwriter. I am delighted to have found it. It's worth your seeking it out, too.

John Lennon wrote a cool F song, addressed to Yoko, called "(Forgive Me) My Little Flower Princess." It was recorded in New York with a great New York band—Hugh McCracken (one of my favourite guitarists), Earl Slick, Tony Levin, and Andy Newmark. A lot of great musicians. This song was released, sadly, after John's death.

With that same band, John recorded a great double F album, *Double Fantasy*. Two especially significant tracks off that album are "Woman" and "Dear Yoko." John referred to "Woman" as a "grown-up version" of his song "Girl," so perhaps it can provide some insight as to how his songwriting had changed over the years. He was also, of course, madly in love. He begins the track with a whispered recitation, "For the other half of the sky," a reference to Mao Zedong's pronouncement that "women hold up half the sky."

"Dear Yoko" (not to be confused with "Oh Yoko!" which is on the *Imagine* album) is a nice bouncy, happy track reflecting, I suppose, that side of his love for Yoko. John was always fond of old-fashioned slap-back reverb on a lead vocal and has sometimes been guilty of overdoing it, but it fits this song perfectly. Also, we were just talking about slide guitar, and there is some terrific slide work on this track—must have been Hugh McCracken, I think.

Let's circle back to Paul. One of his solo F titles, though on the obscure side, is an interesting song. He recorded it with Wings, and it is called "Famous Groupies." I confess that I did wonder whether there was some fascinating (or even lascivious?) story behind the title or the concept, and so I emailed my friend Denny Laine, who was in Wings at the time, and asked what he remembered. His response was not necessarily as enlightening as I could have wished. He wrote back, "Famous Groupies? Don't remind me—I have kids with two of them but that's another story." I think we should rely on our fertile imaginations.

Alan Civil and his French horn.

The Beatles at the peak of their fame succeeded in making some words famous. One of those words, of course, was the abbreviation for fabulous, *fab*. The Beatles were (and forever will be) the Fab Four. I'm not sure who originated the term, whether it was a Beatle or Beatles fans or a journalist or a publicist, but suddenly everything was fab, if you liked it enough. There was a magazine called *Fabulous* that was abbreviated as *Fab,* and the term was widely applied to the Beatles, and to their music and clothes and style in general. George Harrison considerably later wrote a song with Jeff Lynne reflecting on that fact, which qualifies as an F song, called "When We Was Fab." A cool record with some strings, a sitar, some psychedelic sounds, Ringo on drums, and all the proper '60s accoutrements!

We now come to a double F. The first F of this pair is the French horn, an instrument that does not usually feature in rock and roll or R&B arrangements and is more commonly heard as part of a symphony orchestra or as a solo instrument. Based on the original hunting horn, it has a beautiful tone all its own and has become a mainstay of classical music and film music in particular. Paul loved the sound of the French horn, and apparently he imagined it specifically on his song "For No One"—the second of this pair of Fs. He talked to George Martin about it. George wrote out the solo, and Paul said, "Who should we get?" George Martin knew and said, "We will get this new guy who's supposed to be amazing. He's the best. He's played in all the orchestras. He is the premier horn soloist."

His name was Alan Civil, and he was the leading French horn player in the whole of London. He came and did the session, and for a while, the musicians' world in London was abuzz with the fact that apparently, instead of nine pounds, which was regular session scale, he had asked for and received a recital fee of fifty pounds, which made people gasp. But now, of course, it's become one of the most famous solos in any Beatles record, and a brilliant piece of playing it is.

The story goes that Paul wrote a note in the French horn solo that is not officially part of the instrument's range; it's too high. But if you're a great horn player, the way you find notes is a combination of where the valves are set with your fingers but also what your embouchure can get out of the instrument. Alan Civil decided to go for it, and he played this officially unplayable note at the very peak of his horn solo.

"For No One" has been covered many times by many people, but to my ear the best non-Beatles version is by the terrific singer Emmylou Harris, one of Linda Ronstadt's favourite singers, one of my favourite singers, and also one of the favourite singers of someone I work with a lot, Albert Lee, who led Emmy's band, the Hot Band, for many years. Emmy is accompanied on her version by a wonderful group of musicians including Amos Garrett, Herb Pedersen, and one of my favourite pianists, Bill Payne from Little Feat, a band I had the privilege of managing for many years. One tends to think of Bill at his funky best playing "Oh, Atlanta" or "Dixie Chicken," but if you listen to Emmy's "For No One," you will hear exceptionally nuanced piano playing of perfect subtlety and precision. The Beatles did "For No One" in B major but Emmy moves it up to F, and she and the band even make a chord substitution, adding an A minor on the second bar which makes the song even more emotionally intense somehow—and Emmy's vocal will tear your heart out.

An F song which I really love, if we can keep our minds from wandering long enough to pay attention, is the remarkable "Fixing a Hole," another work of collective arranging of great brilliance. Every part merits a close listen. No one plays a shuffle better than Ringo, and this song is a very slow shuffle that could feel soggy in less skilled hands—listen to the unequalled groove of Ringo's hi-hat part. A lot of harpsichord, including the intro—I think both Paul and George Martin added harpsichord elements to this record. And some elegant yet rock-solid lead guitar work from George. One tends to take the excellence of some of these tracks for granted (so great is one's familiarity with the finished record), but the more I explore anew the nature of the arrangements, the more my admiration grows. And, of course, "Fixing a Hole" is a wonderfully original song to start with. And no, nothing to do with heroin or about that kind of "fix"—or even about fixing a roof in Scotland. I think it is more about Paul simply enjoying his recently acquired (and very beautiful) house in Cavendish Avenue and about the pleasures of sitting back in one's own home, smoking a joint, and allowing one's mind to wander.

There is no better way for us to end our journey through the letter F than with the last record the Beatles ever released, "Free as a Bird," which came out in 1995, along with "Real Love," as part of *The Beatles Anthology*. The song began life as a cassette from John Lennon which my friend Jeff Lynne organized and produced into a really good record, with contributions from the three other Beatles. George Harrison plays ukulele, among other things. If there had to be a "last Beatles record" at all (unavoidable I suppose), "Free as a Bird" is a good concept on which to end the chapter as we continue our exploration of the music of the best band there ever was.

We've been dealing with Beatles songs, Beatles projects, Beatles ideas, and Beatles people, and now we reach the letter G. Of course, I have no idea what time of day you're reading this book, but whatever time of day it is, I figure it could do no harm to wish you all a very good morning, with the Beatles' "Good Morning Good Morning"—a great John Lennon song. I love the weird rhythm of it. I don't know if any of you noticed or if anyone's counting, but there are various missing beats all over the place, which really keeps you on your toes. John was quite dismissive of the song in various quotes that are ascribed to him, but I like it a lot. He supposedly was inspired by a Kellogg's cereal commercial which was on the television one day while he was toying with song ideas, and that led him to write "Good Morning Good Morning."

Let us suppose it is morning for the time being. The sun is out, the sky is blue, and all one can say is "Good Day Sunshine," another

Paul and me in the studio with Mary Hopkin.

fine song, this one written by Paul and one of my favourite tracks off the brilliant *Revolver* album. Inspired to some degree by John Sebastian's lovely "Daydream," this song ended up as a truly wonderful record in its own right. From Ringo's immaculate triplet snare fill at the beginning to the surprise modulation and vocal round at the end, it is full of delightful surprises—all built around a seemingly effortless seductive slow shuffle.

I've mentioned before that Beatles songs can be very hard for other singers to cover effectively. But there is a really great cover version of "Good Day Sunshine," and I discovered that it is not very well known. I distinctly remember an R&B cover version being played all the time in the clubs in London around 1967. There was a small selection of London clubs where we all used to hang out at night, sometimes making a round of several of them in one evening. I specifically remember the Ad Lib, the Speakeasy, the Scotch of St. James, Dolly's, Tramp, and the Cromwellian. They all had excellent sound systems, and they all played this record, and it sounded terrific—but now it is largely forgotten. It is a brilliantly made, very American-sounding record, sung by Roy Redmond and produced by one of my musical heroes, Jerry Ragovoy, a very successful songwriter and a brilliant producer who is not as well known as he should be. He wrote "Time Is on My Side," first recorded (curiously) by the jazz trombone maestro Kai Winding in 1963, then by Irma Thomas in 1964, and later that year covered extremely well by the Rolling Stones. He also co-wrote, with Bert Berns, "Piece of My Heart," sung most famously by Janis Joplin. But to me, his towering achievement is that he co-wrote and produced a song called "Stay with Me," recorded by Lorraine Ellison. If you get a chance, listen to it. It's a classic R&B record. Lorraine Ellison is an amazing singer. What makes Jerry Ragovoy's achievement with "Stay with Me" all the more astonishing is that he co-wrote the song and created the complicated arrangement on a day's notice. Frank Sinatra had pulled out of a recording session at the last minute, and it was too late to cancel the large and excellent orchestra which had been booked. So Jerry jumped into the breach and made a classic record rather than let the musicians' skills and time go to waste.

We have been talking about Beatles songs that begin with the letter G, and there is a very important one that we cannot miss. And that is "Get Back," which was pretty much recorded as a live track, as I understand it. John played the guitar solo live, with Billy Preston playing some really cool piano stuff. There has been a lot of discussion about the song's lyrics—*Who was Jojo?* and so on—but my understanding is that Jojo is a compilation of various people. There is no specific Jojo. All the people running around claiming to be Jojo were not. I do believe, however, that the Tucson reference may have actually come from my assistant at the time. I was working at Apple as the head of A&R, and a remarkable and charming woman named Chris O'Dell was my assistant—and remains a friend to this day. She is from Tucson, and she talked about her hometown a lot, so I think she may be able to take credit for the Tucson reference.

Sadly, I missed the famous performance the Beatles gave on the rooftop of our office in Savile Row which included "Get Back"—I was working out of Apple's Los Angeles office (in the Capitol Tower) at the time. Despite my protestations to the contrary, I am frequently told that I can be seen in the video—but it really is not me! A fellow redhead by the name of Kevin Harrington was working as an assistant to Mal Evans, dealing with band equipment on that day, and he can be seen in several shots. I think that must be the cause of the confusion. I certainly wish I *had* been there.

Another very important Beatles G song, one that I hope applies to all of our lives, is "Getting Better," from *Sgt. Pepper's Lonely Hearts Club Band*. I heard at one time that "got to admit it's getting better" was based on a phrase used by the drummer Jimmie Nicol, who substituted for Ringo for about a week during the Beatles' Australian tour in 1964, when Ringo was ill with tonsillitis. He later also played with Peter & Gordon for a while. He was a very good drummer, but apparently his whole life after briefly being a Beatle got kind of odd. I think he is still around somewhere, and I hope he is okay. I have fond memories of him and his drumming.

"Getting Better" was mostly a Paul song. He says that he wrote the lyrics walking his dog Martha on Hampstead Heath one day. That was the origin of the song, and I guess things felt as if they were getting better for Paul. But then, of course, John inserted a few slightly less uplifting lyrics when he put in the bit about, "I used to be cruel to my woman," which, sadly, John occasionally was. He owned up later in his life to having been someone who did not always treat women particularly well. He also added a more realistic note to the song; when Paul said, "I've got to admit it's getting better," it was John who added the lyric "It can't get no worse," putting a cynical turn of phrase on things, which Paul loved. They ended up making a great song out of the contrast between their two attitudes.

Another G song, "Got to Get You into My Life," features one of the best horn sections assembled for a Beatles record. Paul, in particular, loved brass sections, like those on some of the best R&B and jazz records, and he used it to great effect on this brilliant song. George Martin worked closely with Paul on the horn arrangement, and it is exceptional.

There was a relatively small pool of incredibly talented saxophone players, trumpeters, trombone players, and so on, in London at that time, whom everybody used when they needed a horn section. Many of them also played on Peter & Gordon records such as "Black, Brown and Gold," our only attempt ever at a jazz track—with an all-star horn section and an arrangement by John Paul Jones, later of Led Zeppelin. These musicians formed the core of the British jazz scene, which was very healthy. Like the London rock and roll scene, the London jazz scene was based around our admiration for (and emulation of) our American idols, but there were some truly wonderful players in their own right.

The Beatles have often been accused of writing so many songs that are drug related, when very frequently they were not. People were reading things into them that were not there. I do not believe that, for example, either "Fixing a Hole" or "Lucy in the Sky with Diamonds" were *about* drugs, though I concede that the imagery in the lyrics might well have been influenced by the occasional consumption of such substances.

But at least in this one particular case, I know for a fact that "Got to Get You into My Life" *is* a drug-related song. It is a humble ode in praise of marijuana, about the fun of getting high and the temptation to get high every day. Take the line, "I was alone, I took a ride, I didn't know what I would find there." If that line is about a woman, it's meaningless. If it's about a joint, it means a lot.

We've been talking about Beatles songs beginning with the letter G, and a great one that we couldn't possibly leave out is "Golden Slumbers." The lyrics for this song apparently derive from lyrics written in 1603 by a man called Thomas Dekker. He wrote "golden slumbers kiss your eyes," and I have read that Paul saw those lyrics at his father's house. I don't know this to be true, but I gather there was sheet music lying around the house, and these lyrics caught his eye, and he used them and adapted them and set them to music. It had been set to music a couple of times before, but clearly never as successfully as in the version that the Beatles recorded for the *Abbey Road* album.

"Golden Slumbers" calls to mind another golden song that you may not know quite as well. It's a Ringo record that I had the honour of producing, and it is called "Golden Blunders." It was originally a Posies song, and I suggested to Ringo that we might try a cover of it. He liked the idea of "golden blunders," and he played and sang it extremely well. It was certainly fun working with Ringo in the studio—he was most cooperative and obliging, but it was never possible to forget that we were collectively making music with a Beatle and with one of the most important drummers in the world. When I mentioned to Ringo how good the hi-hat was sounding, he casually responded that he had brought the same one he had played on *The Ed Sullivan Show*. The other musicians and I were transfixed with a kind of awe to which he must be thoroughly accustomed. I am very proud to have worked with Ringo in the studio and equally proud to know him and his beautiful wife, Barbara, as friends.

We have moved into the territory of individual Beatles and away from collective Beatles, so let us turn to George Harrison. Possibly his most well-known G song is not a song he actually wrote. It was written by Rudy Clark and first recorded by James Ray. George's version, which was a huge hit all over the place, was co-produced by George with Jeff Lynne. It's "Got My Mind Set on You," with a rocking production and a truly invigorating and lively vocal from

George—more aggressively rock and roll than much of his solo work, and in some sense a reversion to his Beatles vocals. The song is also a bit more live sounding, perhaps inspired by the very crisp and precise track which Jeff constructed, as he does so well. And let us not forget the very creative Gary Weis video which was played everywhere and helped the record become extremely successful.

Paul McCartney wrote at least one really excellent G song which the Beatles did not record, and indeed he didn't write it for the Beatles at all. He wrote it for a production client of his by the name of Mary Hopkin. She was one of the first singers signed to Apple, shortly after James Taylor. The story of how we discovered her starts with Twiggy, who was of course a supermodel back when there was only one supermodel in the whole world. She is a brilliant woman of indefatigable charm and determination and a dear friend of mine and of Paul McCartney. As it happened, one night she was watching a TV talent competition called *Opportunity Knocks*. This beautiful Welsh girl named Mary Hopkin was on with her acoustic guitar, singing a Joan Baez song. Twiggy called her friend Paul and said, "You have to turn on your television. This girl is amazing. Listen to her." Paul thought she was amazing, too, and he called me, told me to watch, and then we all decided that Apple should try to sign her. So I drove up to Wales with Derek Taylor, who was one of the key people at Apple, to meet Mary Hopkin. Her father was understandably suspicious of these rock and roll types arriving from London trying to sign his daughter away.

But we did in the end succeed in signing her to Apple Records, and Paul had already decided what song he wanted to produce for her. He had heard the song "Those Were the Days" in a club called the Blue Angel some months earlier, sung by the American duo Gene and Francesca Raskin, and made a mental note of it. The melody was based on a Russian folk song, and Gene Raskin had written lyrics for it. When we signed Mary, Paul said, "We have to find that song 'Those Were the Days.' I want to do that song with Mary." And we did. Paul produced a beautiful version of it. I helped him put it together, and I was in the studio the day it was cut. Paul had a specific sound in mind which involved finding a cimbalom (a kind of Hungarian hammered dulcimer) and someone to play it—both of which I found. Mary sang a brilliant vocal, and Paul had his first No. 1 worldwide hit as a producer.

Paul then wrote a follow-up song to "Those Were the Days," a G song called "Goodbye," which Mary Hopkin sang beautifully. "Goodbye" featured an arrangement by Richard Hewson, whom I had brought to Apple to work on James Taylor's album. Paul and I used him for "Those Were the Days" and Paul stuck with him for "Goodbye." The arrangement Richard did for "Goodbye" incorporated many of Paul's favourite elements. The trumpet doing pa-pa-pa-pa eighth notes is very much a Paul kind of idea. Indeed, the little pitter-patter noise that Paul put in there for percussion is very Buddy Holly influenced, another of Paul's favourites. Paul McCartney, by the way, also played the bass on that record.

Around this time I produced my first record, at EMI Studios. The artist was Paul Jones, an amazingly good musician who used to be the lead singer of Manfred Mann, and the song was "And the Sun Will Shine," a Bee Gees composition I really like. As it was my very first production, I wanted to hire an incredible band—and that's how I ended up producing a record that has a definite Beatles connection. The band I hired was Nicky Hopkins on piano, Paul Samwell-Smith from the Yardbirds on bass, Jeff Beck on guitar, and on drums an aspiring young player of considerable ability by the name of Paul McCartney, who played some really good drum fills on the track and set a great groove.

G, of course, also takes us to the great country of Germany. And Germany is important in the Beatles' lives for many reasons, as you know. Before I ever met the Beatles, they had spent a lot of time in Germany. I was never there for any of those gigs, but I have been to the Reeperbahn subsequently, which is where the clubs were located. And as you may have read in some of the Beatles books or Beatles biographies, the Reeperbahn was and is a fairly naughty district. And we have it on good authority that the Beatles indulged in a bit of naughtiness themselves while they were there, as one does. It is kind of a weird fun place, and if you are there playing multiple sets at clubs every night for a few weeks, what on earth you might get up to one can only imagine. The Beatles obviously became fond of Germany and even learned some German as well. Which is probably why somebody had the idea of re-recording some of their songs in German. They re-recorded two of their biggest early hits, "She Loves You" and "I Want to Hold Your Hand," over the same musical tracks to create two new versions called "Sie Liebt Dich" and "Komm, Gib Mir Deine Hand." Their pronunciation sounds reasonably good to me, but I am certainly no expert. In time they found that their German fans would buy the English records anyway, so that saved them a lot of effort down the road.

Another interesting thing about Germany is that it is the only place where Gordon and I got to play with the Beatles on tour. I hung out with them on other occasions obviously and worked for them for a couple of years, but we toured with them only once, on the German tour, and it was extremely exciting.

We traveled on this extraordinary train that had been built for visiting heads of state, among them the Queen of England, when she did a royal tour of Germany years earlier. One of the carriages of the train, one full car, had been turned into four separate luxury bedrooms, thus providing one for each Beatle, of course. And I think there were a couple of other bedrooms, too—Brian Epstein certainly had one—each with twenty-four-hour room service and many other extraordinary conveniences that one would not expect on a train. Each Beatle could pick up the phone in his little cabin and order anything he wanted. I remember that attached to that coach was a huge dining room/conference room with a kitchen (a coach on its own) and next came a couple of first-class coaches with seats for everyone else (other acts, crew, and so on). Peter & Gordon's official seats were in that carriage, of course, but fortunately, being friends, we got invited up to the Beatles' elite carriages, so we were there in the big dining room, ordering food and drink, and playing poker. I distinctly remember playing poker with Brian Epstein and the Beatles sitting around one end of a very long table in these luxurious surroundings on this magic train whizzing across Germany, thinking, "This is pretty cool," and it was.

There is actually a video of that tour because one of the shows

Peter & Gordon on tour with the Beatles in Germany.

we did was filmed for a German TV show. Our set included several songs that Paul McCartney had written, not only "A World Without Love" but also "Woman." Paul had asked that "Woman" be released under a pseudonym, with the songwriting credit given to the imaginary "Bernard Webb." The reason for doing this was that some of the press were suggesting that the Beatles' stature had reached a point where anything with their name on it, or anything with a Beatle's name on it, would inevitably be successful, regard-

less of its intrinsic merit and quality. And I think this pissed Paul off a bit, because nobody likes to be thought of as resting on his laurels or relying on his name for success. The "Bernard Webb" deception worked for about three or four weeks before somebody found out that it was really Paul, and the cat was out of the bag, but in truth, "Woman" became a big hit very quickly, so even those few weeks were enough to prove that the success of the song did not depend upon the record having Paul's name on it.

Gordon and I went on, I recall, right before the Beatles did. While we were onstage in Germany singing this song, the Beatles were sometimes at the side of the stage, listening. Then when they went on, I cannot tell you how impressed I was with the vigour, precision, and musical excellence of their live performance. What is amazing is that they really could not hear one another; none of us could hear much of anything onstage. They really just had to guess where they were in the song and what everyone was playing and singing. I wish we had a live recording of the songs they performed in Germany. Had the concert been more recent, everyone would have had their phones up, and the concert would have been videoed and recorded from every angle. But sadly, we do not have any recordings. I just know that I watched from backstage with amazement.

Before we leave our discussion of the letter G, I'd like to acknowledge a sentiment that the world needs now more than ever, "Give Peace a Chance." This was John Lennon's first non-Beatles single, credited to the Plastic Ono Band—a name that John and Yoko coined for their joint projects. They described the band as more of a concept than a group of specific musicians—indeed, they were in the habit of assuring whatever audience members were in attendance that they, too, were members of the Plastic Ono Band for the evening! As years go by, John and Yoko's seemingly simplistic plea for peace and friendship seems more relevant and less laughable than ever—though the press at the time preferred to see it as mere silliness.

We began our journey through G by saying good morning, so the obvious way to end is to ask Ringo to be gracious enough to wish us all "Good Night." This beautiful John Lennon song (credited to Lennon & McCartney, of course) was recorded and released officially as a Beatles track but featured only Ringo, singing over an orchestra playing a lush and traditional George Martin arrangement.

The letter H is an extremely rich, productive letter in terms of Beatles stuff. So let us start with a song that opens with a legendary, instantly recognizable chord.

There are no prizes for guessing which song I am talking about—it is, of course, "A Hard Day's Night." I'm cheating a little bit by leaving off the "A" and considering this an H song because I think of it as "Hard Day's Night." The title is allegedly based on something Ringo said, and "It's been a hard day's night" does indeed sound very Ringo-ish. It was also the title song of the brilliant film

Al Coury presenting a platinum record to Linda Ronstadt and me.

directed in such an original way by the amazing Dick Lester. It is interesting that the reason *A Hard Day's Night* was shot in black and white wasn't to be cool—though it was. It was because of the parsimonious budget. United Artists didn't want to spend the money to shoot it in Technicolor because they were certain that the Beatles were going to be a wholly ephemeral phenomenon, here today, gone tomorrow. But, of course, it has now been tomorrow and tomorrow and tomorrow, and they are very far from gone. And the black-and-white film now looks timeless.

But let us return to the song, and the incredible chord that begins it, which has been much discussed. One can find tons of information and speculation online. Exactly what notes are or are not in that chord? The Beatles and George Martin have each answered that question slightly differently, and the reality seems to be that there are several instruments involved, and they each may be playing slightly different chords. There is a G7 with a suspended fourth at the heart of it, but George Harrison described it once as an F major with a G on top, which is not the same thing. I am convinced the truth is that no one is quite sure. While sonically speaking the Rickenbacker twelve-string is certainly the primary ingredient that gives the chord its intense and aggressive tone, harmonically it is more complicated because other guitars were overdubbed, plus George Martin's piano and Paul's bass, not all playing precisely the same chord, and it all gets mixed together. Who can be sure that everyone remembers exactly what they played all those years ago? One can find numerous claimants online and in books to a total understanding and successful untangling of "the chord," but they are not all the same. I prefer to allow the chord to keep its air of mystery! To imagine that somehow several musicians and several instruments combined to create a sonic and harmonic miracle which survives to this day. One way or the other, it is one of the best beginnings to a record that anyone ever invented, and it was the Beatles who did it.

If we are talking about the letter H and about Beatles movie songs, we can stay on both these subjects and find ourselves conveniently positioned to consider another great song that was also the title of a Beatles movie. Just a couple of days short of a year after they recorded "A Hard Day's Night" (April 16, 1964), on April 13, 1965, they recorded "Help!"—the title song for their next movie.

John sang lead on this song, of which he was the primary composer. It apparently began life as a slow mournful cry for help, but it ended up as kind of an almost jolly cry for help and certainly a big hit cry for help. But it was Paul who introduced this song to me. He played it for me before the Beatles recorded it, and I learned it just for fun because I thought it was a brilliant and unique song. I sat next to him while he played it, so I was able to figure out the chords—though it is not so easy learning from a left-handed guitarist! A little while after that, before the record was released, Gordon and I were on tour in the United States on the Dick Clark Caravan of Stars with the Shirelles, the Drifters, and a whole bunch of other American acts. And I couldn't resist shamelessly showing off to this busload of stars and saying, "Look, let me play you a bit of this. This is going to be the Beatles' next single!" I am not sure they believed me. I confess it was kind of cheesy of me, but as I said, I couldn't resist.

I played as much of "Help!" as I could remember just to show off that I'd heard it ahead of time. And then when the record came out and it was all over the radio, they said, "Oh, it was true. He really had learned one verse of the next Beatles single." That was a big deal because everything the Beatles did was so magical.

Not a story I am entirely proud of (pathetic, really), but it does at least accurately recall the intense and almost desperate anticipation with which the world waited for *any* new music from the best band in the land.

Help! is generally considered not quite as great a movie as *A Hard Day's Night* but still a good one and very funny and entertaining. Ringo was the star, and he was terrific. Ringo had a total naturalness on-screen that made him stand out and, in some ways, grounded the whole movie, however fantastical it became. The film also featured Leo McKern, a favourite actor of mine who finally became famous in the U.S. years later as Rumpole of the Bailey.

The Beatles had talked about various other ideas for a second movie including, strangely, a brief discussion about *The Hobbit* or *The Lord of the Rings*, in which they would have played the four hobbits. It was just an idea that floated about for a while—Stanley Kubrick was even mentioned as a possible director—but it does have a certain fascination, though who knows whether the Tolkien people would ever have entertained the concept. That certainly would have changed the future of the movie business. Peter Jackson might not have been able to make his fantastic series of blockbuster movies. You never know.

I also recall a meeting at Apple with the actor and producer Patrick McGoohan to see what ideas he might have because we were all committed fans of *The Prisoner*, the brilliantly surreal TV series he created after he initially came to TV fame via *Danger Man* (*Secret Agent* in the U.S.). You might even remember that in the very last episode of *The Prisoner* there was a long and mysterious underground corridor filled with jukeboxes playing "All You Need Is Love"—so the admiration was clearly mutual!

So, let's be fair now and turn to a George Harrison song. One of George's very best and most loved and most famous songs begins with the letter H: "Here Comes the Sun." He wrote it in Eric Clapton's garden while waiting for Eric, and it was recorded at EMI Studios in July and August 1969. George deserves our unstinting admiration for the brilliantly original acoustic guitar part alone—quite apart from the beautiful song for which it became the foundation. Astonishing in its chord changes, its unexpected harmonic leaps and apparent modulations—all while actually remaining in one key and one tempo. And George proves himself again to be the master of the well-placed arpeggio. He also made brilliant use of one of the very first Moog synthesizers. A huge and unwieldy machine (the term "user friendly" had not been invented), and yet George coaxed some perfectly beautiful sounds from it—in celebration of those rare moments when the sun makes an appearance in an English country garden.

And to complete the picture, we must include Ringo. I've mentioned him in this chapter as an actor but not as a musician. He made a good record of a song beginning with H—"Hey! Baby," produced by Arif Mardin and written by Margaret Cobb and Bruce Channel, Bruce being the artist who originally recorded the song.

I confess that when Ringo's version opens, I do pine ever so slightly, if momentarily, for the Bruce Channel signature harmonica intro (always the danger in covering a hit everyone knows), but once Ringo's version kicks in for real, I love the giant and boisterous singalong quality it has. And Arif's horn arrangement is superb.

Another very cool H track in the Beatles' world is "Helen Wheels," an excellent song written by Paul and Linda McCartney and recorded by Wings. Apparently, they came up with the idea for the song while driving to London from their house in Scotland in a Land Rover to which they had given the nickname Helen Wheels. I was never in Paul's place in Scotland; it is in the middle of nowhere and supposed to be spectacular. I am very fond of the Scottish landscape myself, bleak and even jagged in some ways but in beautifully muted colours and with an overall starkness that I find very appealing. An interesting thing about the song "Helen Wheels" is that it was apparently admired and chosen for a single by a promotion guy at Capitol Records called Al Coury, a brilliant man who ended up becoming the president of the company. Al and I first became friends back in the '60s, when Al was a local promotion guy and I was on tour with Gordon. He was always really good at picking hit records, which I witnessed personally years later when he picked a song called "You're No Good" which I had just finished producing with Linda Ronstadt and about which we were all very excited. Al was in the studio with us, and I played him the track. He said, "I will make that record number one, I promise!" And he was correct. He did it, and apparently he did the exact same thing for Paul McCartney with "Helen Wheels." Al was one of the greatest promo men in the history of the record business. Paul McCartney and I both owe him a debt, and we thank him.

Now, you may not be reading this chapter at the right time of year, but I do have to mention a very important H song that John Lennon wrote: "Happy Xmas (War Is Over)." It is extremely hard to write a brand-new Christmas song that stands up alongside all the classics and becomes a regular part of a lot of people's Christmas repertoire, but John managed it. This was a majestic and appealing song in the first place, and John made a great record of it.

Lots of people have covered it since, and at Christmastime lots of people sing it live. I produced a cover version of it myself. I was cutting a Christmas album with the amazing Neil Diamond, a terrific singer and songwriter and one of the most charming, smartest, and self-effacing artists with whom it has been my pleasure to work. I thought "Happy Xmas (War Is Over)" would be a good choice for Neil because it would suit his huge and majestic baritone. When making a record for Neil, one never has to worry about dwarfing his vocal with too much accompaniment—it is impossible! His voice is utterly commanding, so I went for size and added many layers of powerful stuff, and it just made his voice sound bigger and better. Finally, I added a children's choir on top because such is the nature of Christmas, and it suits the message of the song. The one I used was, not surprisingly, the choir at my own daughter's school, so it included my daughter, Victoria Asher, at the age of about eight. This was actually her first appearance on a record but by no means her last. As some of you may know, she ended up in the band Cobra Starship, making some hit records with them and being on the radio quite a bit. Now she writes, co-writes, and records on her own as Vicky-T, as well as working in film, her first love.

Turning from a song that John Lennon wrote, I'd like to mention one that John did not write but did sing. We all know that Ringo recorded a version with the Beatles of Carl Perkins's great song "Honey Don't," but until somebody pointed it out to me, I did not realize that John also sang it—and sang it very well. He performed it live during one of the Beatles' sessions at the BBC. The BBC did many live sessions with the Beatles and other bands in the '50s and '60s because there was a time limit on playing records (what was called needle time) each week, so the only way that the BBC could actually broadcast much pop music was to invite the bands to sing live in the studio. Fortunately, they had very good studios and equipment and engineers, which is why the BBC has ended up with this treasure trove of fantastic artists from back in the day. I had the pleasure of attending a few of the Beatles' live

BBC sessions—one of the only possible opportunities to hear the Beatles play and sing live without screaming girls drowning them out—and they sounded truly amazing. In accordance with Malcolm Gladwell's theory that it takes ten thousand hours to master a skill, I realized immediately how hours and hours of hard work and live gigs under fairly brutal circumstances had forged the band into an invincible musical quartet of singular synchronicity and style with four powerful singers.

While we are exploring the letter H, I have been thinking about the Beatles' friends and people they really admired, one of whom was certainly an H and a good one. That was Harry Nilsson, a terrific guy, an amazing singer, a brilliant musician with an astonishing brain.

John, because he admired Harry so much, produced an album with him called *Pussy Cats*. It was a generally good album, especially considering that they were both pretty much going nuts at the time. This was during John's "Lost Weekend," a period when he was overdoing everything a bit and perhaps having too much fun. And that affected the record, I guess, because, to be honest, some of the tracks do not sound quite as good as they should. For example, they recorded the classic rock and roll song "Rock Around the Clock," made famous by Bill Haley and His Comets. Considering that the track was produced by John Lennon, with three amazing drummers playing on it—Ringo, Jim Keltner, and Keith Moon—it should have sounded incredibly huge, impressive, and sonically miraculous. But I've got to say I was a little disappointed with the way the record came out. Three drummers (especially *those* three drummers) should sound earth-shattering, but this team did not end up with this result. Drugs can be fun, but they can also be destructive to any sensible organization of the creative process and can sometimes make you think you are accomplishing more than is in fact the case. I still like the *Pussy Cats* album and recommend giving it a listen while keeping these caveats in mind!

Around the same time, in that same group of sessions that John was producing, he was also beginning work on his own album *Walls and Bridges*. And that of course had a huge No. 1 hit on it—also, by the way, promoted and forecast for No. 1 by the great

Al Coury. It was "Whatever Gets You Thru the Night," with Elton John playing piano. John and Elton had become good friends, and in November 1974 John would join Elton onstage at Madison Square Garden in New York, to play a few songs during Elton's concert there. In addition to "Whatever Gets You Thru the Night," they played "Lucy in the Sky with Diamonds," which Elton had just released as a single, and their own version of "I Saw Her Standing There," a song we associate more with Paul McCartney. John even said to the audience, introducing the song, "We thought we'd do a number of an old, estranged fiancé of mine, called Paul. This is one I never sang; it's an old Beatles number, and we just about know it." And what a great version it turned out to be.

While we're on the subject of hard-driving rock and roll numbers associated with Paul McCartney, let's stop for a moment at a big H song, "Helter Skelter." In the studio, this was a conscious effort to make the loudest, dirtiest, crunchiest rock and roll track of all time. To catch up with and to outdo bands like the Who, who could be seen as "heavier" than the Beatles. And perhaps to inadvertently launch metal and punk on their eventual musical course? Perhaps. But certainly nothing to do with inspiring some total lunatic in California to associate the song with the Book of Revelation or some such nonsense, fail to even understand what *helter skelter* means, and embark on a horrifying and insane course of action.

The term *helter skelter* is much more common in the UK than in the U.S. and has two distinct meanings. As an adjective it means "in disordered haste." As a noun it is an old-fashioned fairground ride, of a sort common at the outdoor fairs I used to go to as a child, and I know Paul did, too. A brightly painted wooden tower with a spiral staircase inside and a spiral slide down the outside. One took a mat (like a doormat) from a pile at the entrance and then climbed up the inside staircase to the top, waited one's turn at the entrance to the slide, sat on the mat, and slid down, repeating the process as often as one could be bothered to get back in the queue. Hence: "When I get to the bottom I go back to the top of the slide / Where I stop and I turn and I go for a ride / Till I get to the bottom, and I see you again."

Helter skelter.

Leaving our doormats behind, if you ask people to name their favourite Beatles song beginning with H, I bet this next one might come out very close to the top. It was written by Paul, sitting by John Lennon's swimming pool in Weybridge while waiting for John. A brilliant song, "Here, There and Everywhere." The Beatles certainly made a very fine record of it, the three-part background "Ahhs" (straightforward triads, nothing fancy—no Brian Wilson swoops or anything like that) are lovely, but essentially the arrangement is very simple. "Here, There and Everywhere" is first and foremost a triumph of the art of songwriting—the combination of a beautiful and moving lyric with a delicious and memorable melody.

Now here is an H curiosity, the song "Hello Little Girl." It was written by John Lennon (reputedly the first song he

Henry Diltz took this photo of James Taylor and me just before he shot the cover for Sweet Baby James, *the first American album I produced for James.*

ever wrote) and recorded by the Fourmost, another band managed by Brian Epstein. I am a huge Brian Epstein fan. When James Taylor and I left Apple and we agreed that I would become James's manager, I looked at Brian as a role model. Like me, he had never been a manager before (he ran a record shop, and I was a performer), and his success proved that one did not have to have any specialized inside knowledge of the music business or unique skills; that intelligence, a willingness to learn, an absolute belief in the talent and ability of one's artist, an absolute commitment to their welfare and success, and fierce determination could actually do the trick—and we both had those qualities for sure. This does not mean that either Brian or I entirely avoided any business missteps or artistic mistakes—far from it, I am sure—but we were honest and determined, and we did get the job done. And in each case, we expanded our management operation beyond our original signings (the Beatles and James

Taylor, respectively) to include other acts. One of those, for Brian, was the Fourmost.

The Fourmost were a comedy group as well as a singing group. They were pretty funny, but they had only a couple of minor hits, and "Hello Little Girl" was one of them. John did sing it himself with the Beatles, but they never officially released it—though they did perform it as part of their (unsuccessful) audition for Decca Records in January 1962.

I am going to conclude by addressing two songs that begin with "Hey." The first is "Hey Bulldog," which is one of those songs that is more popular among listeners today than I imagined it would be. On the various SiriusXM listener surveys, it always ranks high. I like it, but it would not be in my top twenty. But allow me to move from a relatively insignificant "Hey" song (in my view) to undoubtedly the greatest "Hey" song ever written. (I think it even beats Hank Williams's "Hey, Good Lookin'," which is a close runner-up, along with Carole King's "Hey Girl" and Bruce Channel's "Hey! Baby.")

And of course that final H song is "Hey Jude." It is one of the best Beatles songs ever written, a magnificent song from Paul, building on a strong piano foundation and featuring great work by Ringo on the drums and beautiful background vocals by John and George. It was also, for those interested in such technical matters, the first song the Beatles recorded on more than four tracks. What is truly astonishing is that everything they had recorded up to that point, including *Sgt. Pepper*, was accomplished with only four separate tracks—recorded on one-inch, four-track Studer machines at EMI Studios—which drastically constricted the way you made records. It's one of the reasons that working in mono was much more practical than working in stereo, because you kept having to bounce things down to one track to free up more space on the next reel of tape. And once sounds were bounced together, they were bound together forever in that specific balance (which could not be changed) and neither could they be spatially separated in a stereo mix. So it was quite an adventure trying to fit things together with only four tracks to work with.

It turns out that EMI Studios had been in possession of an

eight-track machine for about a year that none of us knew about because they were keeping it in a back room and tweaking it to get it up to EMI standards. But another studio, Trident Studios, did have an eight-track, and they had no such qualms—when the studio owners (the brothers Barry and Norman Sheffield) took delivery, they just opened the box, plugged in the machine, and went for it. That is one of the reasons I chose Trident to record James Taylor's first album. Paul McCartney very kindly came over and visited one of our sessions, and he played bass for us on a song for that album called "Carolina in My Mind." Paul realized then how cool it would be to work on eight-track and decided to bring all the Beatles over to try recording a song there. And that's why they all came over to Trident to record "Hey Jude" in an eight-track format.

I had the good fortune of being invited to attend the end of that session. They had pretty much recorded everything, and they were in the process of starting to mix it. I arrived and heard "Hey Jude" on the gigantic Tannoy speakers at Trident Studios, and it totally blew my mind. If you can imagine hearing that song for the very first time, when you have no idea where it's going musically, it was an extraordinary experience. When the whole second half began (where the "nah nahs" kick in), I didn't know that all that stuff was going to happen or that it would go on so long or that it would be so totally amazing or that all of Paul's great sung interjections and soulful licks would appear when they did. I was totally knocked out. The arrangement is so masterful—and as each new sonic element enters (the tambourine! the strings! the horns!), one's excitement level and musical joy escalate exponentially.

"Hey Jude" broke a lot of rules. Everyone thought it was much too long to be a hit single. It changed the way we all made records because we now thought, *Wow, you can get that big, and you can add that many things, and you can stretch things out, and you can break some of the rules about what makes an obvious pop record—and still be successful.* Well, yes, if you were the Beatles, you could. And it was just another example of the Beatles' colossally iconoclastic revolutionary impact.

The letter I gives us plenty of songs to choose from, that's for sure. But first I am going to tell you a story.

When my parents offered Paul McCartney the spare bedroom on the top floor of our family home (next to my bedroom), it became his London residence for the next couple of years. So that allowed me the pleasure of getting to know him, becoming friends with him, and occasionally hearing songs in progress. My mother had a music room in the basement, where there was a small upright piano, a little sofa, and a music stand. When we first moved in, she used to give private oboe lessons there quite often. But as her job at the Royal Academy of Music grew

Mick and me.

more demanding and she spent more time teaching there, she used the room less frequently. She told Paul that if he ever wanted a piano to write on or to practise on, he was welcome to use the piano in the basement music room. And he often did.

Quite soon after Paul moved in, I remember one particular day when John Lennon came over; they were intending to write together that day. And the two of them went down to the basement music room, interestingly with no guitars—the guitars were upstairs, in Paul's bedroom and mine. John and Paul were just playing the piano down there, and they wrote a song. And when it was written, Paul stuck his head out of the door, called up the stairs, and asked me whether I would like to come down and hear the song they had just finished. I said yes. I went downstairs. I sat on the sofa. The two of them sat side by side on the piano bench and played their new song for the very first time anywhere. It was "I Want to Hold Your Hand." Just John and Paul, just one piano, and it sounded great.

I remember very distinctly the feeling of hearing that song for the first time. I remember how much I loved it and how astonishing it was. Hearing them sing together at full voice while both hammered away on the piano was impressive in itself—and of course they were singing this amazing song neither I nor anyone else had ever heard before. I told them how brilliant I thought it was, and I begged them to play it again, which they gladly did. And, of course, it turned out to be the song that would launch the Beatles' astonishing American career.

An almost equally famous I song which preceded "I Want to Hold Your Hand" was "I Saw Her Standing There," a similarly memorable and instantly appealing song. It was one of the first Beatles songs everyone got to hear because it was the first song on their first album recorded in their first sessions at EMI Studios. A song which had not only cool and evocative lyrics and a classic rock and roll melody, but also a defining bass line that Paul invented and played. It has become an iconic bass line; every bass player learns how to play it. I've always thought of it as part of the very essence of that song.

But something interesting happened decades later, when

Neil Young performed at the MusiCares tribute concert to Paul McCartney. He did a great version of "I Saw Her Standing There" with Crazy Horse and made a drastic change to the arrangement: he left out the legendary bass line. And guess what? It's still a great song. I love Neil's version, too. It's much more chunky and punky and simplified; the new bass line is just a one-note part and it totally rocks.

Now, "I Want to Hold Your Hand" and "I Saw Her Standing There" are both happy and optimistic I songs. But there are certainly some miserable I songs as well, including John Lennon saying, "I'm a Loser," and Paul McCartney saying, "I'm Down." These two depressing songs have very bouncy tracks, and yet each outlines unhappy circumstances and even self-doubt. But the nature of their pessimism is different in each song. In "I'm Down," Paul outlines specific situations which could cause disappointment and sadness ("Man buys ring, woman throws it away, / Same old thing happens every day") or profound frustration, both mental and physical ("We're all alone and there's nobody else, / You still moan 'Keep your hands to yourself!'"). Whereas John's song "I'm a Loser" outlines self-doubt of a more existential nature ("I'm not what I appear to be"), and though ostensibly the sentiment is wrapped within a story of lost love, one gets the feeling that John's concerns may be much more general. These same differences can be seen in the songwriters Paul and John might have been trying to emulate (or at least pay tribute to) as they wrote each of these songs—Paul aiming for Little Richard and John for Bob Dylan. Both are worthy heroes for any songwriter but in very different ways.

After wallowing in these depressing songs, let me revive you by assuring you that in reality "I Feel Fine."

I love the feedback at the beginning of this tune, the legendary Gibson J-160E guitar leaning against the Vox AC30 amplifier. (I still have one of each myself and love them.) It may well have been the first use anyone made of deliberate feedback on a mainstream pop record. And all the people who used feedback a lot later, like Jimi Hendrix and the Yardbirds and all the others, might have heard that feedback on "I Feel Fine" and felt inspired or even liberated. Some people used it onstage, but more often than not, feedback happened by mistake, and it was something one usually avoided. One might accidentally lean a guitar against an amp without twisting the volume knob down and walk away—only to be brought running back by a growing crescendo of unpleasant noise as the guitar sound started to loop through the amp back into the guitar and then back into the amp and so on with no end in sight until someone mercifully turned it down. The Beatles made a real virtue out of it, and indeed it became a key element of that song.

In contrast to "I Feel Fine," which has a real rock and roll feel to it, another Lennon-McCartney I song from 1964, "If I Fell," offers a different musical style. I mentioned in the letter B that John and Paul, like so many of us at the time (Peter & Gordon, Chad & Jeremy, Simon & Garfunkel, and others) idolized the Everly Brothers, with their impeccable close harmonies that gave their songs richness and emotional power. And even though the Beatles had four great singers, all of whom sang different parts and sang lead at various times, John and Paul could certainly be said to have comprised a duo within the band. They sang a lot of Everly-style thirds, close harmony singing, and did it exceptionally well. In fact, I would say that John Lennon and Paul McCartney were one of the best duos in the history of rock and roll even as they were also part of the best band in the history of rock and roll. They instinctively found the right notes (sometimes traditional thirds and sometimes more adventurous intervals) and phrased together impeccably, which takes a lot of practice. And perhaps the best example of John and Paul singing together in the Everly style and doing it so well is "If I Fell." The song is a relatively rare example of a brilliant and almost sentimental Lennon ballad—in a way a precursor to the masterpiece "In My Life," recorded a year later. One interesting structural note on "If I Fell" is that the opening section ("If I fell in love with you, / Would you promise to be true") is effectively a kind of preface to the main body of the song—very reminiscent of all those songs from the '50s and earlier which had an introductory "verse" before the song got going properly. Paul has often expressed his fondness for this device, and I think the opening section of "If I Fell" probably constitutes his contribution to what is essentially a Lennon composition.

John and Paul were not the only Beatles to write great I songs. George Harrison also wrote some excellent songs that begin with the letter I, including "I Want to Tell You," from *Revolver*. We all know that the issue of George's songs was, at times, a troubling one for the band—how many songs was he "allowed" to have on any given album? Was as much attention and hard work devoted to non-Lennon-McCartney songs? And so on. Yet hearing a great track like this one makes such concerns seem irrelevant. It is not only an excellent and well-written song but a beautifully executed arrangement and production. George must surely have been delighted with Paul's piano part, which is brilliantly conceived and fits the song so well. The startling half step piano lick F/E/F/E/F/E/F/E/F/E/F/E/F/E/F/E which first occurs after "things to say" is bold, original, and effective. The background vocal blend is precisely right, and Paul's overdubbed bass part perfectly offsets George's inimitable arpeggios. As with so many Beatles songs and Beatles arrangements, the more closely one examines them, the more their originality and collective genius becomes clear.

Another I song from George is "If I Needed Someone." Here George acknowledged a debt to Jim McGuinn—or Roger McGuinn, as he became later—the legendary lead guitar player from the Byrds. McGuinn's electric twelve-string style was in many ways the backbone of the Byrds' sound (along with their great vocal blend) and was something we all admired. George used some of that guitar sound in "If I Needed Someone," and it works very well. Much of the song explores the notes and the spaces around one chord (in this case an A major) in a way almost anticipatory of the Indian music George would come to appreciate and understand so well. The verse drops down to G only briefly (though the bass stays where it is) and quickly comes back up—but suddenly we get a full-on and impressive pop bridge as the lyrics move in a new direction, then back to the drone in A. And great harmonies throughout.

Finally, I would like to mention one more great George song, one of my favourites, "I Need You." A terrific song. There is a cover version of it I like, but I freely admit I am prejudiced because I love the song and the artists, and I produced it myself for a George Harrison tribute record. The singers are Charley and Hattie Webb, the Webb Sisters. You might have caught up with them on the road with Leonard Cohen or with Tom Petty over the last few years, though both these great artists have now sadly left us. The Webb Sisters sing incredibly well on their own, too, as they do in their cool version of "I Need You." On this cover version, though, I did leave out one of the signature sounds of the Beatles version which I do love but which seemed too specific to steal. That is the "mwa mwa" effect with which George's guitar part echoes the "need you" melody. This kind of effect can be created by a volume pedal operated with one's foot—but I am not sure whether George had one at that time. Some guitarists manage to twiddle the volume knob on the guitar itself with their little finger while playing—but the leading theory about "I Need You" seems to be that George played the part and Paul turned the knob up and down at the same time to create the perfect crescendo and decrescendo for each two-note phrase.

There is another pair of I songs that revolve around a particular theme, both of them written by John. After he sings "I'm So Tired," what else is there for him to say but "I'm Only Sleeping"?

"I'm So Tired" is from the White Album, a late-night composition written while John was tortured by insomnia in India and without alcohol or drugs around to address the problem—and it's certainly the only song to curse Sir Walter Raleigh specifically and directly for the introduction of tobacco!

"I'm Only Sleeping" features some brilliant backwards guitar from George Harrison. It is very difficult to record backwards parts because one has to figure out the exact phrase (in terms of both notes and rhythm) one wants to create when the recorded phrase is reversed. Then the notes must be played precisely as specified, after which the tape is run through the machine backwards. Not only does one get this cool peculiar sound of each individual note being reversed in terms of its attack and decay, but the notes now appear in the originally intended order and (if one has got it right) fit the track. George clearly *did* get it right. These kinds of tricks are relatively easy now with the flexibility and speed of digital technology, but back then it meant streamers of tape hanging from various places in the control room (and around one's neck) and could be quite a lengthy and confusing process.

To get to our next I song, I shall have to leave the Beatles aside for a minute and take you to a club in London called Ken Colyer's Jazz Club, where in 1963 and 1964 I used to go every Monday, on R&B night, when it was renamed Studio 51. There I would see another band who became, in some sense, the Beatles' rivals, at least in terms of public perception, and that was the Rolling Stones.

In truth, the Stones and the Beatles were mutual admirers. I remember going with Paul one night to see the Stones at the Scene club in London, and he expressed great admiration. His only complaint was that he was jealous that the Stones were allowed to wear whatever they wanted onstage—they had not been nagged by their manager (as the Beatles had) into wearing matching suits!

The Stones sang songs by Chuck Berry, Arthur Alexander, Jimmy Reed, the Miracles, Muddy Waters, all kinds of Chicago blues, lots of great stuff. But what they did not do at that time was write songs of their own. The Beatles, of course, were writing songs, and at one point, John and Paul wrote a song for the Stones.

It was called "I Wanna Be Your Man," eventually recorded by Ringo with the Beatles but written originally for the Rolling Stones. And the Stones made a very good record of it, which came out before the Beatles' version. The Stones used to perform this song quite often when I saw them live. And I must confess that Gordon and I also used to perform a folk-rock acoustic version of that song—probably just before the Stones started doing it live. We were just a guitar duo playing bars and clubs and pubs and coffee bars. But it was such an infectious song that after I heard Paul sing it (as soon as it was written) and teach it to the Rolling Stones, Gordon and I couldn't resist learning it ourselves. We never recorded it, but we did tell our audiences that it was going to be a Rolling Stones single and eventually it was. Of course, nowadays one could not do that because if one sang the song live, somebody would film it on their phone. It would be up on YouTube the next day and everyone would be furious. But we just did our little private version at our gigs and nobody knew.

I'd like to switch now from song titles and talk about a person whose name begins with the letter I, who has a distinct role in Beatles history, and that is Neil Innes.

You may be aware of Neil because of his contributions to the Rutles, the brilliant and hilarious Beatles parody invented by Eric Idle of *Monty Python*—himself an I name, a brilliant writer, and one of my best friends. Eric has significant Beatles connections, having been one of George's closest friends and a major figure in the "Concert for George" in 2002. But Neil Innes was also a member of the legendary Bonzo Dog Doo-Dah Band, of whom we were all devoted fans back in the '60s, to such an extent that Paul also worked with them in the studio. Their big hit record was "I'm the Urban Spaceman," with Vivian Stanshall on lead vocals. It was an odd but very appealing song written by Neil Innes and produced by Paul McCartney and Gus Dudgeon. It is a cool record and was a hit. If you get a chance, I highly recommend some exploration into the work of the Bonzos ("The Intro and the Outro" is another favourite) and into the fascinating life of Vivian Stanshall, whose brilliance and humour (and adventures with Keith Moon and others) are greatly missed.

Writing these chapters, I admit, can be a little bit nostalgic. Perhaps reading them has the same effect. So, let's take this moment to almost wallow in nostalgia and end the chapter with one of the Beatles' most poignant songs. A great song that begins with the letter I and talks about remembering things that happened in each of our lives.

"In My Life" is a Lennon masterpiece, though Paul did tell me that he came up with the beautiful little guitar and bass intro, which is also used as a turnaround between the two verses. He was apparently inspired by the guitar and bass intro to the Miracles' "The Tracks of My Tears," a brilliant Smokey Robinson song. I find these kinds of revelations so interesting in that one would never make that connection spontaneously—the two intros sound very different—but when the source of inspiration is identified, one can hear a progression from one musical work to the other.

When writing about music, one is indeed often circling around one of the most mysterious questions—where does great art come from? What we learn is that art of any kind, and perhaps music in particular, is in a continuous state of evolution. Musicians borrow from each other and are inspired by each other all the time—and when a great musician does it, the results of that inspiration or homage turn out very different from the original source and become inspirational themselves, opening new musical avenues for musicians of the future. It is abundantly clear that the Beatles belong in that elite company of musicians, including Bach and Mozart and Charlie Parker (to name but three of my favourites), who have changed music forever and opened artistic pathways which we lesser mortals dare to try to follow.

One of the most widely loved Beatles songs (in the general sense) is actually a Wings song that begins with the letter J, and that is Paul McCartney's "Jet," from the album *Band on the Run*. Most of that album was recorded in Lagos, Nigeria, but "Jet" was recorded entirely at EMI Studios in Abbey Road in London. It was the first British and American single to be released from the album, and it reached No. 7 or thereabouts in both countries.

What I didn't know, I confess, was that the title may well have come from the name of a black Labrador puppy. Songs do not always have only one origin and/or one inspiration and the story varies, but Paul has recounted it this way: "We've got a Labrador puppy who is the runt, the runt of the litter. We bought her along a roadside in a little pet shop out in the country one day. She was a bit of a wild dog, wild girl who wouldn't stay in. We have a big

Indica Books, in Southampton Row.

wall around our house in London, and she wouldn't stay in. She always used to jump the wall. She would go out on the town in the evening. She must have made out with some big black Labrador or something; she came back one day pregnant.

"She proceeded to walk into the garage and have a large litter, seven little black puppies and Jet was one of those puppies. We gave them all names. We had some great names. There was one puppy called Golden Molasses." That's a good song title if ever I heard one.

Then there was also one puppy apparently called Brown Meggs, named after a Capitol Records executive. I know that's a really obscure bit of information, but I remember Brown Meggs very well. He was a key senior executive at the Capitol Tower in Hollywood whom I liked very much for his obvious intelligence and for his unusual attitude. Most Americans we met seemed full of boundless enthusiasm, which was impressive—but Brown had a much more sardonic and sceptical approach to the record business, and to life in general, which was unusual, and I suppose came as something of a relief at that point. He was funny as well—and also clearly a man of taste since he was the executive who agreed to release "I Want to Hold Your Hand" as a single in the United States. I can certainly see why Paul would name a puppy after him. Anyway, that's all we know about Jet, the little black dog whom I never met. But I do love "Jet," the song named in his honour.

J is also, of course, the first letter of the first name of the greatest spy who ever lived, at least in our literary imaginations, James Bond. Mr. Bond had quite a bit to do with the British music scene in the '60s in a couple of different respects. First of all, the classic and instantly memorable and evocative theme music was played by a brilliant session guitar player called Vic Flick. Vic also played the lead guitar on "A World Without Love." So, thank you, Vic, a master guitar player for a master spy and for a pair of young and ambitious singers.

Of course, the other connection between James Bond and the Beatles is that Paul McCartney wrote one of the classic James Bond songs, "Live and Let Die." A very exciting movie and a terrific song to match. It may be the most famous Bond song, or perhaps second to Shirley Bassey's dramatic "Goldfinger," but certainly those two would be my favourites among the Bond songs. "Live and Let Die" is also usually one of the highlights of Paul's live show. Those of you who have seen him live know that the song is always accompanied by giant pyrotechnic blasts and explosions and fire all over the stage and is guaranteed to get the audience on its feet.

Now, since the theme of this chapter is the letter J, it would be both unfair and unwise to talk about Paul McCartney for too long because John (the J Beatle) would undoubtedly get jealous. We all know that he was capable of doing so, and indeed he wrote an entire J song on that very subject, "Jealous Guy."

"Jealous Guy" is a remarkably intense and honest song which John began writing in India and kept around for a while, changing the lyrics and adjusting the melody before finally releasing it on the *Imagine* album. The lyrics were originally inspired by a lecture given by the Maharishi.

John cut an excellent track of the song in London in mid-1971 with Nicky Hopkins on piano, Klaus Voormann on bass, and Jim Keltner on drums (one of John's favourite rhythm sections) but adding on this occasion Joey Molland and Tom Evans from Badfinger (who were around Apple a lot at the time) on acoustic guitars.

Lyrically, John acknowledges his jealousy and even his possessiveness—though the way I read the song it could apply not only to John-Yoko jealousy (of the usual marital kind) but also perhaps a little to John-Paul jealousy (of the two-brilliant-songwriters kind). Maybe it began life this latter way in 1968 and morphed into a Yoko-related song over the next couple of years.

Now, before George Harrison turns into a jealous guy, let's turn to one of his tracks, a great J song called "Just for Today," from his *Cloud Nine* album. This album was co-produced by George and Jeff Lynne and was both a critical and commercial success. "Just for Today" is a mournful song, asking not to feel sad and lonely just for today. Starting with solo piano, it is a beautiful and plaintive record. To me it actually has a little of the flavour and wistfulness of "Imagine" to it—even though John's lyrical wishes are more universal in nature and George's more personal.

George, as everyone knows, was one of the most creative and

significant guitarists in the history of rock and roll, but another fantastic guitarist (and an even more spectacular one) whose path crossed that of the Beatles was another J person, Jimi Hendrix.

My story about Jimi starts with Brian Epstein, who at one point in his career leased a theatre in London called the Saville Theatre. He had decided that it would be both productive and fun to have somewhere to put on shows himself. Brian promoted a series of concerts at the Saville Theatre which have become legendary in retrospect; so many great acts played there. Among these shows was one which included a set by the Jimi Hendrix Experience. Jimi himself had played in some of the clubs around London, at the Scotch of St. James and the Bag O'Nails, sitting in with other London musicians, and I'd seen him at one of those, and we had all heard about him. Everyone was talking about him and what an extraordinary guitar player he was. But then he went away for a while, working with his manager Chas Chandler, who was the bass player in the Animals, to assemble this new band, the Jimi Hendrix Experience, with Mitch Mitchell on drums and Noel Redding on bass. And their first London gig was going to be at the Saville Theatre on June 4, 1967.

Every traditional British theatre has a royal box that is reserved for the Queen, should she decide to attend whatever event is taking place there. Inexplicably, and no doubt she regrets it to this day, Her Majesty did not choose to attend the Jimi Hendrix premiere at the Saville Theatre in London, which meant that the royal box was available for Brian Epstein's use. And Brian, of course, invited the Beatles, and the Beatles kindly invited me. So I got to go to this show, sitting in the royal box with George Harrison and Paul McCartney, and watch this extraordinary concert. And no question, the act that we were all waiting for was the Jimi Hendrix Experience, who more than lived up to our sense of anticipation and totally blew our minds.

First of all, Jimi had just heard the Beatles' new album, *Sgt. Pepper's Lonely Hearts Club Band*, which had come out only three days earlier. And apparently he had learned the title song just by listening to it on the radio; he taught it that afternoon to the other members of the band and they played it onstage that night—and brilliantly well. As I recall, they opened the show with it, which completely surprised and astonished Paul and George. And then of course Jimi went on to do his whole show, playing the guitar with his teeth and behind his head, and setting fire to it, quite apart from playing brilliant, virtuosic, and highly original music. We were all totally overcome; to be fair we also had smoked a little hash, I have to admit, in the royal loo attached to the royal box—not the Queen's private stash, sadly, but some we'd brought with us. So we were a little stoned, but my God, seeing and hearing all that for the first time was an experience I shall never forget, and I was very privileged to have been there.

I met Jimi Hendrix properly only once—a conversation rather than just a post-show congratulation. I was at a party somewhere near Marble Arch in London and was quite nervous when I found myself sitting across from Jimi. Somehow, though, we ended up talking about science fiction, of which he turned out to be a knowledgeable devotee. We discussed our shared admiration for Isaac Asimov's *Foundation* trilogy and explored the philosophy and historical theories of Hari Seldon—who would have thought that we would bond briefly over psychohistory and mathematical sociology? But sadly I never saw him again.

When we weren't having our minds blown by the Jimi Hendrix Experience, Paul McCartney and I were both interested in avant-garde literature and plays and music and the experimental arts in general. A lot of it we were turned on to by our mutual friend Barry Miles. One of the writers we learned about from the profoundly knowledgeable Miles was the French playwright Alfred Jarry, whose most famous work was *Ubu Roi*, or *Ubu the King*. I have never seen the play onstage (it is not performed that often), but Paul and I both read it—and it is not easy to describe. Nonsensical, grotesque, and vulgar, it opened and closed in Paris on December 10, 1896, having received a literally riotous reception. In some respects, the story parodies *Macbeth* and some parts of *Hamlet* and *King Lear*, but the dialogue is obscene and childish.

In the course of his writing, Jarry also invented an entire "science," which he called 'Pataphysics (the apostrophe is intentional) and all things pataphysical. Equally hard to explain (because it resolutely makes no sense), it has been said that the science of pata-physics is to metaphysics as metaphysics is to physics. Does that help? It has also been described as the "science of imaginary solutions." Apparently one visitor to the Society of 'Pataphysics (which still exists), on pressing for a clear definition, was handed a list of a hundred different definitions. He was told to choose whichever one he liked. He was also told that most of the definitions were completely wrong but that it would not be pataphysical to try to say which were which. I confess I find all this entrancing—and it would appear that Paul found the world of pataphysics inspiring as well. The word *pataphysical* may, in fact, ring a bell with you, because Alfred Jarry—with a J—influenced Paul's lyrics to the very surreal song "Maxwell's Silver Hammer." Quizzical Joan, after all (and another J), studied pataphysical science in the home.

In addition to turning Paul and me on to avant-garde writers like Alfred Jarry, Barry Miles was part of a larger countercultural scene in London. The whole hippie age was beginning, when everyone seemed to be wearing beads and flowers and smoking too much dope and having a good time, and we all wanted to be part of this, too. We also related the hippie age to the beat movement that had preceded it, because we had all read Jack Kerouac's *On the Road*; I had even recited Allen Ginsberg's *Howl* in the school poetry reading competition at Westminster, which caused a bit of consternation. It is to the school's credit that they let me do it uncensored—and in a really bad fake American accent.

In 1966 Miles and I decided to team up with another friend, John Dunbar, and start a bookshop and an art gallery to try to create a focal point for this new and exciting counterculture. We loosely based it on places like the City Lights bookshop in San Francisco, which we admired very much. In addition to being exceptionally well read, Barry Miles had been a bookseller and knew all about the book business. As I recall, I first met John Dunbar because he was the brother of Gordon Waller's beautiful girlfriend Jenny Dunbar—strange how it all ties together. John had studied art at Cambridge University and knew a lot about the art scene—and the three of us decided to open both a bookshop and an art gallery. We named the enterprise Indica. We chose that name based on the

Inside the Indica bookshop, with Barry Miles and Jane. And at right, Paul's hand-drawn map showing how to get to Indica Gallery.

plant *Cannabis indica*. You may be aware of this plant—it's been in the news a lot lately.

The bookshop itself was at 102 Southampton Row. Miles managed the shop, but whenever I wasn't out on the road, I would go in and help, as did my sister Jane from time to time. And her boyfriend Paul was very helpful as well; I remember the day he helped us install the shelves immediately behind the counter. He was a useful chap to have around, you know—providing hit songs and shelf installations with equal facility. Then when the time came to start the art gallery at a separate location, Paul drew the map that showed customers where it was.

John Dunbar was always on the lookout for cool new artists, and we had several significant and successful exhibitions. In particular

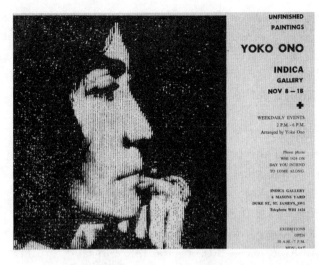

The advertisement in the International Times *for Yoko Ono's exhibition at Indica Gallery.*

John had heard a lot about an innovative Japanese-American artist by the name of Yoko Ono, and we all thought she sounded just right for Indica. So John got in touch with Yoko, and she agreed to do a show for us. We were very excited; she sounded really cool. Dates were chosen and plans were made. We took an ad out in the local underground paper *International Times*—which was actually published from the basement of Indica Books.

We arranged for a normal press opening, but we also invited our friends and family to come and have a look the day before. By this time, of course, the Beatles were included among our friends, so we invited all of them, and John Lennon came.

Here's his account of what happened:

> Yoko was having an art show in London at a gallery called Indica Gallery and I heard this was going to be happening, so I went down the night before the opening. Also the first thing that was in the gallery as you went in, there was a white stepladder, and a painting on the ceiling, and a spyglass hanging down. I walked up this ladder and I picked up the spyglass, and I see teeny little writing that just said *yes*. If it'd said *no*, or, something nasty, like *rip-off* or whatever, I would have left the gallery, but because it was positive, it said *yes*, I thought, okay, it's the first show I've been to that said something,

you know, warm to me. So then I decided to see the rest
of the show, and that's when we met.

Well, of course, being partly responsible for John meeting Yoko
for the first time could be seen by some as making me partly
responsible for the breakup of the Beatles, but I entirely reject that
responsibility and that whole perspective. I think Yoko's extremely
cool—she was then, and she is now.

Picking up our alphabetical journey, another J who played an
important role in the Beatles' career was Dick James. Dick started
out as a singer; he recorded the theme for the 1950s British television show *The Adventures of Robin Hood*, starring Richard Greene
(which also aired in America)—"Robin Hood, Robin Hood, riding
through the glen," and so on. In yet another odd coincidence, I
made several appearances in the *Robin Hood* series myself in my
days as a child actor. Several times I appeared as Prince Arthur
(protected by Robin from the threats of King John and the Sheriff),
and once with my sister Jane as a pair of "peasant children" whose
father had been wrongfully imprisoned by those same villains.
Dick later became a music publisher and through his close friendship with Brian Epstein ended up being afforded the extraordinary privilege of publishing the Beatles' songs.

It was no small thing to co-own the Beatles' publishing—in
conjunction with the Beatles themselves, but Dick controlled it.
And that was the beginning of quite a long story about where their
publishing has ended up, who bought it, who sold it, and so on.
There are various characters involved in this lengthy drama, Dick
James being one of the first, Michael Jackson being another, Sony
Music being another, and so on. Everyone made a fortune out of
it, and many continue to do so. The Beatles have always received
their songwriting royalties, but certainly their business lives would
have been a lot simpler and more profitable had they owned and
controlled their own publishing from the beginning. That said,
Brian Epstein certainly did nothing wrong—he correctly saw Dick
James as someone with connections who could be (and was) a
valuable ally in getting the Beatles' career off the ground and who
was a fellow believer in their music and their talent.

As you may know, Michael Jackson ended up buying John and Paul's publishing, following advice he got from Paul McCartney himself, who told Michael how well he had done owning copyrights. Paul owns the copyrights to many compositions by one of my great heroes, Buddy Holly (along with other major catalogues), and that has worked out extremely well for him.

But when Paul gave Michael Jackson this very sage advice, we can be confident that he was not expecting Michael to turn around and buy the publishing rights to Paul's own songs! And then at one point Michael is said to have declined to sell it back to Paul. All rather complicated and tense. I would imagine their relationship suffered a bit in consequence. But in the meantime, when the relationship was good, they recorded a couple of really successful songs together. And since Michael Jackson is a J, let's look at those tracks.

The first big hit for the duo was "The Girl Is Mine," which was written by Michael and was included on his incomparable *Thriller* album. Paul and Michael recorded the track in Los Angeles (with the legendary Quincy Jones producing), and several members of the band Toto played on the track. They were all seasoned studio musicians and are each famous in his own right. Jeff Porcaro was one the greatest drummers with whom it was ever my pleasure to work—he played on several Cher tracks I produced. The keyboard player David Paich is an all-around musical genius, and guitarist Steve Lukather combines amazing technical skill with the ability to totally rock out. You might have seen him doing so on the road of late with Ringo's All-Starr Band.

Paul and Michael's second hit together was "Say Say Say," which Paul included on his *Pipes of Peace* album. Paul wrote the song specifically to be performed by himself and Michael Jackson, and they recorded it at AIR Studios (with George Martin producing) while Jackson was staying at Paul and Linda's house in London. Some further overdubbing work was done in Los Angeles, and when it was released, the brilliantly catchy McCartney hook did its job and the record was No. 1 on the *Billboard* chart for six weeks. It is almost an R&B kind of groove and in a minor key— and reminds me a bit of the classic "Harlem Shuffle" in that regard.

Another J that you may not immediately associate with the Beatles is jazz. There have been a few great jazz versions of Beatles tunes, and I'd like to single out three of them. The first is by a brilliant jazz legend called Ramsey Lewis. He's an extremely soulful and funky pianist. In fact, he had a big hit record himself many years ago with an instrumental version of the pop tune "The 'In' Crowd," if you remember that, and even though he is a jazz player, I think even a dyed-in-the-wool pop fan can love the groove that he creates and the feel he gets as he does his jazz version of "A Hard Day's Night."

A second remarkable jazz cover of a Beatles song worth checking out is the brilliant version of "Yesterday" by a pianist and singer by the name of Shirley Horn. If you don't know her work, she's really good and well worth listening to. She makes this song almost unbearably sad. This was recorded on her very last album, and she was battling breast cancer at the time and had lost her foot to diabetes. But even in this depressing context, Shirley Horn's artistry gives us a deeply moving version of one of the most beautiful songs ever written.

The third jazz version of a classic Beatles song that I'd like to point out is much more cheerful. In the big band era, there were two killer orchestras, Count Basie's and Duke Ellington's. They had entirely distinctive sounds (one can tell within a few bars which band one is listening to), and they always had remarkable arrangements. Each band also had its own remarkable and distinctive soloists. To a jazz fan, if you hear Lester Young you know it is Basie and if you hear Johnny Hodges you know it is Ellington.

The Count Basie Orchestra recorded an arrangement of "All My Loving" that's truly excellent. It's bouncy. It's happy. It'll cheer you up after that sad version of "Yesterday." Count Basie himself plays the piano and leads the band.

You may have noticed that in this entire chapter, I have not mentioned a single J song performed by the Beatles themselves. That's because there is only one such song, and I saved it for the end. The letter J may have only one Beatles song, but it is one of the most gorgeous, moving, and intense songs that was ever written by anybody, let alone by Lennon & McCartney. It is John Lennon's classic masterpiece "Julia."

The lyrics to this song are very beautiful, and they also provide an example of the breadth of John Lennon's reading and curiosity. The '60s saw a resurgence of interest in a Lebanese-American poet called Kahlil Gibran, who was born in 1883 and first became popular in the 1920s. By the mid-'60s his book *The Prophet* was widely quoted at weddings and so on—and clearly John had read his work as well. The line "Half of what I say is meaningless, / But I say it just to reach you" is only a slight alteration from Gibran's *Sand and Foam*, in which the original verse reads, "Half of what I say is meaningless, but I say it so that the other half may reach you." John also adapted the lines "When I cannot sing my heart, / I can only speak my mind" from Gibran's "When life does not find a singer to sing her heart she produces a philosopher to speak her mind." I see this kind of "borrowing," which happens all the time in all the arts, as a high compliment and a joy—and I also think the words and sentiments in question are even more effective when adjusted and set to music than they were on the page. And it is interesting to be able to see what, beyond John's love for his mother, Julia, inspired this remarkable song.

John always felt that he had lost his mother twice; once when he was sent to live with his aunt (a complicated story) and again when Julia died young in a shocking traffic accident. John's evocation of his late mother is haunting and yearning and vulnerable all at once. It turns out that no one can sing a song of love, or write one, more touchingly than the acerbic and sometimes even angry genius that was John Lennon.

As we continue our roving voyage through the alphabet, we come to the letter K.

I am going to start this chapter by talking not about a song but about a person. Somebody who was very important to the Beatles, a great friend of the band, and a very talented man in so many respects: Klaus Voormann. I like and admire Klaus very much;

Klaus Voormann with some of his artwork.

I remember meeting him back in the day, and we have run into each other on several occasions since. Quite recently I had the pleasure of interviewing Klaus onstage at a Fest for Beatles Fans and was impressed all over again by his understated but intense intelligence and his acute artistic sensibility.

He is a brilliant musician, and he played on a lot of solo Beatle tracks. But his exceptional musical talent has perhaps been overshadowed to some extent by his now legendary achievements as a graphic artist. I am speaking, of course, of the creation of some famously hairy album art—the cover of one of the most famous Beatles albums, and one that many people consider the best Beatles album ever, *Revolver*.

Klaus was a very old friend of the Beatles. He knew them back in Germany. He has been described as a Beatles confidant, inventor of the moptop haircut, and member of the group's inner circle of friends, back when they were playing Hamburg bars and strip clubs—long before I met them. He actually wrote a pretty amazing graphic novel, telling the story of his relationship with the Fab Four in pictures, called *Birth of an Icon, Revolver 50*.

In his book, Klaus recounts that when the Beatles were recording *Revolver*, John Lennon asked him whether he had any ideas for the next album cover and invited him to EMI Studios to hear the album in progress. It was about two-thirds done, and the playback ended with the radical (and almost frightening, at the time) "Tomorrow Never Knows."

Revolver has been described as psychedelic, which some of the music certainly was. "Tomorrow Never Knows" is undoubtedly a track influenced by psychedelic drugs one way or another. But Klaus himself felt that his graphic work was not. He said, "In choosing to work in black and white, I wanted not only to shock and surprise, but I wanted also for the work to stand out in a muddle of colour. But a psychedelic influence on the *Revolver* cover? Well, what is psychedelic? Look at Bruegel, or Hieronymus Bosch. Those guys were far out! I don't know if they ate mushrooms, or whatever. But I know that whatever is inside of you doesn't have to come out through drugs."

I find that very interesting. And let's face it, it is exceedingly rare for an album to be equally acclaimed for the genius of its cover art as for the genius of the music on the album itself. And that's what happened in this case.

Klaus worked in pen and black ink, dotted with cut-out portions of photographs of the band members and forming a "waterfall" of imagery. It apparently took him about three weeks of intermittent work to create the cover. Much of that time was spent with scissors, scalpel, and glue, selecting and arranging fragments of photographs within line drawings of the band members. The result was well worth the work involved. Everyone talked about the cover, and it won a Grammy for album cover of the year. Brian Epstein had been worried about whether the public would be accepting of what, in some instances, seemed to be a very new and interesting and involved kind of music. But when he saw Klaus's cover, he felt that it totally integrated the music into the real world and in a way helped it to "cross over."

Klaus Voormann was not only an extraordinary graphic artist who did that legendary cover—for a fee of fifty pounds, by the way, which was EMI's highest possible rate at the time for an album cover design—he was also a skilled and tasteful musician and still is. A wonderful bass player, he was one of John Lennon's favourite accompanists as well as being someone everyone liked to have around. He was very well liked in every respect and remains so. And his bass playing is extraordinary. He played on tracks for at least three of the Beatles at one time or another in their solo careers.

Perhaps the most notable was John Lennon's immortal "Imagine," on which Klaus played bass and the great Alan White played drums—one of John's most famous tracks, and a brilliant song it is. Sometimes, when it comes to bass parts, less really *can* be more—for certain songs restraint is the name of the game. Some bass players might have wanted to add more melodic lines to "Imagine" (even Paul, genius that he is, might have done so) or to have followed some movements of John's left hand on the piano. But Klaus stuck to the most basic possible part—big fat root notes (in this case mostly C's and F's) and a simple descending line, elegantly leaving all the drama to John's vocal and the lyrics.

Klaus played for Ringo many times; one song that sticks in my mind is "It Don't Come Easy," where he took an entirely different approach from the simplicity of "Imagine" and threw in some cool moving lines and syncopation, especially under George Harrison's solo. And Klaus also played on George's huge hit record "My Sweet Lord," though one of the really interesting and effective things about that production is that the bass and drums do not even start playing until about two minutes into the arrangement—leaving the rhythm entirely to the impressive bank of pounding acoustic rhythm guitars.

Klaus also played for one of the artists we signed to Apple Records, a great R&B singer called Jackie Lomax, who was produced by none other than George Harrison. I went to a couple of the sessions for Jackie's album at EMI Studio Two. On these particular dates, it was Eric Clapton and George Harrison playing guitars, Ringo playing drums, and Klaus playing bass—it sounded truly great, a perfect rock and roll rhythm section. I don't know whether Eric and Ringo had ever played together before because I remember Eric telling me at the end of one of the sessions how impressed he was by Ringo's playing. I think we all sometimes take the excellence of Ringo's drumming for granted—he repeatedly proves that it is possible to be one of the best and most important drummers in the world *without* being a flashy, soloing virtuoso. The fine album that emerged from these sessions was called *Is This What You Want?* and included the single "Sour Milk Sea," on which Paul (rather than Klaus) played bass, making it a rare case of three Beatles playing together on a non-Beatles record.

In the Beatles' catalogue, there are not many K songs at all. One of these, a classic McCartney vocal of undeniable excellence and soulfulness, was a song they did not write. It was written in 1952 by the brilliant duo of Jerry Leiber and Mike Stoller—a really cool blues-based song first recorded by Little Willie Littlefield and called "Kansas City." It became a No. 1 record when it was recorded by Wilbert Harrison seven years later, and it gradually became one of Leiber and Stoller's most recorded tunes, with more than three hundred versions, including a great one by the Beatles with a killer vocal by Paul McCartney. Leiber and Stoller were among the Beatles' favourite songwriters, and the band had probably heard the Wilbert

A Commander of the Most Excellent Order of the British Empire.

Harrison hit—but they also would have heard Little Richard's version live when they toured with him. To my ear, the Beatles' version tops both of those previous recordings—it has a much more urgent feel to it. In this instance, Ringo's unique feel for a rock and roll shuffle is aided by the eighth-note triplets that George Martin added on the piano—a part neither of the other versions included. And the twin electric guitars of John and George are perfectly locked together, providing solid support to Paul's intense vocal.

Of course, we now should call him *Sir* Paul because he was made (by Her Majesty the Queen) a K himself, a knight of the realm. No one actually says, "Arise, Sir Paul," at the ceremony, unfortunately. I think that only happened back in the days of King Arthur. But it is still a fantastic event. I got to watch it up close when I was myself given a CBE (Commander of the Most Excellent Order of the British Empire) at Buckingham Palace—a considerably lesser honour, of course, but one of which I am immensely proud, I confess. The ceremony also included the awarding of several knighthoods and damehoods (the female equivalent). When being created a knight, you do actually get to kneel down on a little raised red velvet cushion (kind of like in church but with a tall handle to make it easier to kneel down and get up again), and the Queen (or a member of her immediate family) does take a sword and tap you on the shoulder, and you are then Sir Somebody, in this case, Sir Paul—whose status was upgraded even further in 2018 when Her Majesty made him a Companion of Honour, an extremely illustrious order of which there can only be sixty-five members at any time. An exceptional and rare honour—which comes with some lovely new bling as well.

This discussion of Sir Paul being a knight keeps our attention on the letter K and allows us to talk about another recent knight in our narrative, Sir Richard Starkey. I think I speak for all of us in congratulating him enthusiastically on this fine achievement. I have seen pictures of Ringo receiving his knighthood in an extremely elegant morning suit, which is the official attire you wear for your audience with Her Majesty the Queen. He was wearing a gorgeous version, made to measure by the great designer John Varvatos. It looked really cool. (See, you even get a little bit of fashion news from Peter Asher.) So in light of his new honour, let us allow Sir Richard to declare loudly and for all to hear without fear of contradiction, "I'm the Greatest." In that song, written by John Lennon, his mama tells him he's the greatest, his friends tell him he's the greatest, his woman tells him he's the greatest, and finally now, by bestowing a knighthood upon him, the Queen, Her Majesty herself, has told Ringo he is officially "the greatest." And, yes, certainly anyone who gives Ringo a knighthood qualifies as a pretty nice girl in my book, so well done, Your Majesty, and thank you very much.

There are a few interesting Beatles-related K songs. One of them is a Yoko song. I confess I sometimes find some of Yoko's music a bit too weird for me. But some of it is really cool. And "Kiss Kiss Kiss," from the *Double Fantasy* album, is charming. I like it a lot and it's a good record.

Sticking with the letter K, we find a slightly obscure Paul track, but one well worth listening to, "Kreen-Akrore," which he recorded on February 12, 1970, at Morgan Studios in London. A percussion-led instrumental piece (or at least with no lead vocal), it features electric guitars, choral-sounding background vocals, and more to create an evocative sonic landscape inspired by the Kreen-Akrore tribespeople of the Amazon rain forest. The song reminds us that, on top of everything else, Paul is an excellent drummer and percussionist.

There is also a really good K song on Paul's album *Pipes of Peace* that people do not seem to know well but which I enjoy, "Keep Under Cover." Paul talks about the joys of staying in bed, among other things. (Perhaps an echo of John's wonderful "I'm Only Sleeping" from *Revolver*.) The song has a fine string arrangement by George Martin, who produced the album.

There is actually another "Keep" song that the Beatles played, which deserves to be better known. This is all to do with a K songwriter whom the Beatles truly admired, and of whom I have long been a besotted fan: the great Carole King. She is certainly one of the best K songwriters of all time—and one of the best songwriters in popular music regardless of alphabet! Carole's story is an extraordinary one. With her husband, Gerry Goffin, she wrote "Will You Love Me Tomorrow" when she was only eighteen, which became a No. 1 record for the Shirelles, and she never looked back, writing hit after hit for a series of acts and becoming very much admired by the Beatles and all the rest of us. When I moved to Los Angeles, I made a point of getting to know Carole, and she did James Taylor and me the honour (at my invitation) of playing all the piano on the album *Sweet Baby James*. This proved to be the beginning of a long and productive musical relationship for the three of us. James sang (and I produced) her song "You've Got a Friend" just as she finished her record-breaking album *Tapestry*, and I managed Carole for a while.

Here I am talking about a K song that Carole wrote which is not that well known. It was the follow-up to the huge No. 1 hit "The Loco-Motion," written by Goffin and King and recorded by Little Eva, who was originally Carole and Gerry's babysitter, strange as that may sound. Carole and Gerry followed it up with a song called "Keep Your Hands off My Baby." Now oddly, even though I know for a fact that the Beatles were giant Carole King fans as well, they did not record many of her songs. I think the only one of which they made a full studio recording is "Chains," and that one everybody knows. But they did sing this other song, "Keep Your Hands off My Baby," in their live set. And we know that because there's a BBC recording of them doing it. It's certainly worth seeking out.

Our only remaining K song from the Beatles is "Komm, Gib Mir Deine Hand," which we already talked about under G for Germany.

You know what? I still think it sounds better in English anyway.

We are now almost halfway through the Beatles catalogue at an alphabetically inspired yet meandering pace, arriving at the letter L. Which may give us a good reason to look backwards and start this chapter at the beginning of the Beatles' success as recording artists, a perfect L song and eventually a big hit even in America, though it happened a bit slower there than it did in the UK.

"Love Me Do" was the Beatles' first single, released in the UK on October 5, 1962, and it was the first time we all noticed them and became aware of how original and how musically remarkable they were. The amazing thing is that "Love Me Do" still sounds

George, Pattie, Ringo, and Maureen (and me) returning from a trip.

much more powerful and memorable than anything else that was around at the time. It is a masterpiece of simple production and instinctive, but by no means simple, musicianship. For example, John plays some exceptionally good (and unexpected) harmonica on this track.

"Love Me Do" is a well-structured song—a traditional verse-verse-bridge-verse structure—but it nonetheless toys with pop-composition norms in that the first verse is effectively thirteen bars long and the second is twelve, where one would expect only eight in each case. Paul apparently began writing the song as a teenager, finishing most of it before he and John ever began writing together. But even the simple lyrics do not detract from the immediate musical appeal of the catchy intro and the beautiful blend of John and Paul's harmony singing—with Paul singing the melody as the high part with John's harmony underneath—another unusual variant.

Before long, Lennon & McCartney began writing together pretty much full-time—often to satisfy urgent delivery deadlines. They wrote so many amazing songs, including many where they sang together as a duo and some on which (with the addition of George Harrison) they made an equally impressive trio. This trio can be heard to great effect on another early Beatles song, "This Boy," a great example of their beautiful three-part harmony, in an arrangement that owes quite a lot to John and Paul's huge admiration for Brian Wilson and the way he arranged harmonies on the Beach Boys' records.

Exploring the letter L means, of course, exploring the Lennon family in all its complexity. Let's start with one of my favourite songs that John Lennon ever did, "Whatever Gets You Thru the Night." I mentioned this song in passing when we discussed the letter H, but here I'd like to linger on it in a bit more detail. Apparently, John got the title from watching the Reverend Ike.

When I first came to America, I was entirely astonished by American television in general. Coming from a country about to acquire only its third channel (when I was a child, we had only one channel, the BBC, with very limited hours and no commercials), I was dumbfounded by the plethora of channels and the frequent and seemingly endless commercials. And when I channel-hopped among the various televangelists on Sunday mornings, I knew for sure that I was in an alien country. They were all so extremely strange! Even so, I rapidly identified the Reverend Ike as my favourite. No less rapacious or nonsensical than the others, he was at least more direct and specific: it was all about money. He was a fine speaker and preached very directly that if you sent him a donation and prayed hard enough, a lot of money would come your way. God wanted him to be rich—God's will was clearly being done in his case, and it could happen to you, too. It was a very interesting theory, that if you prayed enough, you would become very rich and have luxury cars and jet planes. (If only that were true—I might have to take up prayer at this late stage of my life!) But anyway, watching the Reverend Ike expound upon his bizarre philosophy live on TV apparently inspired John to write this very good song. One night when he heard the preacher say, "Let me tell you guys, it doesn't matter, it's whatever gets you through the night." John loved the phrase and wrote it down, and it became a song. Great groove on the record, right from the top, which is not surprising when you consider that Elton John is on piano and sings harmony, along with Jim Keltner and Klaus Voormann and the usual suspects.

Turning from Lennon senior, let's look at the two Lennon juniors, both of whom have written some really good songs and have made some excellent records. We can start with Julian Lennon and one of my favourite tracks that he did, "Too Late for Goodbyes." Kind of a reggae groove, a fine song, and Julian's biggest hit single, going top ten in both the U.S. and the UK. The very brief harmonica solo is by the amazing jazz player Toots Thielemans— possibly the best chromatic harmonic player who ever lived—a little underused in this instance, I would venture to say.

And then we get to Sean Lennon, Julian's younger half brother. If one wants to get a sense of his talent as a musician, one cannot do much better than to listen to his excellent song "Home." It's from the album *Into the Sun*, and it also had a very cool video, directed by Spike Jonze, the brilliant filmmaker. It's worth tracking down and watching.

Now, let's get back to the Beatles' own generation, rather than their offspring, and talk about some great Beatles L songs. There are lots of them. I'll start with a real favourite of mine, "Lovely Rita." I remember when parking meters were introduced in London. It was 1958, and everyone was totally appalled. I mean, before that time, you could park your car anywhere you could find a space for it—and for as long as you liked. And suddenly this horrendous American invention was being imposed upon us. They started putting in these ghastly machines, including several right outside our house. We'd been parking in Wimpole Street with impunity ever since we had moved in, and suddenly we couldn't do so anymore. *Bloody outrage!* we thought, but we couldn't get rid of them.

Then, of course, came the parking wardens, whose responsibility it was to give tickets, and they were widely hated and derided. I remember the English papers having pictures of the uniform, and "Here's what it's going to be like, here's how much the fines are going to be," and so on. It was really very grim, which made the song especially cool when it came out. The idea of a parking meter warden being an attractive woman whom one might ask out on a date was radical. And it is part of Paul's genius that he just finds things to write songs about that no one else would even imagine, like "Back in the U.S.S.R." or "Eleanor Rigby." And this was no exception. Parking meters are here to stay, and maybe one of the only benefits that I can possibly imagine is Paul McCartney's ode to Rita, the lovely meter maid.

Another L song, a Beatles classic that we could not possibly ignore, also from the *Sgt. Pepper* album, is "Lucy in the Sky with Diamonds." When Paul first played me an early version of the song, I remember him telling me about a very young Julian Lennon bringing home a drawing of his friend Lucy against a sparkly sky, and when his father asked him what it was, Julian explained that it was Lucy in the sky with diamonds. And, verbatim, it was an inspiring song title. I may be unduly naïve, but I know that at the time the fact that the initials of the song title added up to LSD never even occurred to me, and I truly believe that it did not occur to John or Paul either. Had they taken acid by that time? Yes. Did that fact influence the lyrics and imagery of the song? Probably, though I think Lewis Carroll and Alice had even more to do with it.

But I do believe that the perceived connection between the song title initials and the drug was a genuine and total coincidence.

Musically, "Lucy" is a remarkable composition, waltzing us through the dreamy verses in 3/4 time only to have our attention riveted by Ringo playing the world's simplest drum fill (three giant quarter notes) and being led thereby into the rocking chorus in 4/4 time.

Another Beatles song that is undoubtedly a classic, but also a source of some dispute and even some anger, is "The Long and Winding Road." As you probably know, the song was originally recorded without an orchestra, but when Phil Spector was brought in to turn the "Get Back" sessions into the album which became *Let It Be*, he decided to add an orchestra, but without the cooperation and approval of Paul McCartney, who had written the song. This was unwise. And even though there are people who like the orchestral version and people who don't, it was at one point a source of some ugliness.

Caught in the middle of the controversy was my friend Richard Hewson, who wrote the arrangement, which is very beautiful. Richard did a perfect job, little realizing that Paul might be pissed off because he didn't know that it was even happening. Richard was a jazz trumpet player and classical composer with whom I played double bass (very badly) in a little jazz group for a while. We rehearsed in the Wimpole Street basement music room from time to time—probably more rehearsals than actual gigs, I would think. Carting the bass around on the tube for a gig which only paid a couple of pounds was barely worth the effort!

When I decided to add some orchestral arrangements to the very first James Taylor album (the one called *James Taylor* and made for Apple Records), I thought of Richard because I knew he wrote classical music and was a master of the orchestral idiom—and I did not want the arrangements to be standard pop. I could have easily gone to someone like Geoff Love (who did all the excellent Peter & Gordon orchestrations), but I wanted to aim for something more offbeat. And that was how I brought Richard into the Beatles' world and how he met Paul McCartney. Paul liked what Richard had done for James's record, so Paul and I invited him to write the arrangement for Mary Hopkin's "Those Were the Days," and he did that brilliantly and much more besides. In that sense, Richard became sort of Apple's favourite arranger at that time, which must be why Phil Spector went to him to write the big string chart for "The Long and Winding Road," Richard being unaware of the fact that Paul was not on board and was not part of this process at all. Anyway, somehow in all that mess, there ended up being two separate versions: the Phil Spector version with a huge orchestra, which Paul did not like, and then, finally, the "naked" version, the original no-orchestra recording that was Paul's favourite. To be honest, it is the version I like better as well. While it is true that Richard wrote a beautiful string arrangement (it is orchestrally superb), there is nonetheless something more emotionally riveting about the unadorned clarity of Paul's vocal without the orchestra.

An interesting story that I had not heard until recently is that Paul McCartney had originally offered "The Long and Winding Road" to Tom Jones before the Beatles recorded it. They were going to record it anyway, but Paul expressed interest in having Tom do a version, and he would have sung it incredibly well. Somehow, it never happened. Tom's record label already had his next single lined up, and the only way to do "The Long and Winding Road" was to do it quickly before the Beatles' record came out. Sadly, this never happened. But that is an interesting Tom Jones and Beatles connection.

If you're looking for another artist's interpretation of this magnificent song, Ray Charles recorded a fantastic cover of "The Long and Winding Road" with the Count Basie Orchestra, which is my personal favourite of Ray's covers of Beatles songs. It's certainly worth checking out.

The next L song on our journey is one that not everyone likes that much, but I am very fond of it: "Little Child." The Beatles themselves apparently looked down on it as being formulaic and not thoroughly creative. It was written for Ringo but ended up being sung by John and Paul, with John playing a strong harmonica part, as he did on "Love Me Do" and so many other early Beatles tracks. I think Ringo could have sung it very well; it's his kind of song, but he never got the chance.

Now let's give George some attention, with a really interesting L song, "Living in the Material World." It was written when George was very much under the influence of the Hare Krishna people, who were all hanging around Apple at the time in their beautiful saffron yellow robes. It is a song that contrasts the material world in which we live with the spiritual world. George actually said that the message of the song is "We are not these bodies. We are in these material bodies in the physical world." I have read that the song condensed lengthy passages from the *Bhagavad Gita* into a dozen or so simple words. Certainly, it's much easier to listen to the song than try to read the real thing.

Some people believe there is a spiritual world entirely separate from (or coexistent with) the material world in which we find ourselves. From my own scientific point of view, I see no evidence for such a belief—but whatever gets you through the night, as someone very wise once said.

An L song that isn't a Beatles song, but is a very good one, is "Last Night" by the Traveling Wilburys, George's spin-off supergroup with Jeff Lynne, Bob Dylan, and the great and much missed Tom Petty and Roy Orbison. They made so many good records, and "Last Night" is certainly one of the best. The Wilburys' music was put together and beautifully produced by my friend Jeff Lynne—another L!—who, thank goodness, is still very much with us and making great music in the studio and on the road.

I haven't talked much about Ringo, but he has a notable L song to offer, one that is historical in nature. Ringo was born and brought up in a very tough area of Liverpool called the Dingle, and he and Dave Stewart wrote a song about it called "Liverpool 8," after the postcode for that area back then. I'm sure by now it's got a lot more numbers and letters attached to it. The song has a bit of Beatles history in it, as Ringo sings about his time with the band, much as George did in "When We Was Fab."

And, of course, we can't leave the letter L without spending some time with two of Paul's classic Beatles numbers, "Lady Madonna" and "Let It Be."

"Lady Madonna" is a terrific song and an example of Paul's excellent piano playing, a brilliant kind of boogie-woogie that he does so well. Paul is one of those people who can pick up any instrument and figure out how to play it in an infuriatingly short amount of time. And he plays piano well. I think some of the earliest piano music he might have heard would have been sort of jazz-ish piano because his father played in a jazz-flavoured band. In England in the 1950s, there was a lot of attention paid to jazz, especially American Dixieland jazz—which we called trad jazz. And indeed, one of those trad jazz bands had a hit record which may well have inspired Paul's piano playing on "Lady Madonna." It is "Bad Penny Blues" by Humphrey Lyttelton and his jazz band. If you listen to the intro, you'll hear the style of piano playing that clearly impressed and influenced Paul and probably inspired him to write that great beginning for "Lady Madonna." Another huge influence on Paul McCartney the pianist was Fats Domino, a brilliant piano player, and you can hear some of him as well in "Lady Madonna," which was a huge hit and a terrific record. It showed off Paul's piano playing in a way that none of the Beatles' records had done previously.

And if we're talking about Paul and his piano, that leads us to the final song in this chapter, the magnificent "Let It Be." It was inspired by a dream Paul had, in which his mother—who had died in 1956, when Paul was fourteen—appeared before him and gave him comforting advice. Of course, as with all great songs, it turns out to mean different things to different people—sometimes with "Mary" being taken to be the Virgin Mary rather than Paul's mother, for example. But we know from Paul that it was indeed *his* mother, Mary, who showed up in a dream. Paul certainly was in the middle of "times of trouble" at that point, with arguments raging among the four Beatles, and Brian Epstein no longer around to offer counsel or consolation—and somehow Paul's genius responded with not only a profoundly comforting dream but also a song which has provided immense comfort as well as musical joy to millions of people the world over. A beautiful record, featuring all four Beatles plus Billy Preston's inimitable organ.

Indeed, "Let It Be" is one of those cases in which it is hard to improve on the original, but two cover versions are worth seeking out, if you haven't already heard them. One is by Nick Cave, who did a really thoughtful and intelligent version of "Let It Be." I love Nick Cave. I love not only his music but also his books. He is an extraordinary writer and a man possessed of significant intellect. His version of "Let It Be" is perhaps less overtly emotional and less *sung* than Paul's—it's almost a recitation in some spots—which I find all the more affecting. It has some of the understated passion of Leonard Cohen at his best.

And then, of course, there's Aretha Franklin. She can take any song and turn it into something remarkable, but give her a great song, and she creates an emotional experience and a musical intensity that are unequaled. She's done that more than a few times, and one of those occasions was when she sang "Let It Be" and really nailed it. They do not call her the Queen of Soul for nothing. She died while I was writing this book, and the outpouring of affection and admiration—and profound musical respect—was deeply and spectacularly well deserved.

We have been on an alphabetical journey with the Beatles, so what better way to start our exploration of the letter M than with a special journey associated with that letter, the double M song "Magical Mystery Tour." It was originally released on the English EP to accompany the TV movie of the same name, which I really enjoyed but which some people find to be confusing or astonishing or even immature and disappointing.

The idea was based on real coach tours that were a feature of British domestic holidays. When you went to a seaside resort for your family summer holiday, very often in the main high street of that town there would be a coach company advertising tours on a blackboard outside its door. And the tours would be along the lines of a jolly trip out to a nearby castle or a museum or a stately home or something, or even just a park, somewhere you could go and visit. They would advertise these tours, how much they would

On the way to the Magical Mystery Tour *premiere party.*

cost, and you would choose one, take your family, and go on this expedition. But often, in addition to all their stated destinations, the company would list a "mystery tour," which was pretty much the same as all the other ones except they just didn't tell you where you were going until you had arrived, so there was a degree of anticipation and excitement.

I don't think there ever was such a thing before the Beatles as a "*magical* mystery tour," but that's certainly what the Beatles created. The coach tours gave them the idea for the song, I think, and the idea for the TV show was to create a coach tour going to various places in England with a curious group of people. They assembled that strange and mixed group of people, put them all on a coach, and went off and had adventures. Some members of the group were specifically cast, and some ended up there by coincidence or accident. There was an overall aim and concept, but the details were left to take care of themselves. I was not on the journey myself, but the closest thing to a script I ever saw (at Paul's house a couple of days before they left) consisted of some lists of people and places and ideas and some elaborate diagrams. Given this methodology, it should not have been a surprise that the resulting film was indeed disjointed and juvenile but also (to me) fascinating, experimentally nonlinear, entertaining, and in some ways ahead of its time. It certainly, though, was not what the BBC had been expecting. They were looking for a jolly, kind of comedic, zany yet fab Beatles special for Boxing Day, the day after Christmas. And what they got was this hour of great fun but considerable strangeness, which they found disconcerting. But I thought it was very cool. If you get a chance to see it, see it. I still like it. And of course everyone loved the music in *Magical Mystery Tour*. There's no argument about that.

America did not know quite what to do with the film, either. Capitol Records didn't put the EP out separately but jumbled in the songs with a whole lot of other stuff and made it part of a full-length album. And the movie itself didn't come out at all until a little while later, when a very dear friend of mine by the name of Nat Weiss, a brilliant man who was the Beatles' lawyer and Brian Epstein's friend and lawyer, had the idea of sending the film out on its own, doing college gigs. They would send a guy with a projector and the reels of film out on the road and play it in colleges and put it on in the canteen or whatever room was available, throw up a screen, put out some chairs, and charge admission. And it did very well; the college audience loved it.

There was also a fabulous party in London when they premiered the movie in the UK—an amazing costume party, what in Britain we call a fancy-dress party. Everyone dressed up in extraordinary outfits. I found a picture of the party—I am just in it, visible over Paul's shoulder, and my father is on the extreme left, as some kind of Chinese mandarin.

I had forgotten until I saw these pictures that Paul had invited the entire Asher family to the event. George and Judy Martin came as the Duke of Edinburgh and Queen Elizabeth, and they looked spectacular. By popular acclaim, they were the best costumed couple.

In reviewing Beatles things from an M-ish perspective, I'd like to turn now to record labels, and one label in particular that we admired above all others. While we loved Stax, and we loved Atlantic, if we had to pick one label where we wanted to own all the records they put out, it was definitely Motown. And one of our favourite Motown records was "Money (That's What I Want)," which was recorded by Barrett Strong and written by Berry Gordy (Motown's founder and owner) with the assistance of Janie Bradford, a remarkable woman who has done a great deal of admirable philanthropic work on behalf of songwriters and others. "Money" became a favourite of many people when the Beatles recorded it in 1963. It is an interesting song—it is at heart a simple twelve-bar blues. The Barrett Strong version was played in F, and the Beatles version is a half step lower, in E. But what makes both versions so interesting is a very rock and roll crunchy discord which happens most notably in the eighth bar of every chorus. This happens because one of the key elements of the song is the two-bar piano riff which one can hear very clearly in the intro and which repeats throughout the song. The result of this repetition is that while this lick fits perfectly over the E chord that starts the chorus, by the time we get to the eighth bar and hear it against a B7 chord, the same notes sound pretty weird and interesting—and under different circumstances could well be considered "wrong" notes. The Beatles kept this arrangement idea in their version, and George Martin overdubbed the piano part. It is to his credit that he resisted what must have been his well-educated musician's instinct to change the lick to fit the chords, recognizing that it is the grind of the discordant repetition that makes the chorus sound so cool.

I also love John's impassioned vocal, and of course the lyrics have perhaps never been more apposite than they are today. Even if it is true that officially money cannot buy you love, it is abundantly clear that it can get you pretty much everything else. Maybe when all the global billionaires have their secret meetings on their giant yachts, they sing this song together after dinner—now that's a conspiracy theory I could get into!

Thinking about Motown brings us to another favourite band of the Beatles, also on Motown and also with an M: the Miracles, led by the great singer and songwriter Smokey Robinson. The Beatles covered one of their songs, making a really cool record of "You've Really Got a Hold on Me." It is an unusual song because the harmonies are all in fourths, which have an exciting, plangent, and sometimes almost ominous flavour to them. The Beatles copied Smokey Robinson's harmonies exactly, and they totally nailed it.

Now the M's really begin to multiply. After "Money" on Motown, and the Miracles on Motown, I'd like to jump forward in time to a triple M, "Mean Mr. Mustard." And it's really a quadruple M, because if you think about it, "Mean Mr. Mustard" is part of a medley on side two of the *Abbey Road* album, which begins with "Sun King" and ends with "She Came in Through the Bathroom Window." (I know that some people think of the medley extending all the way to "The End," but I tend to think of *Abbey Road* as having two separate medleys, one starting with "Sun King" and the other with "Golden Slumbers.")

Another M song, just a single M this time, is one of the best Paul McCartney ever wrote: "Michelle." A remarkable song. Part of it, of course, is in French, and there has been a lot written about where the French came from. Paul is on record as saying that, at parties, he occasionally used to pretend to be able to speak French just to appear cool—and even perhaps played a phrase or two of what became the "Michelle" melody, suggesting that it might be French. As Paul put it, "We all wanted to be Sacha Distel"—he was right about that, and I shall tell you why. It was not so much because Monsieur Distel was cool and handsome, a fine guitarist, and a good singer—it was because he was, at the time, the live-in boyfriend of Brigitte Bardot, with whom we were all hopelessly in love. I maintain to this day that the BB of that era was the most physically attractive woman I have ever seen. I think the Beatles finally did meet her in person (I never had the pleasure) after one of their Olympia shows. So, this may account for at least some of Paul's interest in the French language. But he did not actually speak it, so when he decided to write some cool French lyrics, he needed help. He went first to Jan Vaughan, the wife of a friend, who spoke fluent French, and she made suggestions and translated some phrases for him initially. I also remember Paul conferring with my mother, who spoke very good French, having been educated at the Lycée Français in London. I recall my mother telling me that Paul had consulted her on some French he was using in a song, and it must have been this song because it is the only Beatles song which includes any French words. So, I think my mother had a hand in helping him with the correct French grammar or pronunciation or something like that.

It was a joint effort in several respects. The bridge was John Lennon's idea, inspired by a Nina Simone song that he loved so much, "I Put a Spell on You." That's where the "I love you, I love you, I love you" thing came from. On the recording, Paul does some really excellent finger picking on the guitar, a very different style from the usual rhythm guitar parts that the Beatles played.

Staying with Paul on the acoustic guitar, another excellent M song is "Mother Nature's Son." Apparently, this song was inspired by the Nat King Cole song "Nature Boy," which I would never have guessed. They are both excellent songs yet not very similar at all. Paul's was written mostly in Liverpool, though its inspiration came from a lecture given by the Maharishi about nature—a lecture which also inspired a John Lennon song called "Child of Nature" which morphed years later into "Jealous Guy"! Paul's recording of "Mother Nature's Son" also belongs on a very short list of Beatles tracks on which only a single Beatle is in fact playing or singing.

Now from the comfort of "Mother Nature's Son," which is soft and very pleasurable to listen to, we move to another extreme with John Lennon's song "Mother." A very different kettle of fish altogether.

Back in the late '60s and '70s, a new kind of psychotherapy became fashionable, called primal scream therapy. The psychologist Arthur Janov wrote a very popular book explaining his theories, and he became the psychotherapist du jour for that brief period. His therapy consisted of the patient lying there and thinking of things that made him really angry and then screaming. I chose not to do that. But John thought it would be cool and went through this therapy at Janov's institute in Los Angeles in April 1970, where he spent a certain amount of time reflecting on his relationship with his mother, who didn't raise him herself (he was brought up by his aunt Mimi) and who died when John was just seventeen years old.

During his therapy, he recorded several demo versions of this song, some on guitar and some on piano. He then returned to London and recorded it at EMI Studios, with Klaus Voormann on bass and Ringo Starr on drums. The song ends with some really heartbreaking scary screaming.

I know John had some issues that made him angry, but whether he got them out of his system using primal scream therapy—that I don't know. But it certainly sounds very convincing. The weird, spooky church bell chimes at the beginning, by the way, were added after the initial recording. John apparently had the idea after watching a horror movie on television that employed a similar effect. And they recorded some church bells and slowed them down in a successful effort to make them spooky.

So now let's move on from a scary approach to one's mother— almost a kind of a psycho approach to a mother in that song—to a much more comfortable view of a mother in the song "Your Mother Should Know." Though in my experience it is usually better if your mother doesn't know, in this instance the Beatles made a contrary decision.

"Your Mother Should Know," of course, is also from *Magical Mystery Tour*—the EP and the film. That is one of the only times I think we saw the Beatles do choreographed dance moves, as they came down the stairs in those fabulous white suits. In fact, white tie and tails from top to toe. Pretty amazing look, and they got their dance steps totally right.

I think Paul wrote that song on the harmonium he kept in his house in Cavendish Avenue. The harmonium is an instrument of which Paul and I are both very fond, and we have both used it on records. It is a small organ with a regular keyboard and a free reed for every note, activated by air pumped through the reeds by foot pedals which operate the bellows. I was always impressed when I noticed that the pedals on my old harmonium were labelled "patented mouse-proof pedals" (apparently mice like to crawl in and eat holes in the paper bellows), and the patented system must have worked because I am happy to say that I never had mouse holes in my bellows. The sound created by the reeds can be altered using various stops which physically divert, diminish, or open up the sound. A beautiful and delicate instrument. And I know Paul used the harmonium on "Your Mother Should Know"—you can hear it. A reassuring and jolly song.

Now, we can't consider our discussion of the letter M complete without what may well be George Harrison's most famous song as a solo artist, "My Sweet Lord." A really great record, a beautiful production, and a fine song, from the brilliant *All Things Must Pass* album. One cannot ignore the legal issues raised by the copyright holders of "He's So Fine," the giant Chiffons hit written by Ronald Mack—it was a huge No. 1 record which we all knew by heart, and there is no doubt that having that call and response melody stuck in his head may have inadvertently influenced George's writing. But in the final analysis George's is the better song for sure. In the overall sense, I think the vibe and majesty of the Edwin Hawkins Singers' record "Oh Happy Day" was a more conscious and relevant influence, as George was trying to write an uplifting and all-encompassing hymn and a hit pop song at the same time, and he succeeded magnificently.

I'd like to conclude our time with the letter M by exploring three great Beatles M songs. The first is a Paul McCartney song with an excellent Paul vocal, "Martha My Dear." I think everyone knows by now that Martha was not a woman Paul was in love with; it was a dog he was in love with. I knew Martha. She was a large, floppy, charming English sheepdog. I can picture her now. She was a very pleasant dog, and I remember her hanging out at Paul's house on Cavendish Avenue, and Paul was extremely fond of her. I seem to recall that Martha actually accompanied us on our later trip up north to record the Black Dyke Mills Band and our visit to the town of Harrold on the way home—but that is a story for another time.

To complement that cool Paul vocal, there's an M song with an amazing John Lennon vocal, "Mr. Moonlight." It was written by Roy Lee Johnson and first recorded by Piano Red (as Dr. Feelgood and the Interns) and had become kind of an insider's favourite among British bands; the Hollies and the Merseybeats recorded it as well. It's not one of the greatest Beatles tracks, but they never made a bad record, and this one is totally saved by the declaratory strength and passion of John's vocal.

Finally, I come to a song that both John and Paul sing on, but I hope you don't take this to heart. The song is called "Misery," and I don't mean to end this chapter on a downer. An early song, written on the road while the Beatles were opening for Helen Shapiro and then completed at home in Liverpool. They originally hoped that Helen might record it herself—John and Paul's songwriting ambitions were just as emphatic as their ambitions as a band—but her producer, Norrie Paramor (of Cliff Richard fame), decided it was too gloomy. The song *was* covered by an actor/singer named Kenny Lynch, who was also a friend of the Beatles (and on the same tour with them and Helen, as you can see in the poster on page 53)—a really nice guy but it's not a great record. So, the version we remember today is the Beatles' own version. A simple record in its way, but that is what makes it so right. Rock solid Ringo, without a single fill; tough, masterful, and perfect duet vocals from Paul and John; George adding a key rhythm part but being the quiet Beatle and not even taking a solo; and elegant and restrained piano ornamentation from George Martin. Everything we love about the band!

We have reached the midpoint of our alphabetical journey, arriving at the letter N—N for (among other things) nothingness and nowhere, which takes us directly to one of everyone's favourite Beatles N songs, "Nowhere Man."

It is a John Lennon song, written in his house in Weybridge when he was feeling depressed and at a loose end. He was inspired to write this beautiful song with extraordinary lyrics which are admittedly pessimistic and which John saw as being ultimately as universal as they are personal—like all great songs. The lyric ends by asking whether the Nowhere Man isn't "a bit like you and me." So from me, another nowhere man, to you and to all the other nowhere men and women out there, this is a song for all of us.

Nat Weiss.

Hunter Davies's 1968 book *The Beatles: The Authorized Biography* has a fascinating quote from John.

> I was just sitting trying to think of a song and I
> thought of myself sitting there doing nothing and going
> nowhere. Once I thought of that it was easy. It all came
> out. No, I remember now, I'd actually stopped trying
> to think of something. Nothing would come. I was
> cheesed off and went for a lie down having given up.
> Then, I thought of myself as nowhere man sitting in his
> nowhere land.

"Nowhere Man" is a brilliant arrangement and production as well as a terrific song. Great three-part a capella harmony on the intro and straight into a typical driving Beatles groove: John on rhythm acoustic guitar, Ringo playing a pretty straightforward drum part (with his uniquely relaxed hi-hat feel) set off by Paul's idiosyncratic double-time walking bass part. And George's rippling super-high-end guitar solo, buttoned up with an unexpected harmonic at the end, is masterful.

Moving from a John Lennon N song to a Paul McCartney N song, we come to one which Paul wrote in my family home: "The Night Before." I did not hear it as and when he wrote it—I was on the road myself at the time. But according to all the books, he wrote it in our house in Wimpole Street—and I do remember hearing it when I returned home. And the song ended up in the film *Help!* and on the excellent album of the same name.

The Beatles recorded "The Night Before" in Studio Two at EMI Studios on the afternoon of February 17, 1965, apparently in just two takes, which is remarkable, because it is a very tight and accurate track. Among other things, it includes a guitar solo in octaves, which is played by Paul and George. Playing in octaves that way creates something of the same effect as playing a twelve-string (which is partially strung in octaves itself), but playing it on two guitars in perfect sync makes it even tougher-sounding. And the solo itself is a remarkable composition. The guitars studiously avoid playing on the downbeat of any bar (avoiding the "1," as it were), which is very unusual, and yet Paul and George sculpt a memorable solo melody which they also use later in the track as an ending.

John is playing a Hohner pianet electric piano, which is a great sound. I don't know if anyone owns a pianet now (that would be an eBay question, I suppose), but listening to this song makes me want one! They were more percussive than the Fender Rhodes or the Wurlitzer electric pianos and could cut through electric guitars. I suppose the instrument could be seen as an early ancestor of the Hohner clavinet, which achieved more universal fame. (Think of Stevie Wonder's intro riff on "Superstition"—that's what a clavinet sounds like.)

Looking at the letter N in a Beatles context, I want to mention a person associated with that letter who figured significantly in their lives, and whom I previously mentioned in the context of *Magical Mystery Tour*. That person is Nat Weiss, the Beatles' lawyer in New York. He was Brian Epstein's best friend in that city and one of my best friends in the world, too. He died a few years ago and is very greatly missed by us all. He advised Brian on numerous legal matters and became a trusted adviser to the Beatles as well. Nat also introduced Brian to the thriving gay scene in New York, which changed his life—he had certainly seen nothing like it in Liverpool or even in London! Nat was a brilliant and remarkable man, and when I moved to America with my brand-new client James Taylor, Nat set up my management company and then represented James in our successful negotiations with Warner Brothers. Finally, I remember that in the year Bonnie Raitt won that historic bunch of Grammys, she singled out Nat for special thanks in her acceptance speech—so the Beatles, James Taylor, and I were not his only fans!

And it was at Nat's home in New York that Paul McCartney and Linda Eastman really hit it off.

Paul and Linda had first met at a photo session, and then again at a party. But the first time they really sat down together and talked, and probably the first time Paul got Linda's phone number, was at Nat Weiss's apartment in New York. Nat also had an amazing closet door (auctioned off a while back, I noticed) which all the Beatles signed to Nat in thick black ink. It became a feature of

Nat's apartment, and one of which he was very proud. It is a bit of a digression, I admit, but if we are speaking of N's, Nat Weiss was an important man who ought not to be forgotten by anyone interested in Beatles history.

Seeing that I brought up Linda McCartney, let's move on to a song with Linda on it, a Wings song, also beginning with N, called "No Words," written by Paul and my dear friend Denny Laine. It features Paul on vocals, guitar, bass, and drums; Linda on vocals and keyboards; and Denny on guitar and some background vocals as well. It is from the remarkable *Band on the Run* album and features an excellent orchestral arrangement by Tony Visconti and was recorded at George Martin's AIR Studios in London rather than at EMI Studios. (George and a couple of top former EMI staff producers had opened their own studio at Oxford Circus in Central London, using the name Associated Independent Recording, hence AIR Studios. AIR has since moved to a beautiful old church called Lyndhurst Hall in North London, where it thrives to this day.)

While we're discussing solo Beatle songs beginning with N, we cannot overlook Ringo. Around the time the Beatles broke up in 1970, Ringo recorded and released an album of standards called *Sentimental Journey*, and one of those standards was "Night and Day," written by the immortal Cole Porter, one of my favourite songwriters in the world. And obviously one of Ringo's as well. Now you probably know that Cole Porter was a very famous and successful songwriter, and a lot of people have covered his songs. "Night and Day" has been recorded by Frank Sinatra, Ella Fitzgerald, Tony Bennett, all kinds of amazing singers. And let us not forget that Cole Porter wrote words *and* music, by himself. Songwriting is very often done by teams, some (like Bacharach & David or Gilbert & Sullivan) in which one partner writes the music and the other the lyrics, and some (like Lennon & McCartney) in which they collaborate on both—but Cole Porter was a solo genius. His songs support imaginative and creatively flexible performances, which is no doubt why so many jazz singers take to them with such enthusiasm, but there is a whole other kind of contrary revelation in the way Ringo sings the song totally straight. The phrasing is probably just the way Cole wrote it, before Ella or Frank applied their jazz skills to it—and with a drummer's precision, Ringo sings exactly on the beat, and his definitively amiable singing style gives the song a straightforward and almost childlike clarity.

N also stands, among other things, for "no." Now the Beatles have been accused of writing drug-related songs, even songs that could be construed as pro-drug songs. But Ringo performed at least one song that is unequivocally anti-drug—and in a truly funny and entertaining way. Written by Hoyt Axton and David Jackson, produced by my good friend Richard Perry, it's called "No No Song," with two N's for good measure. It was a big hit, getting to No. 3 in the U.S.

Just say no to drugs. Well, not necessarily and not all the time. But that is the implication of that song. Ringo is firmly suggesting that drugs are not good for you. Ironically, the background vocalists on the record include the brilliant and astonishing Harry Nilsson—a genius who (it must be admitted) did not always say "no" himself.

Sticking with N, and sticking with "no," brings to mind a classic Beatles song, "No Reply." The song was not originally supposed to be a Beatles song at all. John wrote it for Tommy Quickly (another management client of Brian Epstein's), and the Beatles cut a demo from which Tommy learned the song. Tommy did record it, but apparently nobody was very happy with his rendition, and it was not released. But the Beatles' demo was released on *Anthology*. What is interesting about this version is that apparently it is not Ringo playing drums, because he was ill with tonsillitis. Many people think the drummer was Jimmie Nicol because the Beatles had been rehearsing with him earlier that day for the Australian tour that Ringo could not do because of his illness. As I said, I'm not necessarily an expert on all these historical details, but my understanding is that Jimmie, who did go to Australia with the Beatles (indeed, *as* a Beatle), was there rehearsing at EMI. So it seems most likely that he is playing on it. And of course the "real" version was recorded by the Beatles in the fall of 1964 and came out on *Beatles for Sale* in the UK and *Beatles '65* in the United States. John later said that he had been inspired to write "No Reply" by the record "Silhouettes" by the Rays, an R&B quartet from New

York—a song that was later covered by Herman's Hermits. John was taken with the image of knowing someone was home and thus knowing that their failure to answer the door or the phone was deliberate and deceptive.

Another interesting Lennon-related N song—and another "no" song—is "No Bed for Beatle John," from *Unfinished Music No. 2: Life with the Lions*, produced by John and Yoko. And I have to say, I like Yoko's vocal on the song a lot. Every now and then, Yoko does some kind of crazy singing that I'm not always very keen on, but her disarming vocal on this track is very melodic, very in tune, and really sweet. She sounds young and charming. The song is made up of press clippings (sung by Yoko) from her stay in Queen Charlotte's Hospital in London, where she was pregnant and unfortunately lost the baby. John was staying there with her the whole time. A bed was needed for an emergency case, so John gave up the bed and slept on the floor because he didn't want to leave Yoko by herself. The press clippings all tell that story, and they comprise the lyrics to this song.

Now the album title, *Life with the Lions*, you may think was just some kind of surreal concept that came to John. Not at all. To everyone in England at the time, it would have been a phrase they remembered from the '50s, when *Life with the Lyons* was a hugely successful radio sitcom. The Lyons were a family of American actors, a real family, who had moved to London and found various bits of work as actors and somehow were eventually given a weekly radio show of their own. We were all already fascinated by America and by American people and things in general. Meeting real Americans who lived in London was endlessly interesting to British listeners. Ben Lyon and his wife, Bebe Daniels, settled in London during the Second World War. It's weird that somebody would move to London in the middle of a war and all the bombing, but they did. They got some work from 1940 onwards and eventually were offered this very successful sitcom to which we all listened. For a few years it was on television as well. I don't remember ever watching it on TV, but I certainly listened to it on the radio.

We've been following a lot of paths to the past in the letter N, from Cole Porter to *Life with the Lyons*, and John provides another one with his song "Nobody Loves You (When You're Down and Out)," from the *Walls and Bridges* album. John changed one word of the title of a famous 1920s song, a bluesy composition called "Nobody Knows You When You're Down and Out." John's song, which was completely new in every other respect, was written during his "Lost Weekend" period, when he was in L.A. doing a bit too much of everything. But he did make some good records, and this is one he recorded with Klaus Voormann on bass, Nicky Hopkins on piano, Kenny Ascher on organ, and Jim Keltner on drums. The song also featured Jesse Ed Davis, who was a Native American guitarist of very considerable skill and charm—a really remarkable musician.

Let's hope none of us has to find out if it's actually true that nobody loves you when you're down and out. John apparently wanted Frank Sinatra to sing this song. "I always imagine Sinatra singing that one," he once said in a radio interview. "He could do a perfect job with it. If you're listening, Frank, you need a song that isn't a piece of nothing. Here's one for you. The horn arrangement. Everything's made for you." A good song, though a sad one. And perhaps even sadder that Frank Sinatra never gave it a try.

There's an interesting N song called "Not Guilty," written by George Harrison, that might have gotten onto the White Album but ultimately did not. The Beatles recorded 102 different takes (probably a record for them) and fiddled about with the arrangement and so on before giving up on the session. There is one recorded version which survived and was included on *The Beatles Anthology*. Years later George recorded his own version, which I think is fantastic, for the album *George Harrison*. I was very impressed when I recently listened to it—I hadn't heard it for a while—especially by the Fender Rhodes electric piano part, so I looked it up to see who had played it. It was Neil Larsen, a terrific keyboard player who also played on the last few Leonard Cohen tours. I had the pleasure of being out on that tour for a number of dates, and I got to know Neil and to admire his playing very much—though I did not realize that he had played on George's album.

In fact, the whole band on George's version is colossally good. The other keyboard player is Steve Winwood, Willie Weeks is on bass, Andy Newmark plays drums, and Ray Cooper is on congas. A killer band and finally a great version of the song by the composer himself.

I'd like to circle back to the Beatles as a foursome, having spent quite a lot of time in this chapter on their solo work, specifically to look at two great Beatles songs that begin with the letter N. The first is "Not a Second Time." This was the song which inspired the now-famous article in *The Times* newspaper in Britain. William Mann, the classical music correspondent of that lofty and distinguished journal, published a musical analysis of the Beatles music. That fact alone was remarkable enough; in that era the classical music world had a pretty snooty attitude to popular music in general and rock and roll in particular. Yet here was *The Times* taking the Beatles very seriously and praising their inventiveness, using this one specific song "Not a Second Time" as an example. Mann pointed out the "Aeolian cadence" it contains, adding that this cadence also occurs in the final movement of Mahler's "Das Lied von der Erde." John said later, "To this day I have no idea what Aeolian cadences are. They sound like exotic birds." If anyone is interested, it is generally considered that the Aeolian cadence occurs at the end of the line "No, no, no, not a second time" when (on the word "time") the chord is an E minor rather than the G major which the preceding D7 would lead one to expect. The term derives from the fact that the Aeolian mode is rooted in the sixth step of the major scale—in the key of G that would indeed bring us to an E minor.

And we cannot call any discussion of the Beatles and the letter N complete without mentioning "Norwegian Wood (This Bird Has Flown)," a brilliant John Lennon song with mysterious lyrics and the first use of a sitar by George Harrison on a record and so much more.

Not long ago I was looking at *Many Years from Now*, Barry Miles's excellent book about Paul McCartney, and Paul had some interesting recollections about John's song.

I came in and he had this first stanza which was brilliant. *I once had a girl or should I say she once had me.* That was all he had, no title, no nothing. And I said, "Oh yes! Well, ha, we're there." And it wrote itself. Once you've got the great idea, they do tend to write themselves, providing you know how to write songs. [Easy for him to say because they, of course, "know how to write songs" better than almost anyone I've ever met in my whole life.]

I picked it up at the second verse. It's a story, it's him trying to pull a bird. It was about an affair. John told *Playboy* they hadn't the faintest idea where the title came from, but I do! Peter Asher had his room done out in wood. A lot of people were decorating their places in wood. "Norwegian Wood." It was pine really, cheap pine, but it's not as good a title, "Cheap Pine," baby.

That's all very well, and I am certainly very proud if I or my room even made a contribution, but I cannot honestly remember ever doing out my room in wood. I have to ask Paul at some point what exactly he remembers. Maybe it was a different room in our house. I do remember something about putting up some pine paneling in a downstairs room where we sometimes had parties. But my bedroom had weird, geometrical '50s wallpaper and no wood at all that I can recall.

So, it's a bit mysterious, even to me. But anyway, I suppose the whole song ends with him setting fire to her bedroom with its wooden walls in revenge for her making him sleep in the bath. A bit much, I must say—but that is what it means. Not lighting a fire in the fireplace or lighting a cigarette or any of the other theories. I am sorry to say that it is certainly a song which ends with arson being committed by our hero.

Before we close this chapter, I realize that it wouldn't be right to omit my own connection to the Beatles in conjunction with the letter N, in the form of a song called "Nobody I Know."

The story starts soon after Gordon and I recorded "A World Without Love." Sometimes, for any artist, finding a follow-up song to a big hit can be really difficult. There's a sense in which one is trying to live up to one's previous achievement and expectations, and we had just had a record that was No. 1 all over the world, so that was kind of scary. But when one is following up a big hit, one gets sent an awful lot of songs—and numerous songwriters sent us songs they hoped would be our next single. Luckily, one of those songwriters was Paul McCartney, who had written a song called "Nobody I Know," which he played for me as soon as we returned from our first U.S. visit—and I loved it.

John and Paul took their songwriting duties seriously. They understood the responsibilities of being successful songwriters, which meant knowing how to get the right song to the right artist at the right time. If you wrote a big hit, you wanted the follow-up to also be written by you. You didn't want someone else cashing in on your brilliant success. So when we came back from America after our first tour, Paul had already written "Nobody I Know" specifically for us. If you look at the Beatles' early interviews, they were often asked, "What are you going to do when this is all over?" Indeed, this was one question which we could all count on being included in every interview. There existed a universal and confident assumption that a rock and roll career would last two years at most. John and Paul always responded, "Oh, we'll be songwriters." They wanted to follow in the mold of Leiber & Stoller, Goffin & King, and the other great songwriting teams whom they admired so deeply.

As for Gordon and me, we were delighted to record "Nobody I Know," the arrangement extensively featuring the big, beautiful, red sunburst acoustic twelve-string guitar that Gibson had recently made for me. It became a hit, and we sang it on the road, and that was it, thank you very much.

Having reached the letter O, I'd like to start with a song that almost sounds as if it starts with the very word *oh*. And that's "Ob-La-Di, Ob-La-Da."

There is some question in my mind about where the phrase came from. Paul has said that he heard it from a Nigerian conga-playing friend of his, Jimmy Scott, whom he met down at the Bag O'Nails, which was a very happening club in London at the time. It was a musicians' hangout in Kingly Street, which runs parallel to Carnaby Street, on the western edge of Soho. It was well known for great music and for heavy drinking (or so I dimly recall!), and Paul is to be congratulated on remembering the phrase the following day and turning it into such an excellent song. But I think I also remember Paul telling me once that it was someone making a delivery to the studio who had used the phrase "ob-la-di, ob-la-da" at some point, and Paul had liked it and incorporated it into a song. I cannot be sure. But in the final analysis, I assume Paul is right; if he remembers the Bag O'Nails, that must be it. Of course, most people would just hear the phrase and let it slide by, thinking, "What a cool expres-

The oboe.

sion," whereas Paul clearly thought, "What a cool expression, let me write a brilliant song using it." And that's what he did.

I particularly love "Ob-La-Di, Ob-La-Da" because it is one of Paul's songs about imaginary people, and he is so very good at that. By the end of the song, you feel you really know Desmond and Molly Jones even though they are not real people. Paul just made them up as he so often did—like Eleanor Rigby or Jojo from Tucson, Arizona, or Maxwell Edison or so many others. People often try to relate Paul's songs to real friends or real people, but he was like a great novelist or a perceptive poet—while no doubt drawing from the real world, he invented people and places and created wholly credible short stories, and that is what makes the songs so cool. Desmond and Molly Jones will live forever courtesy of "Ob-La-Di, Ob-La-Da," and let us hope they are indeed still happy ever after in the marketplace.

Another song that starts with O is a later Beatles recording but a much earlier Beatles song. By that I mean that John wrote it, or at least the beginning of it, when he was about fifteen, but it was recorded during one of the later Beatles sessions for the *Let It Be* film and album. And that song is "One After 909." Paul explained later that it was an attempt to write an American railroad song in the style of their musical heroes. A bluesy kind of freight train song with a Hank Williams vibe, like "Midnight Special" and all those other great train songs. Perhaps the most famous railroad song of all, at least to us at the time in England, was "Rock Island Line," because that had been a huge hit for our skiffle hero Lonnie Donegan. The skiffle craze was an interesting and vital precursor to the so-called British Invasion which followed. It seems as if everyone who owned a guitar was a member of a skiffle group, and I (like Paul and John) was no exception. A couple of guitars, a washboard and some thimbles, a tea-chest or washtub bass (with broom handle and string), and some simple American folk/blues tunes and you were off and running. "Rock Island Line" was an old song going back at least to the railroad yards of the '30s, captured by the devoted musical explorations of Alan Lomax, made his own by the great Lead Belly, and finally recorded by Lonnie Donegan, the banjo player in the best British jazz band of the day, the Chris Barber Band. With his fake American accent, his master-fully intense vocal, and his devotion to American music, Donegan led a British Invasion of his own ("Rock Island Line" went top ten in America in 1955!) almost ten years before the Beatles and the rest of us caught up. We all thought that there was nothing more quintessentially American than a great railroad song—the trains that Hank Williams or Sonny Terry or Johnny Cash sang about had a romance and mystery to them that ours at home seemed to lack entirely.

"One After 909," I guess, refers to the train that leaves after the 9:09. That doesn't sound very American to me. It sounds a bit more like British Railways at their worst. The 9:09 was prob-ably cancelled and you had to wait for the next one. The song has John Lennon on vocals and rhythm guitar, Paul McCartney on vocals and bass, George Harrison on lead guitar, Ringo Starr on drums, and Billy Preston playing electric piano. George Martin, Glyn Johns, and even Phil Spector contributed to the production and engineering of the track over the course of several attempts to get it right. With so many drivers, one can only be grateful that the one after 9:09 arrived safely and on time.

I've talked about a Paul O song and a John O song, so to be fair, here comes George wearing his "Old Brown Shoe" while play-ing the piano—a rare instrument for him. He also overdubbed a guitar solo and erased John Lennon's rhythm guitar in favour of a Hammond organ part. "Old Brown Shoe" was also, by the way, the B-side of "The Ballad of John and Yoko," a song on which George didn't play at all, so it's only fair that he played multiple instru-ments on this one.

"Old Brown Shoe" came to life one more time because it was featured in the legendary "Concert for George," which took place in London in 2002, a year after his shattering death at the age of fifty-eight. It was an amazing concert, and this was one of the very fine performances that are in it. Gary Brooker from Procol Harum, a terrific pianist and a soulful singer, performed "Old Brown Shoe" with the amazing band that was put together for that concert, including Eric Clapton, Jim Keltner, Dhani Harrison, and Albert Lee. Eric Idle from *Monty Python* was there, too, and helped put the whole thing together. It was a killer event and an amazing band of good friends and inspired musicians.

Ringo is also well represented in the letter O, so let's add him to the mix with his solo track "Oh My My." This song was produced by Richard Perry, and it also has some very cool people playing and singing. The background vocalists are Merry Clayton, who is famous for doing the female vocal on "Gimme Shelter" and many other amazing tracks, and Martha Reeves, who is, of course, the Martha of Martha and the Vandellas. Ringo wrote the song with his friend Vini Poncia, Billy Preston plays keyboards on it, Ringo and Jim Keltner both play drums, Klaus Voormann plays bass, and Tom Scott plays the saxophone solo. It is a catchy and energetic song. It was a big hit, and it is always a key part of Ringo's live show with his amazing All-Starr Band.

Now that we've given each of the Beatles a taste of the letter O, I'd like to go in a different direction and talk about an instrument that starts with the letter O: the oboe. There isn't a lot of oboe on Beatles records, which is kind of odd. And I'll tell you why. While Paul was living at our house, he heard an awful lot of oboe. And that's because, as I have mentioned, my mother was a professional oboe player. I learned the oboe myself for a bit. I could probably tootle out an ugly and quacking C major scale right now, but that's about it. And one of the weirdest coincidences in all of this is that somebody else who was an oboe player is a key figure in our story, the Beatles' brilliant producer Sir George Martin. From whom did George Martin learn to play the oboe, you may well ask? The answer is, amazingly, my mother. Long before my mother met George Martin as the Beatles' producer, she had met him as a pupil of hers. She was teaching at the Guildhall School of Music and Drama, where George was studying, and she taught him the oboe, which was his primary instrument along with the piano.

The oboe is a hard instrument to play. It is a member of the family of double-reed instruments, which means that unlike a clarinet or a saxophone, which has a single reed sitting on a little bit of wood, it has two reeds squished together, just like when you blow through a blade of grass or an actual reed as a kid and make that squeaking noise. The rest of the double-reed family goes from the bassoon (or even contrabassoon), which is super low, up through the oboe d'amore, the cor anglais, or English horn, up to the oboe, which plays the highest notes. My favourite is the cor anglais, a kind of lower-pitched oboe. It is very mournful and beautiful. Now as I say, there isn't an oboe solo as such on a single Beatles song. There are oboes in a couple of the orchestras for sure. Certainly, there are oboes in the big Richard Hewson arrangement on "The Long and Winding Road" and in the orchestra for "A Day in the Life," and so on. But if you want to hear what a cor anglais sounds like, you can find one on the B-side of a big hit Paul McCartney had as a songwriter. That big hit was "A World Without Love," recorded (as you know by now!) by Peter & Gordon. On the B-side is a song Gordon and I wrote called "If I Were You" featuring the cor anglais. So, if you have your old 45 of "A World Without Love," flip it over and play it. And if not, you can find the song online, of course.

Moving back to the Beatles and away (reluctantly) from the oboe, here is a curious fact related to the letter O. In their solo careers, John Lennon and George Harrison wrote and recorded two songs that have almost identical titles—as close to an identical title as one can get without actually being so. There is two letters' difference: "Out the Blue" and "Out of the Blue." Two completely different pieces of music, written by different Beatles, but with very similar titles. The first one is from John's *Mind Games* album, the excellent song "Out the Blue," a gem that is not always given its due. A beautiful ballad about Yoko—and even directed to Yoko, I suppose, since it was released at a time when they were sepa-rated. A song about the suddenness and intensity of love, full of adventurous lyrical twists such as "Like a UFO you came to me and blew away life's misery." Some might see that as over the top— but when John met Yoko, she probably *did* seem a little alien and unidentified, certainly not like any woman he had met before. And it is a record full of cool musical moments as well—the elegant and restrained (almost folky) finger-picked acoustic guitar intro, the sudden and fierce groove of John's American rhythm section, and a rich and complex piano solo from Kenny Ascher, all happening over a very original set of chord changes which are convoluted without being distracting.

By contrast, "Out of the Blue" by George Harrison is an instrumental track, pretty much a jam featuring George's incredibly talented musician friends. George is playing guitar as usual. Klaus Voormann is also on the record, but this time he is playing guitar rather than bass because the bass part is being played by Carl Radle. I seem to recall this as quite a long jam, probably just about the right amount of time to make a martini or whatever you fancy as you listen to it. George always seemed interested in the idea of sitting on one chord for a long time and seeing where an in-depth exploration of that single chord (in this instance C minor) can lead.

Let's move on to a very famous O song performed by the Beatles as a band—one that I'm sure you have been expecting, and I shall not disappoint. This is the great Ringo song "Octopus's Garden," which he not only sang but wrote.

I have been reading about octopuses lately and discovered that they do actually have gardens of a sort, technically called middens. An octopus will collect little bits of glass and shells and whatever treasures it can find (often including the bones or shells of its prey) and build a little fence around the midden and make a comfortable "garden" for itself. It ends up as something between a rubbish dump and a private den, and some can be quite beautiful.

Octopuses turn out to be extremely intelligent animals and startlingly strong. One weird thing I did discover, though, which is a bit disconcerting, is that an octopus has sex only once in its lifetime. Octopuses mate once, and the female has about ten thousand eggs. Shortly after the mating ritual, the male rapidly declines. He loses the sharpness of his camouflage. His eyes cloud over. He stops eating and soon dies of starvation. I mean, goodness me! We have all been guilty of rolling over and going to sleep, but that's taking things a little far. And while we are on the subject of octopus porn, I should mention that the one time they do mate, apparently, it's quite spectacular. According to a *New York Times* article, "Their mating is frenzied and violent, [and looks like] a writhing bowl of spaghetti." What could be more exciting than that?

So anyway, I didn't mean to get you too worked up with all this octopus sex talk. But now you know what really goes on in the garden!

To cool down, there's only one thing to say, and that's "Ooh! My Soul," a Little Richard song that the Beatles performed in one of the BBC sessions. It's a fairly obscure song, though I do remember it and obviously Paul McCartney did, too. Several of Little Richard's compositions sound quite similar, but both he and Paul McCartney sing them so well that I can hear as many of them as they care to sing, and as many as Richard Penniman (his real name) cared to write.

We cannot talk about the Beatles and the letter O without paying homage to an artist whom the Beatles very much admired and to whom one Beatle in particular became very close. And that artist is Roy Orbison. Roy stands out in the world of rock and roll in so many ways. His extraordinary voice was evident even in childhood, as was his quiet, diffident, and self-effacing manner. He grew up listening to all the country greats like Lefty Frizell (hence his Wilbury name of "Lefty"), Hank Williams, and Jimmie Rodgers, as well as rhythm and blues and the orchestral music of Mantovani, all of which made its mark. And when the hits started coming (from "Only the Lonely" onwards), all of us in the UK fell under his spell. There was no other singer like him. When he hit the operatic and ineffably beautiful high A at the end of "Running Scared," we were all moved, delighted, and even jealous. So when the Beatles got to tour with Roy in 1963, they were thrilled. Each night he would stand there motionless on the stage, almost hiding behind his big thick glasses and his dyed black hair and singing with a unique and magical genius. I never had the honour or pleasure of meeting Roy myself, but by all accounts, he was as charming, considerate, and intelligent as he was perhaps withdrawn and cautious when thrust into the role of celebrity rock star.

Like John, Paul, and Ringo, George was a big Roy Orbison fan. And in the 1980s, as I'm sure you know, he and Jeff Lynne were able to incorporate Roy into the brilliant combination of players and singers that was the Traveling Wilburys. Whenever Roy sings a solo or even a harmony, his voice is clear and distinctive, as in their debut single, "Handle with Care." On another Wilburys song, "End of the Line," one can hear Roy's beautiful voice very distinctly towards the end of the track. Roy Orbison is one of the best, purest, most influential, and most instantly recognizable singers in the history of rock and roll, and he is dearly missed.

To wrap up the letter O, let us turn to Paul McCartney's brilliant song and a great vocal from *Abbey Road*, "Oh! Darling." The song has an almost '50s feel to it, and the chord changes have a doo-wop-era flavour. And yet if we compare Paul's vocal to some of the Roy Orbison vocals we just considered, which owe allegiance to that same era, we find them to be entirely different, and it makes for an interesting contrast. Whereas Roy chose to pay homage to singers like Hank Williams, whose skill lay in making every note seem effortless (though in no way dispassionate), on "Oh! Darling" Paul is emulating singers like Little Richard or Wilson Pickett, who apply maximum effort to every single note they sing. Paul has said that he wanted the vocal to sound as if he had been singing to an audience with all his might every night. He walked over to EMI Studios from his house nearby several days in a row and did just one maximum-power full-energy take of the song on each day until he got what he needed—a fervent vocal that takes us back in time to the extreme energy of "Long Tall Sally" or "I'm Down." This vocal style is more often associated with Lennon than with McCartney, and no doubt the unspoken competition between the two of them (John was known to hint that he could have done a great job on "Oh! Darling") played a role in Paul's extraordinary efforts and the remarkable result.

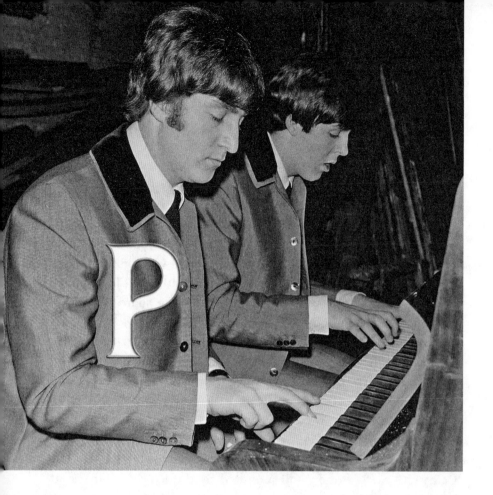

For the letter P, I am going to start at the very beginning, as it were, or very close to the very beginning, with a double P song, "Please Please Me." This was the Beatles' second single in the UK, but in the U.S., no one paid much attention to it at the time. It is an innovative and remarkable record and worth talking about at some length. Among the many interesting facts is how this record came to be.

"Please Please Me" was originally written at a much slower tempo than that of the finished record we know and love. When John wrote the song, it was almost ballad-like; John later recalled that he was inspired by a Roy Orbison song. "I remember the day

John and Paul at the piano.

and the pink coverlet on the bed," he recalled, "and I heard Roy Orbison doing 'Only the Lonely' or something." And that inspired him to write this lovely song, "Please Please Me," in a sad mode. But George Martin had a different idea. "I think it would be better speeded up," he said, and when the Beatles played it that way, they instantly agreed. And that is how they cut the record. If John was originally using "Only the Lonely" as his archetype, that would be a tempo change from the Roy Orbison tempo of about 122 bpm (beats per minute) to the final "Please Please Me" tempo of about 140 bpm—a significant increase and one that makes the final arrangement work brilliantly. George Martin was right. There is great playing from the whole band, including Ringo at his creative best. The way he plays that elegant little rolling snare phrase on each of the background vocal "Come on" responses is beautifully bouncy, and his fill into the bridge (three little one-beat mini-fills, the first played on the snare and the second and third on the tom-tom) is a masterpiece of restraint and precision but takes the song exactly where it needs to go.

"Only the Lonely" may not have been the only classic record which inspired or influenced the creation of "Please Please Me." I am convinced that the vocal arrangement was influenced by "Cathy's Clown," written and recorded by the Everly Brothers. At the beginning of that wonderful record, Don and Phil sing "Don't want your love" in unison but on the word "love" the high part stays on a single note while the low part descends away from it: Don goes down while Phil stays where he is. That makes for a beautiful musical moment, and I have no doubt that John and Paul admired it as much as I do. At the opening of "Please Please Me," John and Paul start on the same note, but John sings the quarter-note descending melody of the song ("Last night I said these words to my girl") while Paul stays up on the original note—an E, as it happens—all the way through the whole line, thus creating a very catchy descending cadence effect which is the heart of the song.

I certainly do not mean to suggest that "Please Please Me" is anything less than a wholly original song—this is just an exchange of ideas. When a record sounds really good, one takes the trouble to listen and to analyze—to figure out *how* it was done and *why* it sounds so delicious. The Beatles certainly did this to the music of their idols—and *everyone* has done it to the Beatles!

"Please Please Me" was also the title track of the Beatles' first album, the one with that very cool picture of them peering down from the staircase in the EMI Records building on Manchester Square. Those stairs are no longer there (the whole building was demolished), though I once read that some piece of the iconic stairwell was saved, but I have never noticed it when I have visited EMI's new building. Perhaps it is hidden away. Back then, of course, EMI House was *the* place to be—as soon as Gordon Waller and I had our own record deal with the same label, we were thrilled to be there. That was where our meetings took place and so on, that was the headquarters of everything, and that's where the Beatles posed for that famous picture. Actually, quite a number of photo shoots were done in and around the building—and even in the little garden that is at the centre of Manchester Square itself. A cheap and convenient location made legendary and iconic by the magic of the Beatles.

The album *Please Please Me* has so many great tracks on it— one of which is a P song which takes us even closer to the beginning of the band itself: "P.S. I Love You," which was released in the UK in October 1962 as the B-side of "Love Me Do," their very first record. It was produced by Ron Richards, not George Martin. I am not sure why George was not there himself, but the staff producers at EMI certainly thought of themselves as a team, and it would not have been unusual for George to give Ron some advance guidance as to what he wanted to achieve and leave the session to him to get it done. This was also the session for which Ringo arrived only to find a session drummer (Andy White) had taken over his role in the studio. Andy played drums on "Love Me Do," and Ringo shared percussion duties with Andy on "P.S. I Love You," no doubt a difficult (and, in retrospect, wholly unnecessary) moment for all concerned. Andy was a fine drummer, but no one now has the slightest doubt as to Ringo's brilliance and his extraordinary importance to the very essence and history of rock and roll drumming.

As with so many Beatles tracks, there are a few particularly distinctive elements which elevate the song and the record from being very good to being uniquely brilliant. On the "you" of "P.S. I love you," instead or returning to the tonic D chord your brain is expecting, the song makes a quick diversion to a B-flat chord and makes you wait two bars for delicious resolution. And Paul's descant part late in the song ("You know I want you to remember") is sublime.

John gave Paul all the credit for this song, saying that Paul was trying to write a letter song like "Soldier Boy," by the Shirelles. Paul wrote "P.S. I Love You" in Germany, on the way to or from Hamburg. The idea of a letter song was not new, of course; such songs have been around a long time. There was even an old song with the title "P.S. I Love You." Ron Richards said that he didn't think the Beatles' "P.S. I Love You" could or should be a single, in part because of this preexisting hit record. But that version was from a long time ago. Rudy Vallee recorded the song sometime in the 1930s. It is not a bad song and worth listening to if you are curious, as I was. The earlier version of "P.S. I Love You," performed by Rudy Vallee and his Connecticut Yankees, was not (of course) written by Lennon & McCartney but rather by the very distinguished songwriting team of Johnny Mercer (lyrics) & Gordon Jenkins (music), which leads us to an unexpected coincidence. Gordon Jenkins subsequently wrote the beautiful string and orchestral arrangements for Harry Nilsson's album of standards, A *Little Touch of Schmilsson in the Night*, an album which each of the Beatles admired and loved. A strange and interesting connection.

The letter P also takes us beyond the Beatles' breakup to what I think is one of the best records and best-written songs that any individual Beatle ever did beginning with P. This is Ringo's song "Photograph," which was written by George Harrison and Ringo himself. The song was recorded in Los Angeles, produced by my friend Richard Perry and engineered by Bill Schnee, a legendary and highly skilled recording engineer. And it does sound extraordinarily good. Great band, great vocal by Ringo, and a huge hit.

Ringo also sang it at the "Concert for George," a performance which was one of the emotional highlights of that event given the nature of the song and that it was sung so recently after George had left us. A couple of additional credits I should throw in because they are important: Bobby Keys played that cool saxophone solo, and the orchestra was arranged by Jack Nitzsche. I don't know if you know who Jack is, but he did a lot of work with Phil Spector. The Wall of Sound was as much his invention as Phil's, and he deserves appropriate credit. He is a terrific arranger, and he did excellent work on "Photograph."

I cannot mention Phil Spector—another P—without spending some time talking about his work with the Beatles. Phil was one of the great geniuses of the record business, produced some of the finest records in the history of rock and roll, but also was (and presumably still is) mad as a hatter and usually heavily armed—though I must assume the latter attribute no longer possible since he is incarcerated. I met him a couple of times, and it was an intimidating and scary experience, most notably at a Linda Ronstadt concert at the Universal Amphitheatre in Los Angeles. Linda, with whom I was working as producer and manager at the time, knew Phil better than I did. I was the one saying, "Oh, we should let him come backstage and visit us after the show." I was a huge fan, and Phil was a legend. But she responded, "No, no, don't! He'll have guns; he'll have crazy people. I've met him, and he is mad!" I thought she was overreacting, so he did come backstage, and oh my God, it was terrifying. He leapt out of this huge car with various bodyguards and holding clearly visible large and dangerous weapons. Linda very sensibly ran away and hid in her dressing room, and I had to get rid of him with the help of the people at the Universal Amphitheatre. But anyway, apart from that (and the fact that he eventually did murder someone), he was a nice enough chap, I guess, and certainly made some truly incredible records. My favourite Phil Spector production, strangely enough, was a huge hit in the UK but not a big hit in America, which I never understood because it is an amazing record. That is "River Deep—Mountain High" by Ike and Tina Turner. A true masterpiece of arrangement and production. An extraordinary song written by Jeff Barry and Ellie Greenwich along with Spector, with a stunning vocal from Tina Turner. (Ike was included in the credits but was paid to stay away.) I consider "River Deep—Mountain High" to be the greatest possible example of Phil's genius—his Sistine Chapel, his *Mona Lisa*, his *Four Seasons*, his *Messiah*—record production as high art and commercial success at the same time.

Phil Spector (along with Jack Nitzsche, of course) created the Wall of Sound, the essence of which was having an astonishing number of first-rate musicians in the band, several of them often grouped together on the same part, to create this gigantic sound. It had a very powerful effect on listeners and led to a string of hit records. Phil was a genius of a record producer, and some records he made during that period have become classics that producers all agree are some of the best-made, best-sounding, most revolutionary records ever.

Phil came into the Beatles' lives to salvage the 1969 "Get Back" sessions and turn them into the *Let It Be* album, in many cases without much input from the Beatles themselves. I've already written about his adding an orchestra to "The Long and Winding Road," and he put his stamp on the rest of the project as well. Even though Paul was unhappy with Phil's additions, the other Beatles continued to work with him after the band broke up. Phil produced George Harrison's "My Sweet Lord" and John Lennon's "Instant Karma!" He and John became friends for a while until he drove even John crazy—Phil was at least as unpredictable and infuriating as he was brilliant.

But as we all know, the Beatles—together or individually—did not need Phil Spector to make hit records, beginning with P or any other letter. In 1966 and 1967 they saw two of their P songs climb the charts, both of them Paul songs. One was about one of Paul's fictitious but richly imagined characters, the unnamed but certainly eager "Paperback Writer." Again, a perfect record. I could dissect it in detail—but allow me to suggest something else. You already know the whole record and you love it. So next time you listen to it, concentrate on one part at a time. Listen to the background vocal arrangement. Listen to the electric guitar lick. Listen to the unstoppable groove of Paul and Ringo as a rhythm section.

One of the curious things about "Paperback Writer" is that it is the only tune that the Beatles ever did live on *Top of the Pops*, which was, as you may know, a huge weekly television show in England that continued to exist until relatively recently. It was the show on which *every* band appeared, with the solitary exception of Led Zeppelin. If you had a hit single, you did *Top of the Pops.* Generally, you did it as a live broadcast, unless you were the Beatles, who were permitted to make videos and send them in to be broadcast. The one exception, apparently, was "Paperback Writer."

Top of the Pops used to be broadcast live from Manchester on Thursday nights, and it was a very exciting process because you had to wait in a state of anticipation until Monday when that week's top forty was published. If your record had entered the charts or made an upwards move, you knew you would be doing *Top of the Pops* on Thursday. You'd get a train up to Manchester in the morning, appear live on *Top of the Pops,* and then the great thing was that you could then go out clubbing that night. And I mean, how could you fail to have a great night? You were out and about in Manchester having just been seen by everyone on live television, singing your hit, and you would walk into some cool club where they were playing records (sometimes even including yours), and there would be lots of charming girls anxious to dance with you at the very least. So, it was always fun and something to look forward to. The BBC later moved *Top of the Pops* down to London, and it eventually became a taped show, not a live show, so all that instant fun disappeared. But we had a great time in Manchester back in the day, staying in the dowdy Victorian elegance of the old Midland Hotel.

I also read recently that the BBC's tapes of the Beatles performing "Paperback Writer" live on *Top of the Pops* were reused to save money, so there is a silent amateur video of the broadcast, which is both sad and pathetic. "Paperback Writer" went to No. 1 in the U.S. a little later but in an odd way. It topped the charts for two weeks, but they were not consecutive weeks. The song was No. 1, then it was knocked off by a very good record by a very good singer, and then that record in turn dipped down a bit, and "Paperback Writer" went back to No. 1. Who was this mysterious interloper? A man by the name of Frank Sinatra, with a record called "Strangers in the Night." Two generations of excellence, sharing the top of the charts.

The second of Paul's hit songs in the letter P category also features imaginary characters, but they inhabit a real place: Liverpool's Penny Lane. The barber, the banker, the fireman, and the nurse were all ordinary people from the Beatles' hometown, and in the space of a few notes and a few words, Paul brings them to life. The song features a wonderful trumpet solo, on a Bach trumpet (also called a piccolo trumpet), which plays in a higher register than an ordinary trumpet.

When I was writing about the letter O, I spent some time discussing the oboe because I like to throw a few musical instruments as well as songs and people into our alphabetical journey. So now I would like to turn our thoughts to the most prominent P instrument, the piano. The piano is incredibly important to every musician. Almost every one of them, amateur or professional and regardless of whatever else they play, can tinkle away a few chords and notes on the piano, and it is often the primary instrument of songwriters, composers, and arrangers. That said, it is a relatively new instrument. The piano—or to give it its full name, the pianoforte—was invented for a particular reason. Up until about the middle of the eighteenth century, the main keyboard instrument available for personal use was the harpsichord.

The harpsichord sounds really cool, with a jangly, pointed sound. One of the best uses of a harpsichord in a Beatles song was when George Martin played it on "Fixing a Hole." When you listen to George Martin on the harpsichord, you can hear that it has a very specific and distinctive tone. When you press a key on a harpsichord, what you are actually doing is lifting a little kind of pick under the string, until you apply enough pressure and suddenly, *ping*, it plucks the string, just as a pick does when you use one to play the guitar. The string then makes a fixed percussive sound, but it has only one volume level. Whether you press a key hard or soft, the strength and volume of the note produced is the same. This gives an almost mechanical consistency to all the notes you play.

The problem was that musicians could not play sensitively and softly on the harpsichord—they could not play with dynamics. They wanted an instrument that could go from soft to loud, or in Italian from *piano* to *forte*. And so, they invented an instrument to do this. Instead of plucking the string with a pick, the new pianoforte hit it with a hammer. That way, if you hit the key softly, the hammer hits the string softly and plays the note quietly. If you bang the key hard, if you Jerry Lee Lewis on it, it plays it loud. And that is what was revolutionary about the piano and why it is the most used keyboard by far, even in the age of electronic keyboards—it is incredibly and uniquely responsive. P for piano leads us to a great variety of songs. I must first acknowledge one legendary John Lennon piano song. You know what it is. He wrote it on the piano. There is a video of him playing that beautiful white piano. It is a song that has been covered many, many times. It is a masterpiece. It is "Imagine." Listen to it again, if you haven't done so recently. You will be glad you did.

There are many Paul piano songs but I realize I have already told you about the best of them. The letter L was particularly rich in such songs, with "Lady Madonna," "Let It Be," and "Lovely Rita." And there are many others as well, like "Martha My Dear" and "Good Day Sunshine"—on the latter of which George Martin played the piano part, as he also did on John's song "In My Life."

Before we leave the letter P behind, I'd like to include one last song in our piano discussion. Mysteriously, on the recorded version of this song there actually is no piano. Paul does not play piano on the record. No one does. However, the song is inextricably linked in my mind to a particular piano and will be so forever. I have told the story before, so I shall not repeat it here. Suffice it to say that even though the song is perfect for guitars, I still hear in my head that miraculous and astonishing piano and vocal duet version I heard in my family's basement music room all those decades ago of "I Want to Hold Your Hand."

We have arrived at the letter Q.

I am sure some of you may have been wondering, *What is Peter going to do when he gets to some of the difficult letters?* Well, the answer is that I did have to think a bit harder. There is only one Beatles-related song that begins with Q, and I shall get to it shortly. But Q does open up a whole other range of possibilities. So, do not worry; there is plenty of interesting Q-inspired stuff to come.

I am going to start by talking about a very early recording of

The "True Love Ways" guitar, given to me by the Buddy Holly Educational Foundation.

the Beatles when they were not even the Beatles. They were a skiffle group called the Quarrymen, a fine name, beginning of course with the letter Q. And, better than that, they were playing a song by one of my very favourite singers and songwriters, the great Buddy Holly. The amateur recording, which was made on one microphone in 1958, was of Buddy Holly's "That'll Be the Day." John was the first nascent Beatle to be a member of the Quarrymen, then Paul joined in October 1957 and George in early 1958. The skiffle craze was at its peak at the time; in his excellent book on the subject, Billy Bragg estimates that there may have been as many as fifty thousand active skiffle groups in Britain in the '50s. The Quarrymen were obviously sliding from skiffle into rock and roll already (in terms of both instrumentation and arrangement) when they made the recording of "That'll Be the Day"—John throws in a couple of great Buddy "hiccups" and George's solo is very close to the original one Buddy played, while still following the skiffle tradition of keeping the arrangement very simple. In fact, they made "That'll Be the Day" into a genuine three-chord song (in A major) by leaving out the B7 chord which would have preceded the E7 on "that's some day when I'll be through"—and they also omitted the heavy triplet accents on the last "you make me cry." And yet one can still hear hints in John's excellent vocal, in the harmonies and in the solo, of rock and roll greatness to come.

Buddy Holly was, of course, a huge influence on the band, in so many ways. As you probably know, one of the reasons they considered "Beatles" as a name in the first place was that they were inspired to do so by the Crickets, Buddy Holly's band. This allowed them to consider the entomological world as a possible source for cool name options. An irony is that they also thought the Crickets was an extra cool name because it comprised a pun by referring to both the insects and the game. They found out later that the Crickets themselves had no knowledge whatsoever of the game of cricket, so the pun factor was invisible to them and played no role in their choice of name. But that didn't stop the Beatles from incorporating a pun on "beat" into their own name.

The Beatles were great fans of all the brilliant songs Buddy

Holly wrote—as I am myself to this day. Gordon and I had a big hit with our duet version of "True Love Ways," and I produced a couple of Buddy Holly songs with Linda Ronstadt ("That'll Be the Day" and "It's So Easy") and one with James Taylor as well ("Everyday").

I mentioned that there is only one actual Q song that I could find in the catalogue of the Beatles, the Quarrymen, John, Paul, George, Ringo, or any of their projects. So, I am going to talk about it right away. It is almost like throwing away your high cards in a game of high-stakes poker. But what the hell, perhaps it will compel us to get more adventurous as we delve deeper into the Q's.

The only Q song I could find is called "Queenie Eye," and it comes off Paul McCartney's excellent 2013 album *New*. Apparently, queenie eye is a street game popular in Liverpool. It never reached London, I guess, because I never played it or heard of it, but maybe my friends and I weren't on the street and the future Beatles were. Who knows?

The name Queenie brings something else to mind, too, which is that Queenie was the name of Brian Epstein's mother. He spoke of her often with great affection. I never met her, but I know she was incredibly important in Brian's life and probably the only person in the world whom Brian loved more than he loved the Beatles.

So now that we've exhausted the Quarrymen, "Queenie Eye," and Queenie Epstein, let's really explore the letter Q. It is the beginning letter of quite a large number of musical terms, the most important of which, for our purposes, is *quartet.*

Now what that word probably brings to mind is the idea of a string quartet, and the Beatles did indeed love and use string quartets. One might well imagine, if one had to guess, that a string quartet would consist of a violin, viola, cello, and bass, just as a vocal quartet would consist of soprano, alto, tenor, and bass. But a string quartet does not work that way. A traditional string quartet is first violin, second violin (playing a part a little bit lower), viola, and cello. And that lineup, the traditional and perfect classical lineup, is what one hears when one listens to Vivaldi's *The Four*

Seasons or any of the other great string quartets that have been written, some of my favourites being Bartók's, which are a bit less obviously melodic and more intense, even punkish in their attitude. But I digress. The string quartet the Beatles used most famously appeared on the song "Yesterday." That has become the exemplar of how to marry a pop song and a string quartet.

No one did it better before, and I do not think anyone has done it better since. It is a masterpiece of a record and a great string arrangement by George Martin, who was essentially following direction from Paul McCartney and then applying his own genius and skill for orchestration. Once Paul figured out what a string quartet could do, he was clear about which lines and melodies and countermelodies and chords he thought would work with his song, and he was right.

I am sure you all know the story of the song, but if not, it is well worth repeating. Paul woke up with the melody in his head fully formed but without any lyrics. First, he thought it must be something he was remembering and asked everybody what tune it was. And when I say everybody, I include my mother, who was one of the first people he saw that day since he was living in our house. I was not there, but my mother (a musician herself, of course) told Paul that she did not recognize the tune and had never heard it before. After many other people said the same thing, Paul finally realized that he had written it magically in his head. Initially, he titled it "Scrambled Eggs" because he just wanted a temporary phrase that would fit that da-da-da scansion scheme, and eventually he came up with the brilliant lyrics about yesterday.

A string quartet has a beautiful, subtle, and emotional sound. But for "Eleanor Rigby," also to be arranged by George Martin, Paul wanted a more intense sound. As I have mentioned earlier, they accomplished this by close-miking a double string quartet. This is why the song sounds a lot less smooth than "Yesterday" and more crunchy and in your face. A brilliant arrangement. "Eleanor Rigby" combines a touching story, a great vocal, and above all eight extraordinarily good string players playing so beautifully and attacking each quarter note—or each crotchet, as we used to call them back in England—with a brio and precision that gives the song such extraordinary presence.

Speaking of quartets, there is, of course, a quartet sitting right in front of us. As plain as the nose on our face, as it were, and that quartet is the Beatles themselves. Now, of course in the records they made, the Beatles frequently overdubbed instruments, doubled their vocals, and did extra work, which could be seen as taking them above and beyond the quartet concept. But the essence of a rock and roll band is often a quartet. And in this case, it is two guitars, bass, and drums and a couple of singers. So here, I thought I'd track down a great pure quartet version of a Beatles song, and I chose the BBC recording of "Ticket to Ride" because it is just the four of them playing the song once—no overdubs, no studio adjustments or tricks, nothing beyond the four instruments and the live vocals. It is the Beatles at their "quartet-est" for the letter Q.

As we can hear on "Ticket to Ride," the Beatles sang very strongly. I imagine that this was something they picked up in Hamburg, where the clubs were undoubtedly noisy every night, and sound systems were not very good. Hearing them live in a regular unamplified environment was certainly very impressive. I distinctly remember sitting with John and Paul when they were learning something on the guitar or at the piano in our house, and their vocals were spectacular. Not just loud but intense, heartfelt, and accurate.

At the opposite end of the scale, it did occur to me to wonder, since we are dealing with the letter Q, what one might consider the quietest Beatles song. I suppose "Julia" would be a contender. It is hard to choose, but in the end, I would go with a different track from the White Album. So, becoming extremely quiet with the letter Q, my choice is "Blackbird." Paul's gently tapping feet, an almost classically restrained finger-picked guitar part, and a contemplative vocal—and an exceptional song, of course.

It has also occurred to me that the letter Q stands for the word *question*. And so I started to wonder how many Beatles songs pose a question. And the answer is that quite a few do so. The list makes for an interesting selection from all the different eras of their career. I'll start with an early one, and a very obvious question, posed this time by George Harrison as he asks, "Do You Want to Know a Secret." John Lennon (the primary composer) did not specifically create it with George in mind, but once the song emerged, John thought it would be a good one for him. John has gone on record with his view that at that time George was not an experienced singer, having concentrated on his guitar playing, and had only a limited range—which would make this song an ideal choice. I have always wondered myself about one of the catchiest bits of the song, the descending chords in the very first bar (after the word "Listen"), curious as to whether John was inspired by hearing that very same sequence (in a key a half step lower) in a song they covered, "Till There Was You" (under the words "heard them at all")—it works brilliantly in both instances.

Turning to the years immediately after the breakup, I shall give John a turn at posing a question. And he asks this one, "How Do You Sleep?"—a question directed to Paul McCartney in a very public way. By this time, the friendship and incredibly fruitful partnership between these two extraordinary musicians had decayed utterly, and their only communications were via lawyers, occasionally in the press—and in song. John was convinced that Paul had sent him multiple "coded" (and insulting) messages in his 1971 *Ram* album, and so he felt entitled to respond vigorously.

I remember not long before that, when there were still in-person meetings at the Apple offices, there were a couple of occasions when the Beatles would have extremely heated discussions among themselves (we could hear shouting through the door), but at least they were communicating. I suppose resorting to the music press and song lyrics was even worse.

Now, of course, to be fair to Paul, I must give him a turn. And the song I would choose is "What You're Doing." I know that if you listen to the beginning of the song, you might not think the song poses a question; he's just saying, "Look what you're doing." But he then goes on to ask, "Would it be so much to ask of you / What you're doing to me?" Suddenly, an important question.

Ringo gets in on the question game with "What Goes On." This song actually dates back to the Quarrymen era; John had written most of the song back then, and it was resurrected (changing perhaps from a folky skiffle track to more of a country song in the process) with help from Paul and even from Ringo. In fact, this song is the *only* one ever credited to Lennon, McCartney, and Starr.

Paul McCartney asked a very significant question in another song, to which the honest answer is probably, "Because we'd be arrested!" The question is, of course, "Why Don't We Do It in the Road?" Very much a Paul effort—John's feelings were hurt that Paul recorded it alone with Ringo and did not involve John at all. Paul has said that it just happened that way circumstantially and was not a deliberate slight, and, of course, John did a similar thing with "The Ballad of John and Yoko," which excluded Ringo as Paul played drums. I have no idea how George felt about either of these songs. "Why Don't We Do It in the Road?" is a brilliantly fierce bluesy vocal from Paul, recorded during the final sessions for the White Album. The track features Paul's extraordinarily intense and passionate singing, with a remarkable octave jump into falsetto and back; Ringo's brilliantly minimalist drum part that fits perfectly around the handclaps and percussion; and Paul's turn at some Elmore James–style slide guitar work. Apparently, the question came to him while in Rishikesh, when he saw a monkey couple doing it in the road without any qualms about the public nature of their location. I suppose only an evolutionary biologist could really answer the question as to why we don't (usually!) do the same thing. In the meantime I shall settle for a quote from the turn of the last century from the legendary actress Mrs. Patrick Campbell, who asked, "Does it really matter what these affectionate people do—as long as they don't do it in the streets and frighten the horses?" And modern motorists might be equally distracted—so perhaps that answers Paul's question for now.

Not all the Beatles' questions were plaintive. Their questions came in all varieties. Sometimes they do not even ask a question as such but rather instruct someone else to do so, as they do on "Ask Me Why," a track recorded in 1962 but with a sound more reminiscent of the '50s. It features a quintessentially American and doo-wop-flavoured vocal from John with harmonies from Paul and George which owe much more to the wonderful harmony arrangements of Smokey Robinson and the Miracles than to any early British rock and roll or skiffle.

Before I close out this querulous part of the chapter, I'd like to pose two questions that the Beatles picked up from others. The first is a very straightforward question to which the answer is usually yes. That is the early Beatles song "Ain't She Sweet." I describe it as a Beatles song, but it actually derives from an even earlier era. "Ain't She Sweet" was written in 1927 by Milton Ager and Jack Yellen in honour of Ager's daughter and was a giant hit back in the Roaring Twenties. It is a cool song and an interesting choice by the early Beatles.

Sticking with the "ain't" theme, Fats Domino wrote a song probably twenty-five years or so after that, which was a favourite of all of ours, including the Beatles. John Lennon recorded it on his *Rock 'n' Roll* album, and that song was "Ain't That a Shame." I confess that if I had to choose one version for the proverbial desert island, I would choose the original Fats version, but I do admire the almost experimental bravery of John's effort. The Lennon version changes the groove completely, removing the triplet feel of Fats's piano part and replacing it with a more "straight" piano part—still a New Orleans kind of thing but without the swing. And I am such a fan of John's singing that the compulsion to load his vocal down with effects (as is the case here) is one I question.

That brings us to the end of my list of question songs. Hope that was not too annoying in that I gave you lots of questions and very few answers, but that's what Q will do.

The letter Q also leads us to a term in classical music, one that is quite rare. It is a Latin term, *quodlibet*. And what it means is "as you please." It is the name for the use of little musical quotations from other composers in one's work. Such use is quite common in classical music and also in rock and roll and jazz. Johann Sebastian Bach was very fond of quodlibet, and a family game in the Bach household is reputed to have been a game of quodlibet in which Bach would play the organ and interpolate into his piece sixteen or so little quotations from other composers. It was up to his children and the rest of the family to guess and identify those composers and the piece of music from which the quotation came. Probably not terribly easy, but I don't imagine being the children of a genius like Bach was particularly easy anyway. Evidently, when he wasn't in his study writing another hit, or when he wasn't on the road doing a gig or something, that's how he would unwind when he was home with his family. When I say "gig," of course, you probably know that Bach was a highly skilled organist as well as a brilliant composer, and he would play gigs, mostly in churches. So (to make a silly modern comparison) I guess he was not only the Lennon & McCartney of his day but the Billy Preston of his day as well.

In the Beatles catalogue I can think of one prominent use of quodlibet. But maybe somebody else will think of another one. The Beatles song which I know contains quotations from other works is "All You Need Is Love," in which there are quotations from "La Marseillaise" and "She Loves You," to name but two—one right at the beginning and one at the end. It is interesting to note that the two quotes are probably equally familiar to a general audience. I think it could certainly be suggested that you know you have made it as a songwriter when you write a song which is as famous, as distinctive, and as instantly recognizable as one of the major national anthems of Western civilization! Each can be named by most listeners in only a few notes. Their use in the global live broadcast of "All You Need Is Love" in June 1967 increased the universality and significance of the event and even added a certain Charles Ives–like sense of everything happening at the same time musically as the song heads towards its dramatic end.

I am very happy to have reached the letter R because it gives me the opportunity to talk about one of my very favourite Beatles songs, and that is "Rain."

I love that track. Everything about it is incredible. An extraordinary song, a great arrangement. Amazing bass part. I mean a highly original and specifically McCartney-esque bass part, and, as I've mentioned earlier, Ringo's drum fills are equally astounding, as is the sound of the snare drum itself on this particular track. Whatever formula Ringo, George Martin, and Geoff Emerick concocted for the snare sound is terrific. And Ringo uses the snare and the hi-hat as part of each one of his brilliantly composed fills, which is what makes them so highly original. I think it is some of Ringo's very finest work.

The Beatles with one of their idols (and mine), Little Richard.

It might be interesting to explore how something like this usually happens in the studio. The way a snare drum finally sounds is the result of a whole series of decisions. First of all, it depends upon which snare drum is used. There are big ones and small ones, wooden ones and brass ones, and many variations and options. There are different kinds of drum heads which can be used, thick ones and thin ones, real calf ones and synthetic ones. Then the heads can be tuned—turning the various bolts which attach the head to the drum tightens or loosens the skin of the head itself, raising or lowering the frequency of the sound it makes.

The resonance of the drum can also be changed by putting something on the head to dampen the vibrations—a wallet sitting on the head is quite a common trick; and Ringo would sometimes drape a tea towel over the whole head to dull the resonance almost completely. The drum can be played with light sticks or heavy sticks or even brushes. And the engineer has numerous options as to the choice and placement of microphones. Each drum can have its own microphone or sometimes two—one above and one below. The kit as a whole can be miked as well by one mic (mono) or two mics (stereo) above it, known as the overhead mics. When the signal from these microphones reaches the control room, it can be processed in multiple ways, the most common applications being "equalization" (EQ) and "limiting and compression." These mysterious terms actually refer to very simple ideas. EQ is a fancy and infinitely flexible version of the treble and bass tone controls you find on home equipment—the engineer can make the sound as crispy or as boomy as one could ever want, with every subtle variation in between. Limiters and compressors are devices that (in the simplest terms) automatically turn down the loud bits and turn up the soft bits in order to fit all the parts together properly. In the right hands, the use of these techniques is an important art throughout the process of recording and mixing.

Yet none of these techniques makes as much difference as who is playing the drums in the first place and what the drummer decides to play. When I previously described Ringo's fills as "composed," I chose the word carefully. Whether he made some up on the spot or thought them up in advance, there is nothing random about them.

The brilliant way he integrated the hi-hat and snare into what would usually just be tom-tom fills was perfect, elegant, and highly original.

As it happens, I had a conversation with Ringo recently on this very subject. I told him that I had been writing admiringly about his drum fills, and he expressed curiosity as to which were my current favourites. When I mentioned "Rain" he told me that it was indeed a special case: he had played differently in a stylistic sense (which drums he used and in what order) on that track than on any other Beatles record before or since. Still very hard for me to choose a favourite—even if "Rain" gets its own category, there are still so many great fills to choose from!

Another interesting thing about "Rain," as I have mentioned before, is that it was slowed down somewhere in the mixing or mastering process. So, if you try to figure out what key the record is in, it is kind of F-sharpish, but I assume it was recorded in G, or possibly even A, and then slowed down. This would not only change the tempo but also lower the pitch and the actual tone of each instrument. Somehow every move the Beatles and George Martin made in the recording and production of "Rain" and every choice they made as it neared completion was perfect.

"Rain" is a John Lennon track, and it shows how experimental and creative he had become by 1966. Of course, John never forgot his rock and roll roots, which we can hear in an early Beatles cover track in the R category, written by one of their great heroes, Chuck Berry: "Rock and Roll Music." The band recorded it in one take, with a live vocal by John. And then they overdubbed three pianists all playing the same Steinway piano at the same time.

The pianists were John Lennon, Paul McCartney, and George Martin. I have no idea who played which particular bits of the piano part. It would be really interesting to hear the piano track soloed and try to figure out who played what because, in levels of piano proficiency, it would be John Lennon at the bottom of the list, Paul McCartney in the middle, and George Martin at the top. The complicated stuff would likely have been played by George Martin, the intermediate stuff by Paul, and the basic stuff by John. However it was, their efforts combined to create an extraordinary piano part and a great track.

Now I'd like to move on to another song that the Beatles also covered, where both the song and the artist use the letter R. The song is "Rip It Up" by Little Richard, which the Beatles sang in their live set, and there are recorded versions of them doing it. But honestly, the original version by Little Richard cannot be beat. He was a brilliant pianist, yet oddly there does not seem to be any piano on his first version. It is a sparse arrangement: beautiful horn parts and a terrific vocal. When you listen to it, check out the scream going into the solo, a scream that certainly influenced Paul McCartney. It is a great song, too.

"Rip It Up" was co-written by someone of whom I am also a huge fan and that is Robert "Bumps" Blackwell. He wrote and produced a lot of Little Richard records. He produced "Tutti Frutti." He co-wrote "Long Tall Sally" and "Good Golly Miss Molly" and "Ready Teddy" as well as "Rip It Up." He also produced "You Send Me" for Sam Cooke, one of my very favourite records and an amazing vocal. And then he produced several songs for a Bob Dylan album. Who knew? Sadly, he died too young, in 1985.

Back to the Beatles themselves, and a double R song, which we could not possibly omit: "Rocky Raccoon." It starts off like a Woody Guthrie talking blues, and it has the clever Gideon's Bible reference and so on. You still find those in hotel rooms all across America to this day. Someone must still be going around putting them in all those bedside drawers.

As I have said, I am a real sucker for those McCartney tunes that tell a story—they form an interesting literary collection of short stories or one-act plays or something. It is very cool. It would be interesting to make a list at some point (I'm sure someone already has) of all the characters that Paul has invented over the passage of time. I mean the girl whose real name was Magill, who called herself Lil, and she was known as Nancy, or her man Dan, or Rocky Raccoon himself. So many people Paul just conjured up who now have real characters and identity and are virtually part of our lives. Not to mention Vera, Chuck, and Dave. I guess they are all grown up now. Where are they? How did they turn out? I hope everything is okay.

Having visited Paul's world for a while, let's go back to John and look at a song that he apparently did not rate highly, "Run for Your Life." He later expressed considerable dislike for this track, saying it was one of his least favourites. And indeed, he has got in some trouble, retroactively, for the line, "I'd rather see you dead, little girl, / Than to be with another man," which is not currently considered an acceptable sentiment. And correctly so—though in John's defence we must point out that he borrowed that particular lyric verbatim from the Elvis Presley recording of "Baby Let's Play House," written by Arthur Gunter. And despite John's disdain, I find much to like about "Run for Your Life." On top of John's usual pounding Gibson J-160E acoustic part, I love the two intersecting electric guitar parts—the intro guitar riff, which reoccurs later in the song as well, along with the slide part. Even though both are out of tune by any traditional standards (as are many of the old blues records to which they owe musical allegiance), they combine to create a mood of rocking melancholy which matches the vocal. And I love the chord structure and background vocal arrangement in the chorus—especially in the last three bars. After alternating between a B minor and an E major a couple of times, the song ends with a descending G major, F-sharp major, and B minor with an added high part in the background vocals (Paul, I feel sure) which rings beautifully and is the kind of vocal arrangement no one can create or execute as well as the Beatles did.

The Beatles also explored the letter R in their post-Beatles days. Wings recorded an excellent R song, "Rock Show," from the *Venus and Mars* album. It features Denny Laine playing the Moog synthesizer, quite early in the Moog's life, and playing guitar and sitar as well. We also get to hear Allen Toussaint on the piano. I hope you recognize the name. Allen Toussaint was a brilliant songwriter and producer, a stalwart of the New Orleans music scene, who wrote and produced all those Lee Dorsey songs like "Ride Your Pony," "Working in the Coal Mine" ("whoops!"), and much else besides. His remarkable body of work is well worth exploring.

George also has some R songs in his catalogue, so allow me to mention a fairly obscure one I like. It is called "Ride Rajbun," and it is a children's song, with George singing along with a fully Indian instrumentation. He recorded it for a multi-artist charity album called *The Bunbury Tails*, which also served as the soundtrack for a British animated television series of the same name. I understand that the Bunburys were a bunny rabbit cricket team. And George got interested in cricket through his friendship with Eric Clapton, who was (and remains) a cricket fan and player, and they played in the grounds of Friar Park, George and Olivia's extraordinary home.

Musically, there is much about "Ride Rajbun" that is of interest. The sitar introduction was played by the great Ravi Shankar while the rest of the sitar parts were played by his student George Harrison. George visited his friend and mentor at his hotel in London and recorded the introduction there. The other singer on the choruses is Dhani Harrison, George's immensely talented son.

I confess that I cannot help but wonder whether David English, the creator of *The Bunbury Tails*, might not be (as I am) a devoted Oscar Wilde fan. The original Bunbury tales are from Wilde's masterpiece *The Importance of Being Earnest*. In the play, Bunbury is a fictional friend whose name gave rise to the word *bunburying*, which is the art of using such an invented friend (in urgent need) as an excuse for not showing up at an event one has committed to attend but wishes to avoid. But I've gotten way off subject here. So far as I know, George Harrison's "Ride Rajbun" and the Bunbury cricket team had nothing to do with Oscar Wilde officially—but the two will always be conjoined in my imagination. Though I rather doubt that Oscar Wilde played cricket!

Staying in somewhat obscure mode, I would like to pull up an R song from Paul McCartney. Paul is a fan of Noël Coward, as am I. Coward, as you may know, was a multifaceted genius, a brilliant English actor, playwright, performer, pianist, and songwriter who was born in 1899 and whose career spanned six decades of the twentieth century. Paul liked his songs very much. A few years back, a tribute album to Coward was produced, and Paul contributed his version of a classic Noël Coward song called "A Room with a View." Paul was certainly an admirer of Coward's style. Coward is terribly English and a little bit affected, but I love the way he sings. I recommend him very highly—the more you read about him or listen to or watch or read any of his works, your admiration will grow. Paul clearly shared my views, even if he did not go as far as the silk dressing gown and elegant cigarette holder that defined Coward's look. I can certainly hear echoes of Coward's clipped and almost staccato delivery, and his very English restraint and precision, in Paul's lovely version.

Another cover of an R song that Paul McCartney recorded was with Wings. On this track, Denny Laine sings lead, but you can hear Paul singing some great harmonies. This is a song called "Richard Cory," written by Paul Simon and originally performed and recorded by Simon & Garfunkel. It was based on a poem by Edwin Arlington Robinson, written in 1897, about a man who had everything—riches and success beyond his dreams—but was nonetheless miserable. The last line of the song, echoing the poem's last line, is "Richard Cory went home last night and put a bullet through his head." A sad song but a nice version by Paul McCartney and Wings featuring Denny Laine, with excellent harmonies throughout.

So now let us turn to an R song that Paul McCartney did write himself. He not only wrote it, he co-produced it with Linda, who also sang the background vocals, and he played every instrument: piano, Wurlitzer electric piano, ukulele, drums, and percussion. This is from the *Ram* album, a record with a pleasingly homemade feel to it, and is one of the best songs on it: "Ram On." Lyrically and musically simple, but a fine song and a good record.

I mentioned that *Ram* has a homemade flavour to it, but in fact the album wasn't really homemade at all, and many of the tracks were *not* recorded using the "Paul plays everything" method. Many of the excellent tracks on it feature all kinds of fine musicians, including the great guitar team of David Spinozza and Hugh McCracken. *Ram* was also the first time that Paul worked with Denny Seiwell, an amazing drummer who later joined Wings. *Ram* was recorded and produced in New York and even included no less than the New York Philharmonic. So not exactly homemade when you get right down to it, but it captures that flavour nonetheless.

Another good track on *Ram* is a song about an imaginary fantasy drink, "Monkberry Moon Delight." The song that inspired Paul to write about an imaginary drink was the Leiber & Stoller classic "Love Potion Number 9." There are accounts of the Beatles performing this song live, early in their career, but I have yet to come across a recorded version. The big hit version of "Love Potion Number 9" was by the Searchers, but it was first recorded by the Clovers, and that version would have been the one that both the Beatles and the Searchers heard. The Clovers also had an alternate version of the song that had an extra verse: "I had so much fun that I'm going back again. I wonder what'll happen with Love Potion Number 10!" The mind boggles. Ultra-Viagra effect, I suppose.

So now we come to our final R song, which actually consists of three songs with almost identical titles: "Revolution," "Revolution 1," and "Revolution 9." An interesting story about an important piece of music.

A common misconception is that John was more avidly interested in the avant-garde aspects of the arts than Paul was. Of course, I spent much more time in conversation with Paul than I did with John, but Paul certainly shared with my friends and me a very lively interest in contemporary drama, literature, the visual arts, and (of course) music which pushed boundaries and headed into the experimental edges of the culture. So far as music goes, that meant that in addition to our beloved American pop music and R&B, we were listening to Albert Ayler, Ornette Coleman, Don Cherry, Stockhausen, Edgar Varèse, John Cage, and others like them. But then John met Yoko, and his own interest in the avant-garde caught up rapidly. And when John recorded his brilliant composition "Revolution," it was the long version of that recording that ended up being split into "Revolution 1" and "Revolution 9." "Revolution 1" was John's version of the song itself—a slow bluesy version with some excellent "shooby-doo-wop" background parts and a great feel—which was John's suggestion for a Beatles single. And "Revolution 9" was the original continuation of that version which John and Yoko turned into a separate example of experimental music, using musique concrète, various loops, and other elements chosen sometimes at random to create a marvelous sonic landscape that became a unique part of Beatles history. The "number nine" part was derived from an EMI test tape on which a recorded voice declares it to be "EMI Test Series Number Nine."

Meanwhile, at Paul's suggestion a more single-oriented version of the song was recorded at a faster tempo and with a more rock and roll feel. This final version (titled, simply, "Revolution") is notable for the remarkable sounds of the electric guitars—rather than using amplifiers, they fed the guitars directly into the tube preamps in the board (or "direct injection" into the "desk," the English word for "board"). This is the version that was released as the B-side of "Hey Jude."

And as for the Revolution itself—as of this writing, we are still waiting for that to happen!

S

As we turn to the letter S, I am going to kick off our exploration
with a great, classic Beatles song, a double S song, "Sexy Sadie."
I am not going to get too deep into the details of the whole business behind the song because I do not have any inside information; I was not there in India. I only know what we all know from
reading.

John Lennon wrote "Sexy Sadie" about the Maharishi Mahesh
Yogi, whom the Beatles had visited in India in early 1968. John
discovered the Maharishi hitting on some of the female disciples,
and generally behaving like a normal revolting bloke and not like
a guru or a god, which John found disappointing but does not

At The Ed Sullivan Show.

surprise me a bit. "Sexy Sadie" is an acerbic, somewhat bitter song, which was the way John undoubtedly felt about the Maharishi at the time he wrote the song in India. It must be said that if John turned against someone, he could be pretty vehement, as indeed "Sexy Sadie" is.

There are also a lot of excellent non-Beatles rock and roll songs that begin with the letter S, and one of them Ringo covered as a solo artist. It is on Ringo's ninth album, *Old Wave*, but the song itself is a classic from 1965, "She's About a Mover," which was recorded originally by the Sir Douglas Quintet, a significant band. Their other big hit was "Mendocino," also a fine record. "She's About a Mover" is essentially a twelve-bar blues. And it has been pointed out that much of the song is very similar to "Can I Get a Witness" by Holland, Dozier, & Holland, the big Marvin Gaye hit. Sing both titles and you'll see that it's pretty much the same melody. But the original version of "She's About a Mover" is an exceptionally cool arrangement, kind of Tex-Mex, with a great Vox Continental organ sound heavily featured. Ringo very wisely sticks close to the same arrangement (same tempo and key) and does a convincing version—both recordings feature some fine aggressive maracas playing. I like Ringo's vocal very much, but I would give points to the original version for the distinctive and highly effective reverb on the organ part—for anyone, like me, nerdy enough to notice such things.

And on we go with a not unrelated song, this one a Paul McCartney track. It's also a twelve-bar blues and states (somewhat tautologically) that "She's a Woman." I called this a Paul McCartney track, but while it was mostly written by Paul, I think John took credit for the line "Turn me on when I get lonely." John and Paul were always delighted with any kind of even passing drug reference that got past the censors and was played on the radio. For example, in another song about a love interest, "Girl," one of the interesting things about it is the major inhalation that takes place after the word "girl"—and this was indeed a marijuana reference—is the sound you make when you smoke a really good joint. And this sounds as if it was *very* good.

John Lennon was a great rock and roll singer and loved the

classic rock and roll songs, several of which begin with S. One classic (based on an old hymn) that immediately comes to mind is "Stand by Me," the Leiber & Stoller song originally co-written and recorded by Ben E. King, who was formerly with the Drifters. John recorded his own version on his *Rock 'n' Roll* album, along with many other classics, including what could be said to be a double S song, "Sweet Little Sixteen" by Chuck Berry.

I have noted previously that Chuck Berry was a hero to all four of the Beatles, and I suspect they covered more of his songs than anyone else's in the course of their careers. They loved his songs, and I still do to this day. Beyond writing these very funky bluesy melodies, Chuck Berry was an extraordinary lyricist. His lyrics are deceptively simple but literate and wholly engaging. One of his best S songs is "School Days," the lyrics of which I think you'll have to agree are fascinating. First of all, nothing repeats. It is a new song from beginning to end with no repeated verses. The lyrics tell a story, and they scan brilliantly. Concise phrases like "Drop the coin right into the slot / You got to hear something that's really hot / With the one you love, you're making romance / All day long you've been wanting to dance." It's just good stuff. And of course, the end is one of the best rock and roll tributes ever penned: "Hail, hail, rock and roll / Deliver me from the days of old." People often forget that this is one of the things rock and roll does: it takes you out of the past and into the future—or at least that was the way my friends and I felt when we first heard it. To us it was genuinely new and exciting music, even though it derived from African-American musical forms like the blues and jazz and so on. Rock and roll struck us like a giant truck and changed our lives—and made us all the more eager to explore its origins.

S is also for "sad," which brings us to George Harrison and a genuinely sad song of his called, appropriately, "So Sad" (two S's for our collection!) from his 1974 album *Dark Horse*. I think it was written when his marriage to Pattie was falling apart or had already fallen apart, and it expresses the opposite sentiment to "Here Comes the Sun," another George classic. "So Sad" has a bit of doom and gloom about it, but it is a good song and certainly worth listening to.

Another George song that I love—one of my favourites, actually—is "Savoy Truffle." The lyrics are so expertly original in the way he uses all the delicious names of the various species of chocolate confection, like "Montelimar," assigning that particular word an elegant rising chromatic melody. Just brilliant writing. George got the idea for the lyric from the insert in a box of Mackintosh's Good News chocolates that contained a little picture of what each chocolate looked like and listed all the various flavours. And he used pretty much all the real names from that guide to the chocolates and added a couple of his own. What I also discovered is that the song owes something to the fact that Eric Clapton had bad teeth and needed a huge amount of dental work, and the dentist had threatened him with the consequences of eating too many chocolates. So were Eric to have eaten his way through the list as far as the Savoy Truffle, he might've had to have all his teeth pulled out! That is the origin of the line in the song, "But you'll have to have them all pulled out after the Savoy Truffle." I find it hilarious that "Savoy Truffle" is a mixture of the insert of a box of chocolates and an admonition to George's friend Eric about his dental health. But the result was at least a great song. I have no idea as to the current state of Eric's teeth and have no intention of asking him.

A couple of other interesting things about "Savoy Truffle." The track was produced by Chris Thomas, who had stepped in for George Martin while he was away on holiday. Apparently, when Chris came back to his desk from his own holiday, there was a note from George saying, "Dear Chris, hope you had a nice holiday. I'm off on mine now. Make yourself available to the Beatles. Neil and Mal know you're coming down." And there he was, producing the Beatles all of a sudden. And he did "Savoy Truffle." One of the other things I love about that track is the horn arrangement. Very good writing for the brass section and excellent playing. A lot of the best horn players in London at the time played on that track, including two of my favourites, Ronnie Ross on baritone and Art Ellefson on tenor. I like to give those guys some recognition because they do get forgotten all too easily. I used to go to Ronnie Scott's Jazz Club as often as I could to hear their brilliant contrapuntal duet improvisations. The British jazz scene was a thriving one, and the Beatles used a lot of these great musicians on their records. Ross and Ellefson also played on "Got to Get You into My Life," from *Revolver*, and Ross is famous for playing the solo on Lou Reed's "Walk on the Wild Side," a classic rock and roll baritone sax solo.

Now, we cannot give a fair treatment to the letter S without stopping on "She Loves You." When Beatlemania hit America, and the band had the top five records in the Billboard chart, "She Loves You" was No. 3. It helped to begin the Beatles' domination of the world of popular music, but it is an important song in another way as well. This was the first specifically narrative song that John and Paul wrote, a song addressed to (and about) a third party rather than just being a song of self-reflection. In other words, it wasn't about I this and I that. Or even I Want to Hold Your Hand. It was a song telling someone else that his girlfriend loves him. It was about a couple and their relationship, which is an interesting switch because, when you think about it, most rock and roll songs are written about what the singer himself or herself is feeling. And in this case, the singer is telling a story about other people, and this provides an early example of how the Beatles' approach to lyrics was already growing in sophistication and experimentation even in these very early days.

We all know that the Beatles made their first U.S. television appearance on *The Ed Sullivan Show* on February 9, 1964, a performance that changed the American musical landscape forever. This was when American Beatlemania really exploded. It seems that everyone in America watched it, parents and kids. Some parents disapproved violently; some kids went absolutely nuts and thought it was the greatest thing they had ever seen and heard in their whole lives. One way or the other, everyone felt strongly about it, and everyone talked about it the next day. It had a power that I am not sure television has anymore, now that it is so diffuse, because there are so many different choices and so little unanimity about what to watch. Back then there were few channels and few choices—and in this instance, everyone had got the message to watch *Ed Sullivan*, everyone saw the Beatles live, and everyone, one way or another, reacted simultaneously, vigorously, and instantly.

I was not there, of course. I was back in London, and it was right about the time Gordon and I were recording our very first tracks at EMI Studios. So our first voyage to New York was yet to come. The Beatles were enjoying their chaotic first visit and having the time of their lives. Their brilliant, record-breaking, and convention-defying performances on *Ed Sullivan* opened the door for the British Invasion.

The first song that many people in America heard the Beatles sing that famous night was "All My Loving," an energetic tune with great harmonies and chord changes that announced the arrival of a new kind of sound, energy, and youthful intensity. The next song they did was a surprise because one might think they would stick to rock and roll songs to establish themselves firmly in the American genre they so loved. But based on whatever advice they may have been given or discussions they had (I would be curious to know), the second song was "Till There Was You." It was not written by the Beatles, though I guarantee you some of the kids who heard it were not aware of its original incarnation. By the same token, it must have surprised those audience members who *did* know the song.

It was written, both words and music, by Meredith Willson, a terrific songwriter who wrote musicals, one of which, *The Music Man*, included this wonderful song. The Beatles obviously loved the song so much that they figured out the chords and did a very good version of it themselves. The original had been sung on Broadway by the legendary Barbara Cook and in the movie by Shirley Jones. They both sang the song beautifully—perhaps Shirley Jones's version is the best known. It is very different from the Beatles' version, but it is a lovely interpretation. And if the name Shirley Jones rings a bell with those of you who don't remember *The Music Man* and do not know her version of that song, that is likely because she became extremely famous playing the mother on the television show *The Partridge Family*.

After "Till There Was You," the Beatles returned to rock and roll with "She Loves You," and the crowd went crazy. That ended their first set. Later in the show, they came back onstage to do two more songs, "I Saw Her Standing There" and their first American No. 1 hit, "I Want to Hold Your Hand," and all of America got excited when they heard it on *Ed Sullivan*.

Some months later, Gordon and I had our opportunity to play on that same stage, but our appearance on *The Ed Sullivan Show* did not happen the way you—or we—might have expected.

Our first record, as you know, was "A World Without Love," which went to No. 1 in the UK, in Europe, and eventually in America. And for Gordon and me, the most exciting thing about that news was that we would get to go to America ourselves. Now, *Ed Sullivan* was the show that most of the British Invasion acts did first, if they had a big enough hit, but we were not able to do so. And here's why: there was an American manager called Allen Klein, who features in the Beatles' story quite a lot later on, and one very clever thing he did at the beginning of the British Invasion—he was not a stupid man by any means—was to arrange for somebody in London to send him the new releases each week because he knew there were many hit songs coming out of the UK. He had thus heard our record of "A World Without Love" the instant it came out and suggested it to a famous singer he represented, Bobby Rydell. So Rydell recorded "A World Without Love" very shortly after it came out in the UK and quickly released his version in America.

Now, in terms of becoming a hit, Rydell's version got off to a decent start but then slowed down, and I'm happy to say that when ours came out, it knocked out Rydell's record, and we shot past him and went to the top of the charts. However, Bobby Rydell was a regular performer on *The Ed Sullivan Show*, and when he released his version of "A World Without Love," he appeared on *Ed Sullivan* that same week, singing it live. When our agents and managers tried to get us on *Ed Sullivan* for our first American visit, the people who booked it were initially receptive to the idea because they knew we were a new English duo and doing well. But once they realized that the song we needed to perform was "A World Without Love," they said, "Thanks, but no thanks. We can't have the same song on our show just three weeks after Bobby Rydell did it."

It was not until the end of 1964, several months later, that Gordon and I made it onto *The Ed Sullivan Show*, singing one of our follow-up records, "I Don't Want to See You Again," another excellent song that Paul McCartney wrote for us. And one of the things I love about that particular recording is that it features a dual oboe solo—as you know, an instrument dear to my heart.

I've spent a lot of time talking about Ed Sullivan, but he is not the S with which I want to close this chapter. We really need to come back to the Beatles and one of their greatest achievements, *Sgt. Pepper's Lonely Hearts Club Band.* The importance of that album has been so widely documented and discussed there may be little to add, but you cannot imagine the effect it had on all of us when we first heard it. Everyone in the record business, everyone who played a musical instrument, everyone who did not play an instrument but just loved listening to good music, everyone who had nothing to do with the record business—we all knew that this was something entirely different and special. Just like Salieri, who is moved to tears when he reads Mozart's music (and hears it in his head) in those great scenes in *Amadeus*, no one could ignore the radical genius and groundbreaking inventiveness of what the Beatles had accomplished.

It was a concept album before that concept existed. The songs were all tied together in a brilliant way. It was a story. It created an imaginary and mysterious entity, Sgt. Pepper's Lonely Hearts Club Band. I remember distinctly the day that Paul brought *Sgt. Pepper* to our home in Wimpole Street. I had heard only a couple of bits of the album, having visited the studio here and there in the early months of 1967, but now Paul played the whole thing for my family. He had an acetate, which is an individually cut pre-pressing disk, and he played it on our little mono record player in the family dining room. Even on that small built-in speaker, it blew our minds. Both my parents were listening, I was listening, my sisters, Jane and Clare, were listening, and we were all impressed and moved beyond measure. It was one of those occasions when you just *know*, perhaps like when people first saw the *Mona Lisa* or first heard Beethoven's Fifth. You kind of just say, "Wow, this is a game changer. This is a new thing."

Along with the title track (and the reprise late on side two), there are two S songs associated with *Sgt. Pepper*, one obvious and one not so much. The first is the beautiful "She's Leaving Home," one of my favourite Beatles songs. The strings were arranged by Mike Leander, an excellent British songwriter and arranger, who also wrote a big hit for Peter & Gordon called "Lady Godiva"—a very different song, more of a comedy-novelty song. But as much fun as "Lady Godiva" was and is (I still enjoy singing it frequently, as I play along on my banjolele), "She's Leaving Home" was an achievement of a different order, not only for Mike Leander as an arranger but also for John Lennon and Paul McCartney as writers. The lyrics are brilliant, with Paul narrating the action and John singing the parents' thoughts as a musical and emotional counterpoint to the young woman seeking her own path in the world. It's a truly great song.

The other S song never made it onto the album, though it was a big hit on its own, and that's "Strawberry Fields Forever." It was recorded during the *Sgt. Pepper* sessions, but when the executives at EMI told George Martin that they needed a new Beatles single and could not wait for the album to come out, he and the band pulled out "Strawberry Fields Forever" and "Penny Lane" and released them as a double A-side single. I'll talk about the brilliance of "Strawberry Fields Forever" in a later chapter, but it is astonishing and enlightening to realize that its creation stemmed from that same unbelievable outpouring of creativity, unconventional recording techniques, and collective genius that changed forever the parameters of what pop music could do, what artistic ambitions it could realistically nurse, and what effect it could have on music and on the world. And that seismic change took place under the expert baton of Sergeant Pepper—conducting on behalf of his creators: John, Paul, George, Ringo, and George Martin.

It seems a long time since we started this alphabet, so I suppose we are in the last couple of laps of the whole thing. But there is still a lot to discuss before we get to the end, and T is an especially interesting letter. I started, as I usually do, by looking at all the Beatles songs that begin with the letter T. And my favourite on first reading the list is "Ticket to Ride." It is an exceptional and highly original composition and a beautifully arranged and produced Beatles record.

I distinctly remember when Paul wrote it. It is one of the songs I was lucky enough to hear the day it was completed. He played "Ticket to Ride" for me and sang me some examples of little guitar

The Black Dyke Mills Band, with Paul and Martha.

licks that he was planning on adding. And those twisty, bendy guitar phrases, which became Paul's guitar part, create several of the
very cool surprises contained in this arrangement and this record.
George's basic (and incredibly catchy) guitar pattern kicks things
off with that great Rickenbacker twelve-string sound, Ringo's opening fill (pretty much just a press roll) and his whole drum pattern
are both brilliantly original—so that by the time we get to Paul's
surprise guitar licks it has been one exciting change after another.
I remember him composing and practising them at home on his
hollow-body Epiphone Casino and getting the bends just right. And
finally, the totally unexpected double-time ending wraps it all up
perfectly. Three minutes of extraordinary creativity and innovation.
The Beatles' recollections in interviews of exactly who invented
which section do not necessarily coincide, but perhaps that is the
point. At this stage, their musical genius was collective as well as
individual, and so exactly who brought what to the table does not
even really matter—it is the extraordinary and everlasting music that
emerged at the end of the process that counts. "Ticket to Ride" is
one of my favourite Beatles records, certainly my favourite T song.

I usually try not to play favourites, but looking at the T list, I find
myself picking them instinctively. My second choice is the George
Harrison song "Taxman." George was lamenting the outrageous tax
rates in Britain at the time, and it is true to say that "there's one for
you, nineteen for me" was in fact the top tax rate in Britain back
then—referring to the fact that there were twenty shillings in a (pre-
decimalization) pound, so this was a 95 percent tax on the top income
bracket. It was no wonder that some people got a little bit depressed
about it. George includes specific references to Mr. Wilson, who was
Harold Wilson, the Labour Party prime minister, and Mr. Heath, who
was Edward Heath, the Conservative Party leader, who would later
become prime minister himself. They led opposing political parties,
but they both believed in heavy taxation of people making lots of
money. George was one of those people, and he didn't like it.

So we move on to my number-three Beatles song beginning
with T. This is one I apparently like more than the composer did.
When John Lennon wrote "Tell Me Why," he looked upon it as a
bit of a throwaway. Perhaps it is autobiographical—I mean, maybe

John and Cynthia were having a row or something, and it had to do with that. Or maybe he just wrote it as a generic song. Who knows? Anyway, John did not think much of it, but I like it. It ended up, of course, in *A Hard Day's Night* as one of the "live" performances in that movie—actually they were lip-synching to a pre-recorded version.

"Tell Me Why" was recorded on February 27, 1964, in the same session as "And I Love Her" and "If I Fell." Not a bad day's work, one would have to say—three really good tracks in one session. Oddly enough, the version of "Tell Me Why" in the movie is a different vocal take than the one on the record, though I do not know why that decision was made. So when they were doing that "live" scene in *A Hard Day's Night*, they were lip-synching to a different vocal take than the one they had chosen for the record. But it is a good moment in the movie, regardless of which take was used.

I could go on forever finding great T songs from the Beatles. There are plenty of them. But as long as we are addressing that letter, I would like to focus on something completely different: time signatures. I am going to try not to be too didactic and boring here, but I probably should explain what a time signature is. Music has both rhythm and melody; the melody part of any song consists of the notes one is playing or singing, and the rhythm aspect consists of *when* one plays or sings them and for how long each note is held. For convenience, it is customary to think of music in counted bars and giving those bars a time signature. The time signature is how many beats of whatever duration there are in that bar and how the defined notes fit into those beats, not to be confused with the tempo (how fast or slow those bars are to be counted and played), which is a separate consideration.

Now, most rock and roll songs are in 4/4 time. The first number means there are four beats in a bar. The second number means that these beats are quarter notes. The count is a simple one-two-three-four, one-two-three-four, one-two-three-four. That's your standard rock and roll beat. That's 4/4, and it's never better exemplified than by Chuck Berry, who wrote so many great 4/4 songs, and the Beatles recorded several of them. Beats 1 and 3 are called downbeats (1 is the downbeat of the whole bar), but the magic of the groove lies in the backbeats (2 and 4). As Chuck Berry says (when defining "rock and roll music"), "It's got a backbeat you can't lose it."

Now, 4/4 is not the only possible time signature; there are multiple variations. It is just the most common one in rock and roll. In fact, I do find myself wondering if Chuck Berry ever wrote a song that was not in 4/4, straight rock and roll time.

The second most popular time signature in music is 3/4. There are three beats in every bar, which means it goes one-two-three, one-two-three, one-two-three, one-two-three. Of course, that sounds like a waltz because all waltzes are based on this signature. The Beatles wrote several songs in 3/4; "She's Leaving Home" is a good example. Johann Strauss, of course, had a series of giant waltz hits in 3/4 time. I'm sure "The Blue Danube" would have been top of the dance charts forever, if they'd had them back then in Vienna— that is an eternal 3/4 hit if ever there was one. There are variations on the waltz time of 3/4; some songs are written in 6/8, six short beats (eighth notes) in every bar—"Baby's in Black" and "You've Got to Hide Your Love Away" are both normally transcribed in 6/8 or even in 12/8 (pretty much the same thing as two 6/8 bars at a time), as are "This Boy," "Oh! Darling," and "Norwegian Wood." All these time signatures have the same waltzing flavour—in every case (as you dance), you can count along in 3 or 6 or 12, and they all work. Try to do so in 4, and you will fall over in no time!

The Beatles also sang quite a few 3/4 songs that they did not write. An interesting one is "A Taste of Honey." It is very clearly a waltz in the verse ("I dream of your first kiss, and then . . ."), but when it gets to the bridge, something unexpected happens. You will notice that when Paul sings, "I will return, yes, I will return," the song goes into 4/4 time and sounds really cool doing it. And then it goes back to 3/4 for the next verse. If you count along, you'll notice that it starts very clearly in 3/4, and then suddenly it changes to 4/4. The Beatles used this very same trick in a song they wrote a couple of years later, "Lucy in the Sky with Diamonds." The verses are in 3/4 and the chorus is in 4/4.

I hope you don't find all this stuff about time signatures too boring. But I confess that I find it musically and mathematically fascinating. And I should point out, by the way, that Western music has the simplest time signatures of all. When you get into Indian and Asian music, the time signatures can get far more intricate. There are all kinds of crazy fifteen-beat bars and weird stuff going on that is really hard to count and figure out, unless you were brought up listening to that kind of music. Perhaps that is why it was George Harrison who wrote the Beatles song with the most time signature changes and the most confusing ones, because he loved and understood Indian music. "Here Comes the Sun" keeps very odd time. It is usually written out with 2/4 bars, 3/8 bars, 5/8 bars, and they're all kind of muddled up. If you try to count in a normal way, you'll get really confused. But it is such a good song, and I think that this rhythmic confusion is part of its charm and brilliance. Indeed, it keeps your brain on its toes. The next time you listen to this innovative and remarkable song, see if you can figure out the time. It is harder than you think.

Talking about weird mixed time signatures, another Beatles song worth mentioning is "Good Morning Good Morning." The "good morning, good morning" part, that's all normal 4/4 time. But the verses ("Nothing to do to save his life") are in 5/4 time, five beats per bar, and then the song returns to 4/4 and stays there through the bridge ("Everybody knows there's nothing doing") before jumping back to 5/4 for the next verse. It is really amazing what John did there.

I have two more examples of the Beatles' excellent work in unusual time signatures. First is "Happiness Is a Warm Gun." There are bars of 3/4 (our good old favourite waltz time), bars of 4/4, and bars of 2/4. The shifting time signatures make the song fun to listen to because you don't quite know where the time is going, but it feels really good. Happiness is certainly a great time signature, even if "Happiness Is a Warm Gun" is a doubtful proposition.

I now come to one final interesting time signature that the Beatles used, and this one is probably the most famous: "All You Need Is Love." One cannot help but notice that the chorus section is totally normal, in 4/4 time, as one can discover by singing or humming it. But when John gets to the verse ("There's nothing you can do that can't be done"), one gets this cool feeling that a beat is missing every now and then. There are bars of four beats alternating with bars of three beats, so the count is essentially in 7/4, strange but fascinating. And then when the song returns to the chorus, it moves straight ahead in 4/4, the iconic lyric of the title taking over in all its declaratory and dithyrambic joy.

This concludes Professor Peter Asher's lecture on time signatures. I hope you find some of this stuff as interesting as I do.

The letter T also, of course, stands for quite a few significant musical instruments that the Beatles used and loved. One was the trumpet, and while the most excellent example of a great trumpet solo on a Beatles record is without doubt on "Penny Lane," trumpets are also a significant part of every brass section or orchestra playing those brilliant George Martin arrangements. The horn sections on "Got to Get You into My Life," "Martha My Dear," "All You Need Is Love," and more all rely heavily on the power, drama, and musical flexibility of the trumpet.

Another T instrument that found its way onto several Beatles songs is the tabla, a small Indian hand drum that is a key element in most Indian music. George Harrison was very fond of the tabla, which is the instrument responsible for maintaining the unfamiliar time signatures in Indian music that I mentioned before. Another interesting thing is that Geoff Emerick, the Beatles' engineer, miked the tabla very close, the same way he miked Ringo's drums, and the Indian musicians were astonished by the sound he got out of it because they were more accustomed to miking all the instruments at a normal distance. But, as Geoff knew, when you mike something really close you get a lot more low end and a lot more impact. The tabla is a key element in George's song "Within You Without You," and it was probably the most powerful recorded tabla anyone had ever heard up to that point.

In talking about instruments and the Beatles, it becomes increasingly clear that their musical curiosity was never confined to guitars and drums alone. One of Paul McCartney's great interests was in brass bands, which is not surprising for someone who grew up in Liverpool. In the north of England, there is a tradition of old-school brass bands, using some of the same instruments as American marching bands but with less percussion and less boisterous arrangements. Each factory and mill used to have its own brass band, and major competitions were held—the grand final often being held at the Royal Albert Hall in London. It was a major event. These competitions still take place, but many of the sponsoring factories are gone, and some of the bands with them. There is a movie called *Brassed Off*, starring Ewan McGregor, which provides an excellent sense of that wonderful music, that culture, and the sadness of its inevitable decay in the face of economic decline, Thatcherism, and other political and social changes—but the music and the best of the bands continue to survive.

In 1968, just as Apple Records was starting, Paul was asked to write and record a theme tune for a television show called *Thingumybob*, and he had the excellent idea that it should be a brass band piece. So, he wrote an instrumental and named it after the TV show, thus bringing it into our T world for discussion. My colleagues and I set about looking for the best brass band in the land, and when we studied the results of the recent brass band competitions, the clear winner was the Black Dyke Mills Band, sponsored by the factory of John Foster & Son in Yorkshire. We arranged a recording session at a local hall where the band had recorded before, and we all drove up there. When I say "all," it was Paul McCartney; myself; the brilliant and legendary Derek Taylor, who was the head of press for the Beatles organization; Tony Bramwell, another key Apple employee; a reporter called Alan Smith; and Paul's dog, Martha. The session went extremely well—the band more than lived up to their winning reputation and were very excited to be working closely with Paul as he produced the session with his usual expertise and charm, and I did whatever I could to help. He recorded "Thingumybob," the song he had written specifically for the band, and he also recorded them playing a brass band version of "Yellow Submarine" as a B-side, which is also well worth hearing.

We were very happy with the way the session went, and we headed back to London full of excitement. It was on that return journey that a series of events took place which have been written about quite a bit and have become almost legendary in a weird way. We were driving back, and we decided to take a detour off the M1 motorway, which had been the first full-length motorway built in England. We were all hungry, and I studied the map in search of a location for lunch. I chose this village called Harrold, spelled with two R's, because I liked the idea of a village that had a person's name.

We drove to Harrold to see what we could find, but when our driver inquired at a couple of pubs there, he learned that none were serving food. Finally, we were driving down the street (in this big black Rolls-Royce limousine, looking just a little bit obvious), and we saw a man cutting his hedge. We stopped and asked him for some advice, and he actually invited us into his home. He was quite curious about us, and once he realized he was inviting a Beatle plus entourage into his home, his fascination and incredulity naturally grew. I won't bother you with the whole long story, but suffice to say we ended up spending the rest of the afternoon and the whole of the evening in the village of Harrold, in a couple of people's houses and a couple of pubs. At one point, Paul sat at a pub piano playing "Hey Jude," which he had just written, and which no one had heard before, along with various other Beatles songs. Some other villagers came over, and a grand time was had by all. It was an extraordinary night. And of course it was the end to an extraordinary day, which had begun with our recording of "Thingumybob" with the Black Dyke Mills Band. For a more extensive and detailed version of this story, I highly recommend the account in Derek Taylor's brilliant book *As Time Goes By*—an account made all the more vivid and impressive by the fact that Derek had taken a modest dose of LSD as the day began.

While we are on the subject of lesser-known compositions, there are very few Lennon-McCartney songs that were actual flops, but one of them was "Tip of My Tongue," which John and Paul wrote for Tommy Quickly, a T song for a T artist. If you can find it, you'll see that it's not bad at all, but it has to be said it was not a hit.

But enough obscurity. Let's end this chapter by talking about a couple of great Beatles songs that begin with the letter T. Let us end, in other words, as we began.

First up is "Tell Me What You See." It is a terrific song. Paul sings and plays bass and electric piano. John plays tambourine as well as playing the guitar and singing. George plays a guiro, which is a part of the Latin percussion family—a lozenge-shaped hollow wooden tube which has a series of grooves in the surface. One plays it by scraping that surface with a thin stick. Ringo is playing the drums and also the claves, another Latin American instrument, a pair of short wooden sticks that one taps together. In Cuban music (itself extremely important and influential in so many other genres of music), the pattern played by the claves (itself known as "the clave") can define the rhythmic foundation of an entire piece—in pop music the instrument is more often used as decoration and to provide rhythmic variation by filling some of the empty spots in the basic 4/4 pattern—just as Ringo does so expertly on "Tell Me What You See."

Some of the song's lyrics are reminiscent of a religious motto that had hung on the wall of John Lennon's childhood home, the one he shared with his aunt Mimi. "However black the clouds may be, in time they'll pass away. Have faith and trust and you will see God's light make bright your day," which bears a substantial resemblance to the lyrics of that song. John collected brilliant influences from wherever he was, whatever he heard, whatever he read, and added them into his writing, as so many great writers do.

Let us close our chapter with a nod to another of my favourite T songs, "Things We Said Today." One of the remarkable things about this track is that it starts off in a minor key ("You say you will love me"), but when we get to the bridge, it suddenly shifts into a major key ("Me, I'm just the lucky kind"), which makes for a really happy moment. I love that—a simultaneous and joyous change both lyrically and musically.

The letter U is an interesting letter. It came as a bit of a surprise to me when I started to look and found that there are few significant songs of any kind, by any artists, which begin with the letter U. It makes for a more creative exploration.

There is one U song associated with a Beatle, which is a terrific one: Paul McCartney's "Uncle Albert/Admiral Halsey." Because of our focus on the letter U, we are, of course, more interested in Albert the uncle than we are in the eminent naval officer with whom he shares the title.

We do know that Uncle Albert was at least partially inspired by a real person. Albert Kendall had worked with Paul's father, Jim, at Hannay and Company, Liverpudlian cotton merchants. He

The six "courses" of my twelve-string guitar.

later married Jim's sister Millie, making him Paul's uncle—but as far as we know Paul never caused him any pain or had any reason to apologize, as he does in the song! The combined track "Uncle Albert/Admiral Halsey" is astonishingly complex for a No. 1 pop single—sound effects, cleverly executed multiple tempo changes, some beautiful flugelhorn playing, George Martin conducting the New York Philharmonic orchestra, and an overall mood and production verging on the surreal.

I realize that if I am going to compose a whole chapter about the letter U, I am going to have to cheat just a little bit. Though there are not many songs that begin with the letter U, there are plenty of brilliant ones that begin with "You." I can hear you groaning, but to my mind it is an elegant solution.

One of these songs is "You Can't Do That"—an early Beatles song, recorded on February 25, 1964. There is so much good to say about this song, on which John Lennon sings lead and plays lead guitar. The background vocals, for instance, are extraordinary. The "gonna let you down and leave you flat" reply part with the seventh in it is a brilliant vocal arrangement perfectly executed. John also plays one of his rare guitar solos while Paul plays the cowbell, adding the *clang-clang-clang-clang* that gives the song its irresistibly propulsive groove.

Another clever aspect of "You Can't Do That" is that it's a twelve-bar blues which turns into a modern pop song with the addition of a very cool bridge ("Everybody's green"), which is unexpected and brilliant. This is one of the things the Beatles are so good at: taking traditional elements and making them new.

Whenever I listen to the record, I always notice and admire George Harrison playing his brand-new Rickenbacker twelve-string guitar. All that delicious jangling sound. That is probably why John played the guitar solo—because George was busy jangling away on his twelve-string, providing such a great texture to sing and play against.

I have mentioned the twelve-string guitar several times already, and it is one of my favourite instruments. Whereas a normal guitar has six strings, a twelve-string guitar has doubles on all of the strings. Each of what would be a single string on a regular guitar is replaced by a "course" of two strings. The top two courses each consist of two strings tuned to the same note, and the next four courses consist of two strings tuned an octave apart, so every regular string is replaced by a pair of strings, some in octaves, some in unison, and it gives the instrument a great, rich, jangly sound. There are two iterations of the twelve-string guitar, an acoustic version and an electric version, and I love both of them. I have played my Gibson acoustic twelve-string on plenty of records and have used a lot of electric twelve-strings as well—usually a Rickenbacker, but there was a cool British version as well, made by Burns as I recall, and I recently acquired a beautiful Gretsch. There are plenty of twelve-string parts on the Peter & Gordon records—generally played by a studio musician much more skilled than I am! You can hear an acoustic twelve-string on "I Go to Pieces," from the intro onwards, and you can hear an electric one playing the solo on "A World Without Love."

I think the first time I ever knowingly heard a twelve-string was on a record called "Walk Right In" by the Rooftop Singers. They used two acoustic twelve-strings, and the instruments were apparently very rare at the time. The band had one that they got from Gibson, but in order to get the sound of two, they had to wait for Gibson to make them another one. They helped bring that instrument out of obscurity, because I remember that when this record came out, we all wondered what that really cool sound was, and it was the acoustic twelve-string. Turns out it also provided the great sound of the Lead Belly records I already loved so much—he played a Stella twelve-string tuned way down from E to B. As soon as I figured out what it was, I wanted one myself, and quite a few years later, when Gordon and I started actually making money doing gigs, I bought myself a big beautiful Gibson twelve-string which tragically got stolen a few years later, and I had to ask the company to make me another one. But I still have that one to this day and love it dearly.

It was around the time George got his own electric Rickenbacker twelve-string that he started composing songs of his own. And in our "You" category is one of George's early compositions, "You Like Me Too Much." It was the third George Harrison song to be recorded by the Beatles, after "Don't Bother Me" and "I Need You." I imagine that "You Like Me Too Much" is a reference to Pattie Boyd, the woman he was in love with at the time and would later marry.

Another fine "You" song is "You Never Give Me Your Money," written when the Beatles were all in financial arguments with one another, with Allen Klein, and with Apple, and so much confusing and contentious business stuff was going on. And that is when they felt as if "you never give me your money, you only give me your funny paper." I am sure it was true. In my experience, it is the lawyers (who write the "funny paper") who end up with the money. Depressing and infuriating—but in this instance the situation led to the creation of a brilliant song, with an extraordinary arrangement.

Listen to the bass part on the first verse. Paul created these little melodic descending lines that are just amazing. He plays them with such fluency and brilliance, they become moving melodies unto themselves. Then when he gets to the second verse, he plays this extraordinary descending lick into the more normal bass part that the second verse requires. It is a great song and one of so many examples of extraordinarily creative playing and meticulous arranging from all four Beatles and their producer.

Sarah Vaughan did a very cool cover of "You Never Give Me Your Money." She was one of the premier jazz vocalists of all time. Without doubt, America tends to have the best jazz vocalists in the world, and Sarah Vaughan was certainly one of them. For many years, she and Ella Fitzgerald were the joint queens of great female jazz singing. Sarah Vaughan had this huge, deep, lustrous voice, which she used to very good effect on "You Never Give Me Your Money." It is a great example of her work as well as an excellent cover of a Beatles song.

Returning to George Harrison, I cannot help but mention another song of his that fits our category perfectly. There cannot be a more appropriate "You" song than the one called "You."

George's song "You" has an interesting history. He wrote it as a virtual tribute to the girl group records he loved so much when he was younger. And in fact he originally intended it for Ronnie

Spector, a great singer we all got to know back in the day. She was formerly of the Ronettes and eventually the wife of Phil Spector, though she later accused Phil of locking her in his mansion and mistreating her, which I imagine is true. George wrote this song for her, and a session did take place at which she recorded it, but somehow it never went anywhere. George ended up recording it himself with a collection of very eminent musicians—Leon Russell on piano, Jim Gordon on drums, and Jim Horn playing the saxophone solo—and turned it into a really good record.

But let's get back to the letter U and go beyond "You." A musical term most everyone knows is the word *unison*. It refers to a group of voices singing the same part together, rather than singing separate notes in harmony; and unison voices can be very powerful. It sounds very emphatic and authoritative, and the Beatles used it to great effect several times. One of these times was in the opening of "The Continuing Story of Bungalow Bill." You'll notice that right after the elegant and surprising classical guitar intro, a whole group of voices come in all singing the same notes, and that makes a great beginning to the track.

But perhaps the most famous Beatles unison moment is one that doesn't happen until halfway through the song. And that song, of course, is "Hey Jude." One of the shocking surprises and exceptional musical moments is when the main song—what, on first hearing, we took to be the primary motif for the whole record—ends and suddenly this great "na na" part comes in with many people singing very powerfully in unison. And now that we know it is coming, we listen in gleeful expectation for the repetitive unison section and await the joy of hearing Paul's extraordinarily soulful descant part filling the interstices between the repeats with licks we know by heart. It sounds amazing, and it turned the song into a real anthem.

The letter U also leads us to an instrument of which the Beatles were fond and about which one Beatle was particularly enthusiastic: the ukulele. It is an entirely charming instrument, originally from Hawaii, which has spread into every kind of music. George Harrison was a big fan. There is a clip on the *Beatles Anthology* DVD in which George, Ringo, and Paul are seen sitting on the lawn at Friar Park just noodling away on the ukulele with some vocals. They play "Ain't She Sweet" and a Jimmy Reed song, "Baby What You Want Me to Do." George takes a cool ukulele solo as they sit on the lawn together, and his love for the instrument is evident.

George was the best ukulele player in the Beatles, but John and Paul both played it a bit as well, and indeed, it was in honour of George the ukulele player that Paul made a very sweet decision during his appearance at the "Concert for George" in 2002. Paul did a brilliant version of "Something," on which he played the ukulele and rethought the whole song in the ukulele style. It is lovely, and I urge you to listen to it.

Another word that begins with U, and this one may surprise you a little bit, is not a strictly musical one, but it is musically relevant. I am going to talk for a moment—please do not consider me too eccentric—about the uvula. (I have spoken before about the influence of my mother, a musician, but don't forget that my father was a physician, so I absorbed some anatomical knowledge as well!) You probably know that the uvula is the little dangly thing at the back of one's throat, and it has a distinct musical role. Apparently, without the uvula, one's voice would not project out of one's mouth the way it does. The uvula closes off the back of the throat and prevents the voice from going straight up and coming out of the nose. I guess if it did that, we would all sound kind of like Fran Drescher or something—who sounds great, by the way, but that's a nasal voice that we know and love. As a universal trait, it could wear thin.

The uvula also gives one the ability to execute certain pronunciations, especially of foreign languages, like those guttural sounds in French and German. Speaking French without a uvula would be very hard. So we can definitively report that Paul McCartney has a uvula, and he deployed it to great effect when he sang in French on "Michelle." *Sont les mots qui vont très bien ensemble* requires effective use of the uvula. Without the Beatles' uvulas, perhaps the German on "Komm, Gib Mir Deine Hand" and "Sie Liebt Dich" might not have sounded so convincing!

Our last musical reference from the letter U is the uilleann

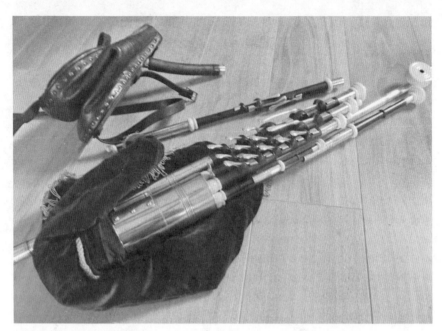

The uilleann pipes.

pipes, an ancient and revered Irish instrument which made many new fans when people fell in love with the soundtrack to the movie *Titanic*. The pipes have long been used to great effect by bands like the Chieftains and all the other legends of Celtic music.

One of these very famous Irish bands is the McPeake Family. Francis McPeake was the leader of that family, and he played the uilleann pipes really well. When John Lennon expressed interest in the uilleann pipes, he bought a set and had a couple of lessons from Francis McPeake himself, who later told his son that John was the best student he ever had, that he learned in a day the real concept of the pipes and would have made a great piper. But I guess John got interested in other things because he eventually just quit practising and gave his set to Francis McPeake. As I understand it, the McPeake family still has John's uilleann pipes.

The Beatles didn't use uilleann pipes on any of their songs, but they did like the sound of the pipes in general. The more grown-up, more serious, more warlike version of the Irish pipes are the Scottish pipes called the Highland pipes. Same principle.

Bigger bag, lower notes, and all that kind of thing. But the same idea. The melody is played on a single pipe called the chanter, and the other pipes are tuned to specific "drone" notes that play along with it. And the drone effect is completed by the fact that rather than blowing directly into the pipes themselves, the piper blows into a bag which provides a reserve of air and allows all the notes to sound continuously, even when one is breathing in.

Paul McCartney fell in love with the bagpipes and used them, the real Highland pipes, on his most Scottish of songs, "Mull of Kintyre." I will close this chapter with all of us imagining the mournful sound of bagpipes floating across the Scottish Highlands. A fine end to any day's music.

As with the letter U, there are not a lot of V songs in the Beatles' world. I am going to start with one which I did not really remember very well, but as soon as I played the track it came back to me—and it is a good one.

It is a Paul McCartney song called "Vintage Clothes," produced by my friend David Kahne, an excellent producer who made the Bangles' best records and worked with a whole list of other cool people. "Vintage Clothes" features the mellotron—apparently the same mellotron the Beatles used back in the day at EMI Studios, an instrument which I guess Paul subsequently bought. So Paul had it and they used it.

The mellotron has a very particular and fascinating sound, but it is also a temperamental and mechanically untrustworthy piece of equipment. Both characteristics can be attributed to how the machine works—it uses actual physical samples of real instru-

Vera Lynn entertaining the troops.

ments playing specific notes, recorded on tape. This was the first time the concept of sampling instrument sounds came to the fore because the mellotron contained within it a multitude of lengths of recording tape. Not continuous loops; each one had a beginning and an ending, and each length was a recording of an instrument (or several of the same instruments in unison) playing a specific note.

The mellotron came with several different racks of these strips of tape, one for each group of instruments (strings or brass and so on). One would lift out the rack of tapes that were inside the keyboard (about the size of an upright piano) and insert a different one as needed. The rack consisted of a whole lot of dangling tapes hanging from little wheels, and the chosen rack would be slotted down into the mellotron. Then, when one hit the relevant note on the keyboard, the machine would play that specific tape—it would play for a maximum of about seven or eight seconds, as I recall—until either that tape ran out or one removed one's finger from the key. As soon as the key was released, there would be this kind of clacking noise, and the tape would whiz back to the beginning as fast as it could in case that same note was needed again. One of the side effects of that instant rewind was that quite often the tape would break, and mellotrons were a bit of a nightmare in that regard. The Moody Blues took a mellotron on the road for a while and apparently had to have three or four available so that one would be working for every gig.

The first time we all fully realized how stunning and magical a mellotron could sound was when we heard the song "Strawberry Fields Forever." The Beatles used mellotron flutes right at the intro, rather than actual flutes, because the mellotron had a sound all its own. The thing about having these little pre-recorded tapes is that by the time the necessary process of recording and playback for the mellotron was completed, the tapes no longer sounded exactly like real flutes but rather like a spooky replica of real flutes. Not quite sonically accurate and not quite in tune or entirely steady in pitch—but in some ways more mystical and inspiring than real flutes would have been in the same context.

The tape would be a bit wobbly, so the instruments would have a weird and inhuman vibrato to them. And of course this weirdness sounded really cool in the hands of the collective musical genius that was the Beatles. When you first hear those flutes on "Strawberry Fields Forever," they don't sound quite like real flutes, but they sound totally fantastic.

Thinking about the mellotron makes me think of all the original devices that the Beatles employed to achieve the sound they wanted on their records. One of these devices begins with the letter V, and that was the varispeed. Now, *varispeed* refers to any method by which one speeds up or slows down a tape. When you speed a tape up, obviously, the tempo gets faster. In addition, the key gets higher until eventually one ends up in Alvin and the Chipmunks world, when it is all very fast and very high. Nowadays, it is different. Digitally, one can change the speed and the pitch of recorded music separately and independently. But back then one's only option was physically changing the speed of the tape, and even that was quite complicated. It was easy to double or halve the speed of the tape (a setting available on the tape machine itself), but more subtle variations were not as easy, and such adjustments became a trick the Beatles pioneered to a considerable extent. They had a machine built (the varispeed) that would change the frequency of the electricity powering the electric motor that drove the tape, which enabled subtle changes in speed (and therefore in pitch as well).

One of the key songs on which they did this was, again, the masterpiece that is "Strawberry Fields Forever." The record is made up of two sections from two different takes. These two takes were different arrangements in different keys, and to make them fit together, Geoff Emerick used the varispeed to lower the key of the higher-pitched take. John's voice in that section thus became low and doomy sounding, which he liked very much. So that's what was used, and varispeed was the key to all of this.

People often ask me about the actual location in Liverpool after which "Strawberry Fields Forever" was named, and I have to admit I have never been there. I have hardly been to Liverpool at all. People sometimes assume that I am some kind of universal Beatles expert, and I have to explain that I am definitely *not* that person. The only visits I have made to Liverpool have been to play a gig and drive back home. My only Beatles expertise is that I have loved their music for so long and happened to have had the extraordinary good fortune to witness some events of that historic period and the pleasure to have known them—an honour which persists to this day.

I mentioned that there are not a lot of V songs in the Beatles' world, and that is true. But there is one thing the Beatles have that begins with V that you must admit is extremely important. And that is their voices. The Beatles' voices were extraordinary! I've mentioned before that they had to be able to sing pretty loud to have any chance of hearing themselves, and I remember being particularly impressed when I went to a couple of their BBC sessions. When I sat in the control room, of course, I could hear everything because it was coming through the microphones and the board and the big speakers. But if I sat in the studio itself, as I sometimes did, I would hear only what was making music in that room, without benefit of any amplification or electronics. I would hear live drums, live guitar, guitar amps, and so on, but the vocals I would hear only from their lips, as it were, as they stood at the microphone. And yet I could still hear everything they sang very clearly.

I honestly cannot remember exactly which BBC sessions I attended, but if you listen to them now, you will get a sense of what I heard when I was sitting on the floor in the little BBC carpeted studio listening to them singing and being extraordinarily impressed.

This vocal strength was clear from their very first recordings. In the studio, they had the advantage of microphones. When singing together, Paul and John would often stand on opposite sides of the same microphone, a Neumann U67, which can work in what they call figure eight, which means that the two opposite sides of the mic can be live at the same time. I love recording that way. Engineers tell me I may be imagining this, but to my mind, the fact that two people are singing into the same capsule means that the same vibrating diaphragm joins up both voices and records that physically blended signal onto tape. That is how John and Paul did most of those early records.

The letter V also stands for violins, violas, and what were originally called violoncellos. The word *cello* is actually an abbreviation. If one wants to be a little bit pedantic, one actually puts an apostrophe before the word *cello* to indicate the fact that one knows it is *violoncello*.

I already wrote about these instruments under the letter Q, as we discussed string quartets, but I would like to ask one new question: When is a violin not a violin? When it's a fiddle. A fiddle is almost a different instrument (while remaining, physically, exactly the same thing as a violin) because great fiddle players—and I think of that category as including bluegrass fiddlers and country fiddlers and Cajun fiddlers—can be just as skillful and equally amazing at what they do as the finest classical violinists. Different styles, different sounds, different songs, and they both use the exact same instrument, but played in very different ways. A rare few musicians excel in both worlds (Mark O'Connor deserves recognition in this regard), but most specialize in one or the other. For my own listening pleasure, I treasure players like Stuart Duncan or Alison Krauss or Sara Watkins in the bluegrass world—and for classical violin, no one can beat Hillary Hahn playing Bach or pretty much anything else.

Another favourite fiddle player is Nicky Sanders of the Steep Canyon Rangers, the great bluegrass band with whom Steve Martin makes records. I have had the pleasure of working on some of them myself as a producer.

One of the records I did not produce is an early album on which Steve Martin and the Steep Canyon Rangers had a guest singer who is relevant to our task. On the song "Best Love," Steve had the idea to invite a singer he thought would sound really good on that particular song. He called Paul McCartney and asked him if he would come in and sing one song—and Paul said yes. If you find "Best Love," you will hear the great fiddle player Nicky Sanders, Steve Martin on the banjo, and the rest of the Steep Canyon Rangers accompanying Sir Paul—it is a great track.

All four Beatles were born during World War II, as was I, and to anyone who grew up in postwar Britain, a very important V singer is Vera Lynn. She is a major national heroine. She sang to the troops throughout the war and had monster hits with "(There'll Be Blue-birds Over) The White Cliffs of Dover" and particularly "We'll Meet Again," which became kind of a national anthem for Britain during the war. Vera Lynn, I am very happy to say, at least at the time I am writing this, is still with us. She is 102 years old. She has always been held in incredibly high esteem throughout the whole of Brit-ain by all artists, including the Beatles. She reciprocated this admi-ration and even covered one of their songs, "The Fool on the Hill."

By the way, in theory, but I am certain not in practice, the Beatles might have actually resented Vera Lynn ever so slightly, because in 2009, when the long-awaited remastered editions of the Fab Four's whole catalogue were finally released, the No. 1 position on the British album chart was claimed by Vera Lynn with a new repack-age of her greatest hits, *The Very Best of Vera Lynn*, released at the same time. She was ninety-two at the time and she kept the Beat-les off No. 1, but I am confident they didn't mind in the slightest.

Paul McCartney seems to be the only Beatle with a fondness for the letter V. In addition to "Vintage Clothes" and "Venus and Mars" (the elegantly melodic prelude to "Rock Show"), he wrote and recorded two other V songs with related titles, "Valentine Day" and "My Valentine." "Valentine Day" is an instrumental, whereas "My Valentine" is a more conventional and traditional song. It is a fine work with some beautiful guitar playing from Eric Clapton. And if you watch the video, you will see the actress Natalie Portman doing sign language.

On "My Valentine," Eric Clapton plays classical lead guitar in something of a departure from his usual style—but clearly, he can play anything! When I had the pleasure of producing a session with Eric, I found it to be a remarkable experience. He came in and played on a charity record I was producing (with Cher, Chris-sie Hynde, and Neneh Cherry) and just ripped off three or four amazing solos, all completely different and all extraordinary, and then he said, "Will that do?" All I could do was respond, "That's brilliant! Thank you very much!" And he packed up and left. He was both efficient and miraculously good—and the record went to No. 1, raising a lot of money for Comic Relief on Red Nose Day.

Let us end our journey through the letter V on a jovial note, because V also stands for vaudeville. Vaudeville is, of course, the American version of what we in England mostly call music hall, but it has the same vibe. Everything is bouncy and happy (except when occasionally it's maudlin and tear-jerkingly sentimental), sometimes adding double meanings and jokes and lighthearted moments. Paul McCartney was a fan of the vaudeville and music hall traditions, as we can see in particular in songs like "Honey Pie" and "Your Mother Should Know."

"Honey Pie" is a clear and direct tribute to ragtime and vaudeville and also very much a collective Beatles recording, proving that the band shared Paul's affection for the genre. John played the old-school guitar solo and George played a perfect bass part which was very much *not* rock and roll in tone or in composition, with Ringo on drums and Paul on ragtime piano, playing with a feel probably more familiar to Paul's father's band than to the Beatles. The arrangement for saxophones and clarinets was a joint effort by George Martin and Paul—and a masterpiece of authenticity. The song also follows a story line not unfamiliar to Beatles fans—an act from the north of England hits the big time in America and off she goes!

Vaudeville and music hall have always included a substantial quotient of nostalgia in their appeal. And "Your Mother Should Know" is heavily laced with nostalgia throughout. From the opening lines which specifically address the past ("Let's all get up and dance to a song / That was a hit before your mother was born") to the visual presentation of the song in *Magical Mystery Tour* (white tails, choreography, and an elaborate set reminiscent of the glory days of movie musicals) to the musical arrangement itself (the lovely old-fashioned "ah"s in the background vocals and Ringo's retro hi-hat shuffle on the second verse), the whole track has a joyous and nostalgic sentimentality which I much admire. Indeed this 1967 song expresses and exemplifies an admiration for the music of previous eras which parallels the respect and love we enthusiastically express for the '60s and the band that gave voice to that decade.

Though we are approaching the end of our quest, we still have some important letters to explore. Quite a few great songs begin with the letter W, which is where we find ourselves.

We start with a favourite, "When I'm Sixty-Four." This is a song that Paul McCartney wrote in his home in Liverpool, on the upright piano in the living room. He was only about fifteen at the time, looking nearly fifty years into the future. The irony of the song today, of course, is that both the composer and I look back on our sixty-fourth year with nostalgia. It occurred to me to look up what Paul was up to when he was sixty-four, and it turns out that that was the year he released "Dance Tonight," one of his best solo singles and a really good record that did well. So Paul, as we

Linda Ronstadt and me visiting Paul and Linda McCartney backstage at a Wings concert.

well know, was flourishing at sixty-four and continues to do so to this day.

In the previous chapter, I wrote about vaudeville and its English cousin, the music hall. "When I'm Sixty-Four" is probably the best-known Beatles song that has this distinct music hall flavour. We should give credit to a brilliant clarinet arrangement by George Martin, beautifully written for three clarinets and skillfully capturing the vaudeville musical spirit with which Paul had already imbued the song with his melody and lyrics.

The lyrics are remarkably evocative and softly charming. Paul is such a master of melodic motifs that he is sometimes underrated as a lyricist, and these are very clever lyrics indeed. "We can rent a cottage in the Isle of Wight," by the way, would be wishful thinking. The Isle of Wight these days is extremely expensive, and the cottage would indeed be "too dear" by far.

For those who don't know, the Isle of Wight is an island about five miles off the southern coast of Britain—but separate in many ways and with a fascinating history. It has always been at the forefront of Britain's defences, both against the Spanish Armada in the reign of Elizabeth I and against any potential German invasion in World War II. They also hold interesting events there of a (thankfully) nonmilitary nature, including a music festival. The most famous iteration of the Isle of Wight Festival took place in 1969. That year it attracted an audience of about 150,000 to see Bob Dylan, the Band, the Who, Free, Joe Cocker, the Bonzo Dog Doo-Dah Band, and the Moody Blues. Bob Dylan was making his first public appearance since his serious motorcycle accident—he had declined an offer to play Woodstock and took some convincing to make his "comeback" at the Isle of Wight. Apparently, it was the poetic heritage of the island—Alfred Lord Tennyson had called it home—that made the difference. And it was Dylan's performance that provided the motivation for George, John, and Ringo (along with Keith Richards and Eric Clapton) to attend.

Before we leave "When I'm Sixty-Four," it is worth noting that the song has been covered by a lot of different people. A cover that I had not heard until quite recently was one by Keith Moon, for the movie *All This and World War II*, and it is an original and interesting version. I like the way he sings it with a slightly affected posh accent, a bit like his friend Vivian Stanshall from the Bonzo Dog Doo-Dah Band. I also like the elegant orchestrated arrangement, including a bunch of marimbas and such alongside the string ensemble. And Keith was a surprisingly good singer, too. The saddest part about it is that Keith himself made it only halfway to sixty-four. He died at the age of thirty-two, which was a terrible loss. He was an amazing drummer and an extraordinarily generous and charming man.

Another miraculously creative drummer and fine singer, of course, is Ringo Starr, and we cannot ignore his exceptional performance of "With a Little Help from My Friends," another great W song. I have discussed Ringo's drumming on this track in the letter D, but here I would like to call attention to his vocals. Ringo sings as he speaks—plainly, without affectation or any licks or decoration— and the performance clearly comes from the heart. Though very straightforward, his singing never sounds in the least pedestrian but rather has the solidity and conviction of someone simply stating a fact—that friends are invaluable and that their support is crucial. And this was the attitude the Beatles relied upon to help hold the band together through difficult times—though in the end, those difficulties proved insurmountable.

And as expressive as Ringo is, this is a song that two other singers have particularly made their own, in very different and effective ways. The first is James Taylor, who in addition to his own songwriting genius has a remarkable talent for taking a song originally written and performed by someone else and making it sound like a total James Taylor song. He did it with "Handy Man," "How Sweet It Is (To Be Loved by You)," and "You've Got a Friend," and that is what he does with a live version of "With a Little Help from My Friends" which he has performed from time to time ever since he first learned the song all those years ago. Listening to James's version, you would never know that it was a rock and roll Lennon-McCartney song. You might indeed think it was his own, as he adds in those James Taylor signature guitar licks and his vocal phrasing.

And the second, of course, is Joe Cocker, who did a version

of "With a Little Help from My Friends" that really brought out something new and entirely different in the song, and between his intensely soulful vocal and the astounding arrangement and production (thanks to the brilliance of Leon Russell and Denny Cordell), his recording adds greatly to one's admiration for the song and to the joy of hearing it.

Joe Cocker performed this famous version at Woodstock, the great festival that preceded the Isle of Wight and is another W to mention, though it is a brief detour from our alphabetical Beatles tour. I was actually at Woodstock. I somehow managed to scam a ride out to the site on a helicopter, which at the time was the only way to get there because, as you may have read, all the traffic was stopped. The roads were closed because people were just abandoning their cars and walking, so every traffic artery was completely clogged. This whole festival was put together in a very hippyish, amateurish way, which was charming and fun, but when all these hundreds of thousands of people showed up, it was complete chaos. But I did manage to see some of it, admittedly from backstage. I was not out in the mud with the masses, which looks fun in the movie, but I am not sure how much fun it would have been in real life. I saw Richie Havens, Country Joe and the Fish, and more, and it was quite an experience.

It was also the closest I ever came to meeting Janis Joplin, whom I had seen perform at the Hollywood Bowl on another occasion. She was at Woodstock, too, but I did not see her perform there. Instead, when we got back to the motel where I had somehow managed to find a room, I was walking along the corridor, and people were sleeping everywhere—one had to walk carefully. I was stepping over a couple of people, and I looked down and saw this woman holding an empty bottle of Jack Daniel's, and it was indeed Janis Joplin. So we never actually met, unless you count meeting while one person was unconscious, because she was lying there passed out or sleeping on the floor in the corridor, and I said to myself, "Oh, that's Janis Joplin, how cool," and went into my room. So that's my Woodstock story.

Returning to the Beatles, we have talked about Paul and Ringo, so turning to George, perhaps his greatest W song was "While My

Guitar Gently Weeps," a musical masterpiece and lyrically accurate in the sense that it was indeed George's guitar doing the weeping but not actually in his hands. As many of you may know, George did not play that lead guitar part. It was played by his dear friend Eric Clapton. George was an amazing musician and created many astonishingly beautiful solos of his own but deferred to Eric on this occasion—and to good effect. This song alone should also be enough to establish George's status as an exceptionally brilliant and imaginative songwriter in his own right.

George also wrote another cool W song that is much less well known but I really do like it. It is called "Wreck of the Hesperus." It does not have much to do with other versions of the story. First, there was a famous poem by the great American poet Henry Wadsworth Longfellow, published in 1842—a tragic poem about a sea captain and his daughter out in the storm, and everyone dies. All very sad. George's song is not sad at all; he is essentially declaring that he is *not* the "wreck of the Hesperus" but rather "the wall of China" and "tall as the Eiffel Tower." And he does so over a seriously rocking track which featured many of George's world-class musician friends—excellent Keltner drums and dramatic blues licks from Clapton—as well as terrific playing and singing from George himself. Check out the great guitar lick played in octaves and mixed hard left and hard right which becomes a solo at 2:25 and continues to the end of the fade. It is also worth noting the reference in the lyrics to Big Bill Broonzy, another example of a great bluesman held in higher esteem in Britain than he has ever been in his homeland. George's songwriting skills, arranging ability, intense vocal, and musical taste are all clearly on display.

Ringo's solo career also features several W songs, two of them unexpected. One is "When You Wish upon a Star," an excellent performance from a Disney-tribute album called *Stay Awake*, which includes a trumpet solo by the legendary Herb Alpert. The album featured artists as disparate as Bonnie Raitt, Sun Ra and his Arkestra, James Taylor, and Harry Nilsson, and was produced by my friend Hal Willner, a New York record producer of great brilliance who has done a number of equally cool "themed" albums, each with a remarkable cast of artists.

Now, I confess, I have been saving what is probably my favourite Beatles W song, one that Paul wrote when he was staying at our house. A brilliant song, a great arrangement, a very well-made record, with excellent production by George Martin: "We Can Work It Out." In many respects this track exemplifies exactly what was so exceptional about the Beatles as a creative team. Paul wrote the verse, a positive sentiment that difficulties can be overcome, set to music in the key of D major—a thoroughly happy key—ending with a triumphant kind of mini chorus of "We can work it out, we can work it out" over two bars of alternating G and D chords. Then John wrote the bridge, which takes an ominous turn musically and lyrically. As it reminds us that "life is very short," it slips down into B minor (the relative minor of D major, where we started) and provides a startling change of mood. And then George suggested the change to waltz time (3/4) for four bars for the "fussing and fighting my friend" section. Ringo created an ultra-solid drum groove on the basic track, and his switch to a four-to-a-bar snare part is one of the elements that makes the chorus so satisfying. John played acoustic rhythm guitar (of which he was a master), and on this occasion it was George who locked the tambourine so accurately to Ringo's drums. Then John overdubbed the imaginative harmonium swells. A genuine group effort, a masterful record, and a huge hit—as half of a double A-side with "Day Tripper."

Before we leave the letter W behind, one of the very important W's in the world of the Beatles is the band Wings—by far the most successful Beatles spin-off project. And, in fact, Wings would be considered a gigantic band even if the Beatles had never existed. They had so many huge hits people forget. To begin with, probably my favourite and possibly the most famous Wings track of all is "Band on the Run," a remarkable record and an unusual hit in many respects. In the first place, it is one of Paul's longest singles at 5:09 and is composed of three distinct and discrete musical segments. It is also worth noting that two members of the band had already run away before recording even began! Paul had decided to make the whole album in Lagos, Nigeria, but both Henry McCullough (guitar) and Denny Seiwell (drums) quit Wings shortly before the planned departure date. So the band was reduced to its essence—just Paul, Linda, and Denny Laine. Paul reverted to playing several instruments on each track—drums, percussion, and much of the lead guitar work as well as bass. This little trio (along with their invaluable engineer, the trusty Geoff Emerick) also had to contend with the various hazards of their chosen location—technical mishaps, health scares, and even a terrifying robbery at knifepoint which involved the loss of lyrics and demos. Eventually, they decided to finish the record at AIR Studios in London. Despite all this drama, both the album as a whole and the song "Band on the Run" in particular have more than withstood the test of time and rank with the very best of Paul McCartney's extraordinary body of work.

Together we have been exploring the Beatles alphabetically, and it is with some trepidation that I have brought you to the letter X. I confess that I have been wondering in advance what on earth I was going to do when I got to X because there unequivocally are no Beatles songs that begin with that letter at all. Some of you must have thought, *Well, he's going to be stuck now! What's he going to do?* But I have come up with a few dodges and cheats and shortcuts which I hope I may get away with. So here we go.

Did you know (I did not) that on December 13, 2009, on the final night of the television program *X Factor UK*, there was a

George at Friar Park.

surprise guest appearance by our very own Paul McCartney? And that guest appearance on the (perfectly named) *X Factor* qualifies instantly for this chapter, of course. Paul sang two songs live: "Drive My Car" and "Live and Let Die." These are songs he often performs—and very well, too. You can find excellent live versions of these songs on his album *Good Evening New York City*, which was recorded over the three nights of the inaugural concerts at New York's Citi Field on July 17, 18, and 21, 2009. A huge gig, but it instantly sold out, and by all accounts it was a great performance. Several friends of mine were there and raved about the music, the energy, and the sheer excitement of the show. It is perhaps worth reflecting on Paul's boundless enthusiasm for performing which does not appear to have diminished at all over the decades. When Peter & Gordon had the privilege of opening for the Beatles more than fifty years ago, I remember watching Paul bound onto the stage as if there were nowhere else in the world he would rather be—and watching him much more recently it is clear that the sentiment has not changed. He plays for far longer now (often three hours straight) than he ever did in the old days and with even greater and more readily apparent joy. He's obviously no longer doing it to make a living or to become a star but solely out of love for music and performing. With all the old problems of sound and staging having found modern technological solutions, with the various issues so clearly outlined in the documentary *Eight Days a Week* happily resolved, Paul can relax and enjoy not only the miraculous body of work upon which he can call but also the musicianship, vocal resilience, audience appeal, and stagecraft which have always impressed us so much.

At the end of his performance on *X Factor*, Paul asked, "Did we pass the audition?" And to everyone's relief, Simon Cowell said, "Yes, you made it through to the next round!" And I am looking forward very much to Paul's "next round" myself, whatever it may bring.

So *X Factor* got me started on the letter X, but it is hardly enough for a whole chapter. I found myself wandering around the house mumbling, "X . . . X . . ." to myself, wondering what on earth to do, and it occurred to me that one X topic we do have is

"Ex-Beatles." And the most famous ex-Beatle by miles is Pete Best. He has not had an easy career, but he is in person a charming man. I have run into him at some Beatles-related events, and he is totally cool.

After he left the Beatles in 1962, Pete went on to have his own group, the Pete Best Band. One of their tracks is a nostalgic song about Liverpool, in the same vein as Paul's "Penny Lane" and Ringo's "Liverpool 8." Pete wrote and recorded "Haymans Green," about an area in which no doubt the Beatles played gigs back in the day in Liverpool.

Pete Best, of course, is not the only ex-Beatle. If you think about it, Paul and John and Ringo and George themselves became ex-Beatles after 1970 and proceeded to make some terrific records in that capacity. So I would suggest that we choose and explore one significant or interesting song that each recorded as an ex-Beatle. For Paul, many people consider his first extraordinary and creative song as an ex-Beatle to be "Maybe I'm Amazed," a track from the album *McCartney*, his first release after the breakup. The music world did not know what to expect from this record and probably *was* amazed (and impressed) when Paul's first solo album turned out to be so terrifically good and to contain such an exceptionally powerful song. Written by Paul and dedicated to his wife, Linda, it was recorded in EMI's Studio Two, with Paul playing every instrument. "Maybe I'm Amazed" was never released as an actual single, but it received a great deal of airplay worldwide nonetheless. Much later, a live version of the song was recorded by Wings as part of the album *Wings over America*, and that one *was* released as a single and became a top ten hit in the U.S. So the power of "Maybe I'm Amazed" was proved beyond any question, and the song can be seen in retrospect as a clear harbinger of the extraordinary solo career Paul enjoys to this day.

Moving on to our second ex-Beatle, John Lennon, who is so profoundly missed. He was an extraordinary man, an intimidating and even mordant intellect, and a brilliant musician. He recorded so many good tracks it is hard to choose just one. In this instance I have chosen a song which shows John in a gentle mood, which was not always the case with him. That song is "Love Is Real"—or so I always call it, though the official name of the song is just "Love." This song was included on John's 1970 album *John Lennon/Plastic Ono Band*. Though never released as a single, it rapidly found a following and received substantial airplay as well. With disarmingly plain but profoundly effective lyrics, with some simple but unexpected chord changes and a beautiful vocal (double tracked, as John so often did), the record has a contemplative elegance to it that I find very affecting.

Then there is Ringo—a brilliant and astonishingly creative drummer, an amazing musician, a charming man, and a valued friend. I picked an odd one here. Not one of Ringo's classics, but a track which I find highly entertaining. The song is called "Wine, Women and Loud Happy Songs." Well, since that time, Ringo no longer drinks the wine, and he found himself one incredibly wonderful and beautiful woman in Barbara, of whom I am a great admirer—but he is still really good at singing loud happy songs, like this one.

Our last ex-Beatle, George Harrison, is also so seriously missed, of course. An extraordinary composer, a wildly skilled and inventive guitarist, and a brilliant and remarkable man. He combined some of the traditional virtues of an English country gentleman (civility, good humour, and a certain traditionalism) with a profound fascination with other cultures, their music, their skills, and their philosophical knowledge. He also felt a deep connection to his own extraordinary and beloved home in the British countryside, Friar Park, so miraculously loved and maintained to this day by the amazing Olivia—just as she maintains every aspect of George's legacy with unbounded love and a precise attention to detail. I do not think there can be a better song to represent George's ex-Beatles years than "Give Me Love (Give Me Peace on Earth)," one of George's biggest hits and a significant change of style from its predecessor, "My Sweet Lord," though both share a spiritual theme. Switching from the pomp and size of a Phil Spector production to a clarity and intimacy more reminiscent of what George Martin might have done, it allows individual instrumentalists to shine rather than building a wall of sound: Nicky Hopkins's irresistibly catchy repetitive piano lick and the perfectly light, almost jazzy, syncopation shared by Klaus Voormann on bass and Jim Keltner on drums. And above it all the sincerity of George's vocal and (my favourite element) the ineffable sweetness of his elegantly written and beautifully played twin slide guitar lines in the introduction and the solo.

At this point, in contemplating the letter X, I decided to take advantage of outside help. On my radio program, I regularly give out my email address (it is peterasher@siriusxm.com, if you're curious), and I do read and answer every email I get. In the course of this correspondence, some listeners graciously send suggestions or requests for particular songs. In relation to the "A to Zed" project, I received a suggestion from two listeners named Mike and Jennifer Brunsberg, who said, "When you get to X, you're probably going to be completely stuck! But here's an idea."

And the idea was one that was silly enough that it appealed to my jejune English sense of humour, and I am going to include it. What Mike and Jennifer pointed out was that John and Paul had actually written a song that was clearly, specifically, and definitively composed from the point of view of an X-ray technician, and thus perfect for addressing the letter X.

"What song could that be?" I hear you ask. "What song could possibly be said to be written from a radiological standpoint?"

Well, the answer, of course, is "I'm Looking Through You." An excellent early Beatles track from *Rubber Soul*, written in Paul's bedroom next to mine. It was the only time I witnessed some actual live writing, because I distinctly remember Paul sitting with his guitar in my bedroom for some reason—trying to finish the bridge and suddenly coming up with the line "Love has a nasty habit of disappearing overnight," which fits so perfectly. And he was done!

Now, to return to an actual musical discussion that fits our topic, there is one famous musical instrument that begins with the letter X, and that is the xylophone. The xylophone is a family of instruments: the name refers to any instrument made out of bits of wood that you hit with mallets. The name comes from the Greek for "wood," which is *xylo* (ξύλο) or *xylon*, and *phone* (also a Greek word, φωνή), which means "sound." So it is literally wood-sound. You hit bits of wood, they make a sound, and you are playing a xylophone! And one prominent member of the xylophone family is the marimba, which the Beatles used quite a lot in the studio. George Martin used multiple marimbas and other xylophones to great effect on his soundtrack for *Yellow Submarine*, most noticeably on "March of the Meanies." If you listen attentively, you will hear many mallets hitting a lot of wood!

I happened to learn classical Greek at school. Perhaps part of the tradition of an old-school English education is that you learn stuff you hardly ever need, but finally, it has come in handy. Who knew that my classical education would prove invaluable when I was searching for Beatles songs related to the letter X?

Let us also consider what other instruments are mostly made out of wood. Rather obviously all the woodwind instruments, of course (the oboes and clarinets and bassoons) along with the strings (violin, viola, cello, and bass). But in the world of rock and roll, we would have to go with the guitar—and the acoustic guitar, in which instance the wood from which it is made is a very important factor in creating its particular tone. The Beatles played acoustic guitars a lot and made them sound really good— and they knew that the sound of each acoustic guitar was affected directly by the kind of wood out of which it was made. When musicians talk about their guitars, they talk about whether the top is made of spruce or the sides are made out of koa or whatever, and they discuss all these different kinds of fancy woods, each of which creates a different resonance and thus a different tone. The Beatles made extensive use of these differences. They used the Gibson J-160E, with a *laminated* Sitka spruce top (essentially fancy plywood), for all their rhythm parts, as in "I Should Have Known Better" and "You've Got to Hide Your Love Away." But they also used different guitars for other songs, for a more varied and effective sound. On "Yesterday," Paul played an Epiphone Texan with a *solid* Sitka spruce top, a mahogany back and sides, and a mahogany neck—and it sounds great.

Paul also had a 1967 Martin D-28, made of different kinds of wood entirely. The D-28s of that year were constructed of Brazilian rosewood for the back and sides, solid Sitka spruce on top, and a mahogany neck. The supply of Brazilian rosewood soon ran low, and Martin changed to East Indian rosewood in 1969, but the Beatles (John had one, too) beat this downgrade by a couple of years. Brazilian rosewood is crazy expensive now. One can often identify Brazilian rosewood by the circular knot patterns in the wood instead of the straighter-line look of East Indian rosewood.

As you can see, one can get seriously nerdy about wood when in a conversation about acoustic guitars, but these woods do make a difference. Compare the sound of the Martin D-28 that Paul plays on "Blackbird" with the Epiphone Texan on "Yesterday," and you will hear what I mean.

I have made it almost to the end of what began as our X chapter and has become kind of our wood chapter. And what better way to end a wood chapter than with a giant fire, the bit of arson that concludes the only song specifically written about wood in the entire Beatles catalogue: "Norwegian Wood."

So as the fire crackles away merrily in the background, I say thank you very much. We made it through the letter X. It is no more. It is an ex-letter.

Welcome to the letter Y, an oasis of plenty in the desert at the end of the Beatles' alphabet. The letter X was hard, as we have seen, and of course Zed could be brutal. But Y is an open house: a plethora of subjects, people, and songs. We have plenty of interesting topics from which to choose. Let us start very simply with the name of the letter itself. It may sound simple but of course when one utters it one is (perhaps inadvertently) posing what may be the most profoundly existential and philosophical question of them all:

"Why?"

But fear not, Ringo wrote and sang a song in which he (in his usual succinct and matter-of-fact way) provides as good an answer as any:

"Y Not"?

The Dirty Mac (Eric Clapton, John Lennon, Mitch Mitchell, and Keith Richards) at the Rock and Roll Circus.

It was the title song of one of Ringo's solo albums—a blues with a strong and entrancing groove, a terrific snare sound, and a very positive sentiment. The record was engineered by Bruce Sugar, and the song was co-written by Ringo with the remarkable producer and songwriter Glen Ballard. You know Glen from his work with Michael Jackson and Katy Perry and (perhaps most significantly) for having produced and co-written the whole of Alanis Morrisette's extraordinary and hyper-successful album *Jagged Little Pill*.

I mentioned "Why?" as perhaps the most obviously existential *question* one can ask (and Ringo's response of "Y Not")—and surely, on the other hand, the most existentially positive *statement* one can make is "Yes It Is," the title of a John Lennon Y song written for the Beatles, the B-side of "Ticket to Ride." John thought he was writing a follow-up to "This Boy," but it stands very well as a song (and record) on its own. It was recorded on February 16, 1965, the same day as "I Need You," and George Harrison seemed to be particularly enthralled by his volume pedal (or his volume knob?), which he used to create those smooth swells, those elegant crescendos and diminuendos on his electric guitar on both songs.

Moving forward through the letter Y, I am now going to head towards a more obscure Beatles track, one that they did not record on any of their albums. As I have mentioned earlier, the Beatles, in addition to being brilliant songwriters themselves, admired many American songwriters, two of whom are Jerry Leiber & Mike Stoller, and another is Doc Pomus. John Lennon in particular was a devoted fan of the remarkable Doc Pomus and famously requested to sit next to him at a dinner in New York, where they spent the whole evening in rapt conversation.

I had not realized that the three American composers (Leiber, Stoller, and Pomus) had written together, but they did collaborate on a song called "Young Blood"—originally a Coasters record, which the Beatles sometimes covered in their live show. Luckily, they also performed it at the BBC, so a recording of their version does exist. I urge you to track it down. "Young Blood" had been the B-side of the Coasters' huge hit single "Searchin'," a song the

Beatles also used to sing live and which they recorded as part of their unsuccessful audition for Decca Records.

Our next stop in the letter Y is a song that is a favourite of many Beatles fans, including me: "You're Going to Lose That Girl." One of the most brilliant things about this song is the way the Beatles put the chords together to get in and out of the bridge. The song virtually changes key for the bridge in a remarkable way. This kind of writing owes a lot to Buddy Holly, who took completely simple "normal" chords—not weird jazzy chords—and used them to move around through the keys in an odd and creative way. The verse ("If you don't take her out tonight") and chorus ("You're gonna lose that girl") are both clearly in E major with a lot of minor chords added (F-sharp minor and G-sharp minor), giving the song a mournful air—almost as if the writer were feeling sympathy for the "other man" about to suffer such a distressing loss. Yet then the bridge leaps from the F-sharp minor of the chorus into a world of major chords, travelling via a D major into the key of G major for a solid eight bars as the singer declares with absolute certainty, "I'll make point of taking her away from you."

This song was, of course, in *Help!*, the movie, as was our next Y song, "You've Got to Hide Your Love Away." This is such a wildly catchy song and a powerful 6/8 groove, carried primarily by John's emphatic acoustic guitar playing and Ringo's bold tambourine. George's twelve-string licks connect the dots as Paul fills out the bottom end. Breathtaking support for John's intense vocal.

As was the case with "You're Going to Lose That Girl," a very important element of the song is the simple but unusual chord structure. There is also an equally simple little guitar motif which renders the chorus unforgettable—after every "Hide your love away" and starting on the "way." Technically it is a Dsus4 and a D and a Dsus2 and back to a D. All that this really means is that the top string of the D chord on the guitar starts up a half step (playing a G rather than an F-sharp), moves down a half step (to play the F-sharp), down a full step (to play an E), and then back up to the F-sharp. Again, brilliantly simple, and it becomes a hook all on its own.

We have spent a lot of time with John, so let us move on to an excellent George Harrison song in the letter Y department. This one is a beautiful love song from the album called *George Harrison*. When the album was released in 1979, George said, "I think that what happened between this album and the last album is that everything has been happening nicely for me. My life is getting better all the time. I'm happy and I think that's reflected in the music." Most of this happiness came, of course, from his wonderful wife Olivia, and their newborn son, Dhani. This song was a perfect reflection of George's state of mind at this time, and it is called "Your Love Is Forever."

Sticking with songs of emotional power and content, there is an excellent Traveling Wilburys song that begins with the letter Y, a song called "You Took My Breath Away." It features great singing not only from George Harrison but also from Tom Petty and Jeff Lynne. I believe that the song was written about Roy Orbison, who had recently died and had been a mentor and idol to the other Wilburys. I am not sure whether I read that or if it just sounds that way to me, but Roy Orbison's singing could certainly take one's breath away! A fitting tribute.

In much the same way, and as a tribute to an even older style of music, there is a sweet Wings song called "You Gave Me the Answer," which sounds as if it could have been written and recorded about fifty years earlier. It features a muted trumpet, clarinet, bassoon, strings, and more—an old-time orchestra lineup surely not dissimilar to the one that was led by Paul's father, who came of age musically in the 1920s. "You Gave Me the Answer" has the kind of Rudy Vallee/Fred Astaire vocal that Paul McCartney does so well—he even used an electronic filter on his voice (removing the lower frequencies) to simulate the lo-fi sound of an old-fashioned recording or even that of singing through a megaphone.

Turning back to the Beatles' catalogue itself, we find many great Y songs to choose from. Of course, I am now forced to pay the price for having cheated in the letter U, where I discussed so many Y songs already. I thought it was so clever of me to talk about songs that begin with "You" under U, but now I question that decision.

But not to fear—the Beatles have many other Y songs, and one of them is "Yer Blues," from the White Album. Back then, in the midst of all the ongoing discussions about the "Blues Boom" happening in the UK, all the questions about why so many young musicians in Britain had fallen in love with the music of a whole other culture, John contributed this fine example of some white boys paying tribute to the blues. Sung and performed with an almost satirical enthusiasm—making fun not of their authentic blues heroes, for whom they had absolute respect, but rather of themselves and their colleagues. It is a standard blues in E major but with a couple of passing chords like a G major making it a bit different. And a time signature switching between 6/8 and a kind of jazzy swing. In some ways it reminds me of the James Taylor song "Steamroller"— itself a parody of the determination of the New York musicians of that era to come up with the "heaviest" blues ever.

I remember witnessing a live performance of "Yer Blues" many years ago when I attended a Rolling Stones event in London called the Rock and Roll Circus, which was being filmed for a TV show. It is out on video now (having been unreleased for many years), and you may have seen it. It looks kind of fun on the video, but I must tell you, the event itself was truly boring because it felt as if it went on forever. Filmed shows can often be like that, but this was worse than most. They kept stopping, they had to do stuff again, there would be giant gaps when something wasn't working. I think I left at two or three in the morning, and they were certainly still going strong—I remember that the Stones themselves were onstage, but some technical hitch or other had brought things to a standstill again, and everyone was looking a bit worse for wear. But they did get some good recordings out of it, including a version of "Yer Blues" with a band featuring John Lennon, Mitch Mitchell, Eric Clapton, and Keith Richards—a one-off supergroup known as the Dirty Mac. The whole show does not seem unduly long in its edited, released version—but I have to say I'm glad I don't have to sit through that again.

Another Y song from the Beatles is not one of my favourites, but it has become increasingly appreciated. It was the B-side of "Let It Be," and it is probably the weirdest record the Beatles ever made. It owes a lot to groups like the Bonzo Dog Doo-Dah Band, particularly with the odd kind of singing and the spirit of parody in which the Beatles approach the whole song. It also reminds me of their affection for *The Goon Show* and Spike Milligan, who worked with George Martin. It is close to being a comedy record itself: "You Know My Name (Look Up the Number)." For me, it's okay, if kind of goofy. I mean, everything the Beatles do is terrific, and I love listening to the record. But a favourite? I am always surprised by how often it is requested.

I am going to end with another Y song by the Beatles that is everyone's favourite, "Yellow Submarine." Children love it. Grown-ups love it. I love it. You love it.

The song was one-half of an extraordinary single that the Beatles released in 1966. It is an indication of Lennon & McCartney's songwriting talent that they put out a single with two songs which have each become true classics, songs that are written in different styles, recorded in different styles, sung in different styles, and could well be from two completely different bands—but they are not. They are separate aspects of the genius of the Beatles. On one side, the humour and sonic creativity of "Yellow Submarine," with its sound effects, its voices, its characters. And on the other side, "Eleanor Rigby."

But for now, I can think of no better way to close our discussion of the letter Y than by joining the Beatles in an underwater singalong as we sail off in what could be the most famous submarine in the world—and I certainly do not have to tell you what colour it is. It is the only colour that begins with Y, anyway!

It has taken us twenty-five chapters, but we have finally reached the letter Zed. For most of this peripatetic musical drift through the alphabet, Zed has felt like a faraway goal; but surprisingly, we have arrived, and I have much enjoyed working our way through the twenty-six letters together.

So here we are at Zed—or "Zee," as you call it in America. And guess what? I did find one song that qualifies as a genuine Zed song, a song called "Zig Zag," by George Harrison. It is on his album *Cloud Nine*, and it was the B-side of "When We Was Fab," an excellent George single. It was also in the movie *Shanghai*

The zebra crossing at Abbey Road, with the Belisha beacons on either side.

Surprise. It is a blues-flavoured number, not officially a twelve-bar blues but more like "St. James Infirmary" or one of those classic jazzy, New Orleans–ish songs, featuring a trumpet, a tenor sax, and a four-string banjo playing rhythm. The trumpet is played with a Harmon mute. The elegant and very authentic arrangement was created by John Dupree, an extremely talented musician and composer who is also Eric Idle's longtime collaborator. He co-wrote much of the music for *Spamalot* and wrote the arrangements for songs like "Always Look on the Bright Side of Life" and other *Python* classics. The song was written and produced by George Harrison and Jeff Lynne and sounds a bit like one of those great old Cab Calloway tunes in which the whole band sings in unison from time to time.

That is the only real Beatles Zed song that I could find. So we are going to have to discover other interesting Zed topics, and I thought we could consider Beatles songs from a zoological standpoint. This Beatles zoo would contain all the animals about which they have ever sung or thought or written. You may think there are not that many of those, but on the White Album alone, I spotted birds, tigers, elephants, bees, and pigs, not to mention a lizard, a dog, an eagle, a worm, and a monkey, along with a notable raccoon. Enough to fill a sizable menagerie.

As we walk into the zoo, first you see the huge building on the right, which is the entomology department: the study of insects. In this case specializing, need I say, in the study of beetles. And, as you Buddy Holly fans will know, a similar department for the study of crickets. Anyway, we walk past that important building, because the Beatles have studied themselves a lot, and everyone else has studied them even more. We walk into the zoo itself. This being an imaginary zoo, every animal has the perfect habitat. There are no bars or cages; it is a luxury zoo, and all the animals are very happy.

For example, immediately in front of us, we see this huge, amazing aviary. What birds are in the aviary, you may ask? Well, think about it. We know for sure that there is a blackbird, and a bluebird, as well. There's also a bird that can sing and a bird that is spectacularly free.

Beyond the aviary, of course, there are many other animals—some of them you'll know about, some of them you may not immediately think of. There are quite a few dogs. Some dogs that have names, some particular dogs, one dog of a specific breed, and so on.

There are also cats, and a kitten.

There is, of course, a horse, with a name.

There are also cows. You may find that one trickier. Where do cows come into a Beatles song?

And there is also a very large and mysterious walrus.*

All these animals are in this miraculous zoo. And as we depart, we see our path marked by another Zed with zoological associations: a zebra crossing.

Zebra crossings are international. There are certainly a lot of them in London, and one is clearly much more famous than all the others put together. Zebra crossings, as you know, are the black-and-white striped markings on the pavement which warn motorists to allow you to cross a road safely.

In London, each side of a zebra crossing is obliged to have a contraption called a Belisha beacon, which consists of a yellow globe-shaped light on a black-and-white striped pole. The beacons were named after the minister of transport at the time, whose name (believe it or not) was Lord Hore-Belisha. Of course the Belisha beacons at the famous crossing under discussion are covered in autographs and dates and many variations on "I love Paul" and "Ringo Forever" and an infinite variety of Beatles graffiti, because, as you have already realized, I am referring to the zebra crossing that spans Abbey Road on the way to what was once EMI Studios, the location for the extremely famous photograph on the cover of the Beatles' *Abbey Road* album.

The name Abbey Road did not have much significance at the time the photo was taken. The Beatles were simply trying to decide what to call their new record and what kind of picture to

---

* I presume many of you will be able to identify the songs from these clues, but if you are stumped, I have listed the songs in the playlist section at the back of this book.

take for the cover, and both decisions were made very quickly. They named the album after the street where they were at the time (sitting in EMI Studios) and took a picture on the nearby zebra crossing that traverses it. That was it—a plan that elevated that particular crossing to long-term iconic status as well as becoming a substantial traffic headache since there are *always* pedestrians walking slowly across as photographs are taken. Taxi drivers have been known to avoid that route during peak tourist times simply to escape that particular delay. The tube is usually quicker anyway.

It is strange, but in talking about zebra crossings at the end of the alphabet, I have returned to our discussion at the beginning of our journey—of *Abbey Road* the album and Abbey Road Studios. I talked about the classical recordings made there and the first rock and roll record made there. I also talked about the first Beatles record and all that followed, including my own introduction to EMI Studios with Gordon Waller in January 1964.

The zebra crossing, which is what got us all here in the first place, is just a few yards from the studio itself. Eventually, of course, they changed the name of the studio to match the road it was on, and to match one of the greatest albums ever made by the greatest rock and roll band of all time—an extremely shrewd marketing move!

As we approach our conclusion, I can think of no better way to honour the Beatles, the studio they thought of as home, and the alphabetical mystery tour we have shared than to turn to two epic tracks, both recorded at EMI Studios in 1967 and both of which were filmed: "A Day in the Life" and "All You Need Is Love."

"A Day in the Life" featured the legendary session during which the Beatles asked the orchestra to put on silly hats and masks and to sometimes play without specific written notes in front of them but with tremendous enthusiasm nonetheless. For the famous ascending crescendo, they were each asked to play their own individually chosen notes, starting with the lowest notes they could play and then following the conductor up to the highest note in their whole range. A classic moment.

For "All You Need Is Love," the track was actually pre-recorded at Olympic Studios, but at the televised event, the Beatles and their numerous friends and guests and many additional musicians all played and sang together live, on top of the track they had previously cut at Olympic, and the result was broadcast live around the world. Millions of people worldwide heard the Beatles put in a plea for the optimistic suggestion that all you need is love.

And so, in exploring the letter Zed and talking about the zebra crossing in front of Abbey Road Studios and some of the remarkable things that happened there, we have come full circle and completed our alphabet. It has been an amazing journey. Thank you so much for joining me.

We are going to stroll back across the zebra crossing to the other side of Abbey Road, walk up to the St. John's Wood tube station, and be on our way. We're going home.

Chapter Playlists

I have listed the artists and songwriters as they appeared on the record labels at the time. If a song appears more than once, even if sung by a different artist, I have not repeated the songwriting credit.

Please note that some of Paul McCartney's solo tracks were released under his name alone, some as Paul and Linda McCartney, some as Paul McCartney and Wings, and some as Wings. Similarly, some of John Lennon's solo tracks were released under the name of the Plastic Ono Band.

Also, during the time the Beatles were together, even those songs written by John or Paul alone were credited to the Lennon-McCartney partnership.

Introduction
Peter & Gordon, "A World Without Love" (John Lennon / Paul McCartney)

A
The Beatles, "All My Loving" (John Lennon / Paul McCartney)
The Beatles, "Across the Universe" (John Lennon / Paul McCartney)
The Beatles, "Lady Madonna" (John Lennon / Paul McCartney)
Eddie Izzard, "Being for the Benefit of Mr. Kite!" (John Lennon / Paul McCartney)
Rufus Wainwright, "Across the Universe"
The Beatles, "Act Naturally" (Johnny Russell / Voni Morrison)
George Harrison, "All Things Must Pass" (George Harrison)
"Pomp and Circumstance March No. 1" (Edward Elgar)

Cliff Richard and the Drifters, "Move It" (Ian Samwell)
The Beatles, "Something" (George Harrison)
James Taylor, "Something in the Way She Moves" (James Taylor)
The Beatles, "I Feel Fine" (John Lennon / Paul McCartney)
James Taylor, "Carolina in My Mind" (James Taylor)
Elvis Presley, "All Shook Up" (Otis Blackwell)
Paul McCartney, "All Shook Up"
The Beatles, "Anna (Go to Him)" (Arthur Alexander)
Arthur Alexander, "You Better Move On" (Arthur Alexander)
The Beatles, "And I Love Her" (John Lennon / Paul McCartney)

B

The Beatles, "Baby It's You" (Burt Bacharach / Mack David / Barney Williams)
The Shirelles, "Baby It's You"
The Beatles, "Twist and Shout" (Phil Medley / Bert Berns)
The Shirelles, "Will You Love Me Tomorrow" (Carole King / Gerry Goffin)
Brian Hyland, "Itsy Bitsy Teenie Weenie Yellow Polkadot Bikini" (Paul Vance / Lee Pockriss)
The Beatles, "Boys" (Luther Dixon / Wes Farrell)
The Beatles, "Baby's in Black" (John Lennon / Paul McCartney)
The Everly Brothers, "Bye Bye Love" (Felice Bryant / Boudleaux Bryant)
George Harrison, "Bye Bye Love"
The Everly Brothers, "The Price of Love" (Don Everly / Phil Everly)
Gene Vincent and His Blue Caps, "Be-Bop-a-Lula" (Sheriff Tex Davis / Gene Vincent)
John Lennon, "Be-Bop-a-Lula"
The Beatles, "Birthday" (John Lennon / Paul McCartney)
The Beatles, "Roll Over Beethoven" (Chuck Berry)
Chuck Berry, "Roll Over Beethoven"
The Iveys, "Maybe Tomorrow" (Tom Evans)
The Beatles, "With a Little Help from My Friends" (John Lennon / Paul McCartney)
Badfinger, "Come and Get It" (John Lennon / Paul McCartney)
Badfinger, "Carry on Till Tomorrow" (Pete Ham / Tom Evans)
Ringo Starr, "Back Off Boogaloo" (Richard Starkey)
Ringo Starr, "Bye Bye Blackbird" (Ray Henderson / Mort Dixon)
The Beatles, "Blackbird" (John Lennon / Paul McCartney)
"Bourrée in E Minor" (Johann Sebastian Bach)
George Harrison, "Beware of Darkness" (George Harrison)
The Beatles, "The Ballad of John and Yoko" (John Lennon / Paul McCartney)
The Beatles, "Back in the U.S.S.R." (John Lennon / Paul McCartney)
Chuck Berry, "Back in the U.S.A." (Chuck Berry)
Linda Ronstadt, "Back in the U.S.A."

C

Plastic Ono Band, "Cold Turkey" (John Lennon)
The Beatles, "Come Together" (John Lennon / Paul McCartney)
Plastic Ono Band, "Give Peace a Chance" (John Lennon / Paul McCartney)
Aerosmith, "Come Together"
Robin Williams and Bobby McFerrin, "Come Together"

Chuck Berry, "You Can't Catch Me" (Chuck Berry)

George Harrison, "Crackerbox Palace" (George Harrison)

Lord Buckley, "God's Own Drunk" (comedy routine)

Paul McCartney, "Coming Up" (Paul McCartney)

Ringo Starr, "Cryin'" (Richard Starkey / Vini Poncia)

James Taylor, "Up on the Roof" (Gerry Goffin / Carole King)

The Beatles, "Can't Buy Me Love" (John Lennon / Paul McCartney)

The Beatles, "The Continuing Story of Bungalow Bill" (John Lennon / Paul McCartney)

The Beatles, "Please Please Me" (John Lennon / Paul McCartney)

The Beatles, "From Me to You" (John Lennon / Paul McCartney)

The Beatles, "Love Me Do" (John Lennon / Paul McCartney)

The Beatles, "I Want to Hold Your Hand" (John Lennon / Paul McCartney)

Peter & Gordon, "A World Without Love"

The Beatles, "Hey Jude" (John Lennon / Paul McCartney)

D

The Beatles, "Day Tripper" (John Lennon / Paul McCartney)

The Temptations, "My Girl" (Smokey Robinson / Ronald White)

The Beatles, "We Can Work It Out" (John Lennon / Paul McCartney)

The Beatles, "Drive My Car" (John Lennon / Paul McCartney)

Bill Haley and His Comets, "Rock Around the Clock" (Max C. Freedman / James E. Myers)

Sting and Ivy Levan, "Drive My Car"

The Beatles, "Don't Bother Me" (George Harrison)

The Beatles, "Don't Pass Me By" (Richard Starkey)

Larry Williams, "Dizzy Miss Lizzy" (Larry Williams)

Swinging Blue Jeans, "Dizzy Miss Lizzy"

The Beatles, "Dizzy Miss Lizzy," BBC Recording

The Beatles, "A Day in the Life" (John Lennon / Paul McCartney)

The Beatles, "Thank You Girl" (John Lennon / Paul McCartney)

The Beatles, "With a Little Help from My Friends"

James Taylor, "Fire and Rain" (James Taylor)

The Beatles, "She Said She Said" (John Lennon / Paul McCartney)

The Beatles, "Rain" (John Lennon / Paul McCartney)

The Beatles, "Doctor Robert" (John Lennon / Paul McCartney)

The Beatles, "Dear Prudence" (John Lennon / Paul McCartney)

Buddy Holly, "Raining in My Heart" (Felice Bryant / Boudleaux Bryant)

The Beatles with Billy Preston, "Get Back" (John Lennon / Paul McCartney)

The Beatles with Billy Preston, "Don't Let Me Down" (John Lennon / Paul McCartney)

The Beatles, "Do You Want to Know a Secret" (John Lennon / Paul McCartney)

From *Snow White and the Seven Dwarfs*, "I'm Wishing" (Frank Churchill / Larry Morey)

E

The Beatles, "Eight Days a Week" (John Lennon / Paul McCartney)

The Beatles, "Everybody's Trying to Be My Baby" (Carl Perkins)

Carl Perkins, "Everybody's Trying to Be My Baby"

The Beatles, "Matchbox" (Carl Perkins)
Paul McCartney with Carl Perkins, "Get It" (Paul McCartney)
Carl Perkins, "Blue Suede Shoes" (Carl Perkins)
Elvis Presley, "Blue Suede Shoes"
Elvis Presley, "Heartbreak Hotel" (Mae Boren Axton / Thomas Durden)
Elvis Presley, "Mystery Train" (Junior Parker)
The Beatles, "That's All Right (Mama)," BBC Recording (Arthur Crudup)
Elvis Presley, "Blue Moon of Kentucky" (Bill Monroe)
The Beatles, "I Want to Hold Your Hand"
The Beatles, "Love Me Do"
The Beatles, "From Me to You"
The Beatles, "Please Please Me"
Ringo Starr, "Don't Be Cruel" (Otis Blackwell)
Elvis Presley, "Return to Sender" (Otis Blackwell)
Elvis Presley, "All Shook Up"
Jerry Lee Lewis, "Great Balls of Fire" (Otis Blackwell)
Peggy Lee, "Fever" (Otis Blackwell)
Jimmy Jones, "Handy Man" (Otis Blackwell / Jimmy Jones)
James Taylor, "Handy Man"
Paul McCartney and Stevie Wonder, "Ebony and Ivory" (Paul McCartney)
The Beatles, "Eleanor Rigby" (John Lennon / Paul McCartney)
The Beatles, "Yellow Submarine" (John Lennon / Paul McCartney)
Ray Charles, "Eleanor Rigby"
The Beatles, "Every Little Thing" (John Lennon / Paul McCartney)
Paul McCartney, "Early Days" (Paul McCartney)
The Beatles, "Everybody's Got Something to Hide Except for Me and My Monkey" (John Lennon / Paul McCartney)
George Harrison, "This Guitar (Can't Keep from Crying)" (George Harrison)
Whitney Houston, "I Will Always Love You" (Dolly Parton)
Ringo Starr, "Electricity" (Richard Starkey / Glen Ballard)
The Beatles, "The End" (John Lennon / Paul McCartney)

F

The Beatles, "From Me to You"
The Beatles, "From Us to You" (promotional jingle)
Helen Shapiro, "Walkin' Back to Happiness" (John Schroeder / Mike Hawker)
Helen Shapiro, "You Don't Know" (John Schroeder / Mike Hawker)
The Beatles, "Flying" (John Lennon / Paul McCartney / George Harrison / Richard Starkey)
The Beatles, "The Fool on the Hill" (John Lennon / Paul McCartney)
The Beatles, "For You Blue" (George Harrison)
Ringo Starr, "Free Drinks" (Richard Starkey / Mark Hudson / Gary Burr / Steve Dudas / Dean Grakal)
John Lennon, "(Forgive Me) My Little Flower Princess" (John Lennon)
John Lennon, "Woman" (John Lennon)
John Lennon, "Dear Yoko" (John Lennon)
The Beatles, "Girl" (John Lennon / Paul McCartney)
Wings, "Famous Groupies" (Paul McCartney)
George Harrison, "When We Was Fab" (George Harrison / Jeff Lynne)

The Beatles, "For No One" (John Lennon / Paul McCartney)
Emmylou Harris, "For No One"
Little Feat, "Oh, Atlanta" (Bill Payne)
Little Feat, "Dixie Chicken" (Bill Payne)
The Beatles, "Fixing a Hole" (John Lennon / Paul McCartney)
The Beatles, "Free as a Bird" (John Lennon / Paul McCartney / George Harrison / Richard Starkey)
The Beatles, "Real Love" (John Lennon)

G

The Beatles, "Good Morning Good Morning" (John Lennon / Paul McCartney)
The Beatles, "Good Day Sunshine" (John Lennon / Paul McCartney)
The Lovin' Spoonful, "Daydream" (John Sebastian)
Roy Redmond, "Good Day Sunshine"
Kai Winding, "Time Is on My Side" (Norman Meade, pseudonym for Jerry Ragovoy)
Irma Thomas, "Time Is on My Side"
The Rolling Stones, "Time Is on My Side"
Big Brother and the Holding Company, "Piece of My Heart" (Jerry Ragovoy / Bert Berns)
Lorraine Ellison, "Stay with Me" (Jerry Ragovoy / George David Weiss)
The Beatles with Billy Preston, "Get Back"
The Beatles, "Getting Better" (John Lennon / Paul McCartney)
The Beatles, "Got to Get You into My Life" (John Lennon / Paul McCartney)
Peter & Gordon, "Black, Brown and Gold" (Michael Lease / Phil Stevens)
The Beatles, "Fixing a Hole"
The Beatles, "Lucy in the Sky with Diamonds" (John Lennon / Paul McCartney)
The Beatles, "Golden Slumbers" (John Lennon / Paul McCartney)
The Posies, "Golden Blunders" (Jonathan Auer / Kenneth Stringfellow)
Ringo Starr, "Golden Blunders"
George Harrison, "Got My Mind Set on You" (Rudy Clark)
Gene and Francesca Raskin, "Those Were the Days" (Gene Raskin / Boris Fomin)
Mary Hopkin, "Those Were the Days"
Mary Hopkin, "Goodbye" (John Lennon / Paul McCartney)
Paul Jones, "And the Sun Will Shine" (Barry Gibb / Robin Gibb / Maurice Gibb)
Bee Gees, "And the Sun Will Shine"
The Beatles, "She Loves You" (John Lennon / Paul McCartney)
The Beatles, "I Want to Hold Your Hand"
The Beatles, "Sie Liebt Dich" (John Lennon / Paul McCartney)
The Beatles, "Komm, Gib Mir Deine Hand" (John Lennon / Paul McCartney)
Peter & Gordon, "A World Without Love"
Peter & Gordon, "Woman" (Bernard Webb, pseudonym for Paul McCartney)
Plastic Ono Band, "Give Peace a Chance" (John Lennon / Paul McCartney)
The Beatles, "Good Night" (John Lennon / Paul McCartney)

H

The Beatles, "A Hard Day's Night"
The Beatles, "Help!" (John Lennon / Paul McCartney)
The Beatles, "All You Need Is Love"

The Beatles, "Here Comes the Sun" (George Harrison)
Ringo Starr, "Hey! Baby" (Margaret Cobb / Bruce Channel)
Bruce Channel, "Hey! Baby"
Paul McCartney and Wings, "Helen Wheels" (Paul McCartney / Linda McCartney)
Linda Ronstadt, "You're No Good" (Clint Ballard Jr.)
John Lennon, "Happy Xmas (War Is Over)" (John Lennon)
Neil Diamond, "Happy Xmas (War Is Over)"
The Beatles, "Honey Don't," BBC Recording (Carl Perkins)
Carl Perkins, "Honey Don't"
Harry Nilsson, "Rock Around the Clock"
John Lennon, "Whatever Gets You Thru the Night" (John Lennon)
Elton John, "Lucy in the Sky with Diamonds"
Elton John and John Lennon, "I Saw Her Standing There" (John Lennon / Paul McCartney)
The Beatles, "Helter Skelter" (John Lennon / Paul McCartney)
The Beatles, "Here, There and Everywhere" (John Lennon / Paul McCartney)
The Fourmost, "Hello Little Girl" (John Lennon / Paul McCartney)
The Beatles, "Hey Bulldog" (John Lennon / Paul McCartney)
Hank Williams, "Hey Good Lookin'" (Hank Williams)
Freddie Scott, "Hey Girl" (Carole King / Gerry Goffin)
Bruce Channel, "Hey! Baby"
The Beatles, "Hey Jude"
James Taylor, "Carolina in My Mind"

I

The Beatles, "I Want to Hold Your Hand"
The Beatles, "I Saw Her Standing There"
Neil Young, "I Saw Her Standing There"
The Beatles, "I'm Down" (John Lennon / Paul McCartney)
The Beatles, "I'm a Loser" (John Lennon / Paul McCartney)
The Beatles, "I Feel Fine"
The Beatles, "If I Fell" (John Lennon / Paul McCartney)
The Beatles, "I Want to Tell You" (George Harrison)
The Beatles, "If I Needed Someone" (George Harrison)
The Beatles, "I Need You" (George Harrison)
The Webb Sisters, "I Need You"
The Beatles, "I'm So Tired" (John Lennon / Paul McCartney)
The Beatles, "I'm Only Sleeping" (John Lennon / Paul McCartney)
The Rolling Stones, "I Wanna Be Your Man" (John Lennon / Paul McCartney)
The Beatles, "I Wanna Be Your Man"
The Bonzo Dog Doo-Dah Band, "I'm the Urban Spaceman" (Neil Innes)
The Bonzo Dog Doo-Dah Band, "The Intro and the Outro" (Vivian Stanshall)
The Beatles, "In My Life" (John Lennon / Paul McCartney)
The Miracles, "The Tracks of My Tears" (Smokey Robinson / Pete Moore / Marv Tarplin)

J

Paul McCartney and Wings, "Jet" (Paul McCartney / Linda McCartney)
The Beatles, "I Want to Hold Your Hand"

Peter & Gordon, "A World Without Love"
Wings, "Live and Let Die" (Paul McCartney / Linda McCartney)
Shirley Bassey, "Goldfinger" (John Barry / Leslie Bricusse / Anthony Newley)
John Lennon, "Jealous Guy" (John Lennon)
George Harrison, "Just for Today" (George Harrison)
The Jimi Hendrix Experience, "Sgt. Pepper's Lonely Hearts Club Band" (John Lennon / Paul McCartney)
The Beatles, "Maxwell's Silver Hammer" (John Lennon / Paul McCartney)
Michael Jackson and Paul McCartney, "The Girl Is Mine" (Michael Jackson)
Paul McCartney and Michael Jackson, "Say Say Say" (Paul McCartney / Michael Jackson)
Bob and Earl, "Harlem Shuffle" (Bob Relf / Earl Nelson)
The Ramsey Lewis Trio, "The 'In' Crowd" (Billy Page)
The Ramsey Lewis Trio, "A Hard Day's Night"
Shirley Horn, "Yesterday" (John Lennon / Paul McCartney)
Count Basie Orchestra, "All My Loving"
The Beatles, "Julia" (John Lennon / Paul McCartney)

K

The Beatles, "Tomorrow Never Knows" (John Lennon / Paul McCartney)
John Lennon, "Imagine" (John Lennon)
Ringo Starr, "It Don't Come Easy" (Richard Starkey)
George Harrison, "My Sweet Lord" (George Harrison)
Jackie Lomax, "Sour Milk Sea" (George Harrison)
Little Willie Littlefield, "Kansas City" (Jerry Leiber / Mike Stoller)
Wilbert Harrison, "Kansas City"
The Beatles, "Kansas City"
Ringo Starr, "I'm the Greatest" (John Lennon)
Yoko Ono, "Kiss Kiss Kiss" (Yoko Ono)
Paul McCartney, "Kreen-Akrore" (Paul McCartney)
Paul McCartney, "Keep Under Cover" (Paul McCartney)
The Shirelles, "Will You Love Me Tomorrow" (Carole King / Gerry Goffin)
James Taylor, "You've Got a Friend" (Carole King)
Little Eva, "The Loco-Motion" (Carole King / Gerry Goffin)
Little Eva, "Keep Your Hands off My Baby" (Carole King / Gerry Goffin)
The Beatles, "Chains" (Carole King / Gerry Goffin)
The Beatles, "Keep Your Hands off My Baby"
The Beatles, "Komm, Gib Mir Deine Hand"

L

The Beatles, "Love Me Do"
The Beatles, "This Boy" (John Lennon / Paul McCartney)
John Lennon, "Whatever Gets You Thru the Night"
Julian Lennon, "Too Late for Goodbyes" (Julian Lennon)
Sean Lennon, "Home" (Sean Lennon)
The Beatles, "Lovely Rita" (John Lennon / Paul McCartney)
The Beatles, "Back in the U.S.S.R."
The Beatles, "Eleanor Rigby"

The Beatles, "Lucy in the Sky with Diamonds"
The Beatles, "The Long and Winding Road" (John Lennon / Paul McCartney)
The Beatles, "The Long and Winding Road" (*Let It Be . . . Naked* version)
The Beatles with Billy Preston, "Get Back"
Mary Hopkin, "Those Were the Days"
Ray Charles with the Count Basie Orchestra, "The Long and Winding Road"
The Beatles, "Little Child" (John Lennon / Paul McCartney)
The Beatles, "Love Me Do"
George Harrison, "Living in the Material World" (George Harrison)
The Traveling Wilburys, "Last Night" (Traveling Wilburys)
Ringo Starr, "Liverpool 8" (Richard Starkey / Dave Stewart)
George Harrison, "When We Was Fab"
The Beatles, "Lady Madonna"
Humphrey Lyttelton and His Band, "Bad Penny Blues" (Humphrey Lyttelton)
The Beatles, "Let It Be" (John Lennon / Paul McCartney)
Nick Cave, "Let It Be"
Aretha Franklin, "Let It Be"

M

The Beatles, "Magical Mystery Tour" (John Lennon / Paul McCartney)
Barrett Strong, "Money (That's What I Want)" (Janie Bradford / Berry Gordy)
The Beatles, "Money (That's What I Want)"
The Miracles, "You've Really Got a Hold on Me" (Smokey Robinson)
The Beatles, "You've Really Got a Hold on Me"
The Beatles, "Mean Mr. Mustard" (John Lennon / Paul McCartney)
The Beatles, "Sun King" (John Lennon and Paul McCartney)
The Beatles, "She Came in Through the Bathroom Window" (John Lennon / Paul McCartney)
The Beatles, "The End"
The Beatles, "Golden Slumbers"
The Beatles, "Michelle" (John Lennon / Paul McCartney)
Nina Simone, "I Put a Spell on You" (Jalacy "Screamin Jay" Hawkins)
The Beatles, "Mother Nature's Son" (John Lennon / Paul McCartney)
Nat King Cole, "Nature Boy" (Eden Ahbez)
John Lennon, "Child of Nature" (John Lennon)
John Lennon, "Jealous Guy"
John Lennon/Plastic Ono Band, "Mother" (John Lennon)
The Beatles, "Your Mother Should Know" (John Lennon / Paul McCartney)
George Harrison, "My Sweet Lord"
The Chiffons, "He's So Fine" (Ronald Mack)
Edwin Hawkins Singers, "Oh Happy Day" (Edwin R. Hawkins)
The Beatles, "Martha My Dear" (John Lennon / Paul McCartney)
The Beatles, "Mr. Moonlight" (Roy Lee Johnson)
Dr. Feelgood and the Interns, "Mr. Moonlight"
The Hollies, "Mr. Moonlight"
The Merseybeats, "Mr. Moonlight"
The Beatles, "Misery" (John Lennon / Paul McCartney)
Kenny Lynch, "Misery"

The Beatles, "Nowhere Man" (John Lennon / Paul McCartney)

The Beatles, "The Night Before" (John Lennon / Paul McCartney)

Stevie Wonder, "Superstition" (Stevie Wonder)

Paul McCartney and Wings, "No Words" (Paul McCartney / Denny Laine)

Ringo Starr, "Night and Day" (Cole Porter)

Frank Sinatra, "Night and Day"

Ella Fitzgerald, "Night and Day"

Tony Bennett, "Night and Day"

Ringo Starr, "The No No Song" (Hoyt Axton / David Jackson)

The Beatles, "No Reply" (John Lennon / Paul McCartney)

The Rays, "Silhouettes" (Bob Crewe / Frank Slay)

Herman's Hermits, "Silhouettes"

John Lennon and Yoko Ono, "No Bed for Beatle John" (John Lennon / Yoko Ono)

John Lennon, "Nobody Loves You (When You're Down and Out)" (John Lennon)

Bessie Smith, "Nobody Knows You When You're Down and Out" (Jimmy Cox)

The Beatles, "Not Guilty" (George Harrison)

George Harrison, "Not Guilty"

The Beatles, "Not a Second Time" (John Lennon / Paul McCartney)

"Das Lied von der Erde" (Gustav Mahler)

The Beatles, "Norwegian Wood (This Bird Has Flown)" (John Lennon / Paul McCartney)

Peter & Gordon, "Nobody I Know" (John Lennon / Paul McCartney)

Peter & Gordon, "A World Without Love"

The Beatles, "Ob-La-Di, Ob-La-Da" (John Lennon / Paul McCartney)

The Beatles, "One After 909" (John Lennon / Paul McCartney)

Lead Belly, "Midnight Special" (American folk song)

Lonnie Donegan, "Rock Island Line" (American folk song)

The Beatles, "Old Brown Shoe" (George Harrison)

The Beatles, "The Ballad of John and Yoko"

Gary Brooker, "Old Brown Shoe" from the "Concert for George"

Ringo Starr, "Oh My My" (Richard Starkey / Vini Poncia)

Rolling Stones, "Gimme Shelter" (Mick Jagger / Keith Richards)

The Beatles, "The Long and Winding Road"

The Beatles, "A Day in the Life"

Peter & Gordon, "A World Without Love"

Peter & Gordon, "If I Were You" (Peter Asher / Gordon Waller)

John Lennon, "Out the Blue" (John Lennon)

George Harrison, "Out of the Blue" (George Harrison)

The Beatles, "Octopus's Garden" (Richard Starkey)

The Beatles, "Ooh! My Soul," BBC Recording (Richard Penniman)

Roy Orbison, "Only the Lonely" (Roy Orbison / Joe Melson)

Roy Orbison, "Running Scared" (Roy Orbison / Joe Melson)

The Traveling Wilburys, "Handle with Care" (Traveling Wilburys)

Traveling Wilburys, "End of the Line" (Traveling Wilburys)

The Beatles, "Oh! Darling" (John Lennon / Paul McCartney)

The Beatles, "Long Tall Sally" (Enotris Johnson / Robert Blackwell / Richard Penniman)
The Beatles, "I'm Down"

P

The Beatles, "Please Please Me"
Roy Orbison, "Only the Lonely"
The Everly Brothers, "Cathy's Clown" (Don Everly / Phil Everly)
The Beatles, "P.S. I Love You" (John Lennon / Paul McCartney)
The Beatles, "Love Me Do"
The Shirelles, "Soldier Boy" (Luther Dixon / Florence Greenberg)
Rudy Vallee and His Connecticut Yankees, "P.S. I Love You" (Gordon Jenkins / Johnny Mercer)
Ringo Starr, "Photograph" (Richard Starkey / George Harrison)
Ringo Starr, "Photograph" from the "Concert for George"
Ike and Tina Turner, "River Deep—Mountain High" (Phil Spector / Jeff Barry / Ellie Greenwich)
The Beatles, "The Long and Winding Road"
George Harrison, "My Sweet Lord"
John Lennon, "Instant Karma!" (John Lennon)
The Beatles, "Paperback Writer" (John Lennon / Paul McCartney)
Frank Sinatra, "Strangers in the Night" (Bert Kaempfert / Charles Singleton / Eddie Snyder)
The Beatles, "Fixing a Hole"
John Lennon, "Imagine"
The Beatles, "Lady Madonna"
The Beatles, "Let It Be"
The Beatles, "Lovely Rita"
The Beatles, "Martha My Dear"
The Beatles, "Good Day Sunshine"
The Beatles, "In My Life"
The Beatles, "I Want to Hold Your Hand"

Q

The Quarrymen, "That'll Be the Day" (Jerry Allison / Buddy Holly / Norman Petty)
The Crickets, "That'll Be the Day"
Peter & Gordon, "True Love Ways" (Buddy Holly / Norman Petty)
Linda Ronstadt, "That'll Be the Day"
Linda Ronstadt, "It's So Easy" (Buddy Holly / Norman Petty)
James Taylor, "Everyday" (Buddy Holly / Norman Petty)
Paul McCartney, "Queenie Eye" (Paul McCartney / Paul Epworth)
"The Four Seasons" (Antonio Vivaldi)
The Beatles, "Yesterday"
The Beatles, "Eleanor Rigby"
The Beatles, "Ticket to Ride," BBC recording (John Lennon / Paul McCartney)
The Beatles, "Julia"
The Beatles, "Blackbird"
The Beatles, "Do You Want to Know a Secret"

The Beatles, "Till There Was You" (Meredith Willson)
John Lennon, "How Do You Sleep?" (John Lennon)
The Beatles, "What You're Doing" (John Lennon / Paul McCartney)
The Beatles, "What Goes On" (John Lennon / Paul McCartney / Richard Starkey)
The Beatles, "Why Don't We Do It in the Road?" (John Lennon / Paul McCartney)
The Beatles, "The Ballad of John and Yoko"
The Beatles, "Ask Me Why" (John Lennon / Paul McCartney)
The Beatles, "Ain't She Sweet" (Milton Ager / Jack Yellen)
John Lennon, "Ain't That a Shame" (Antoine Domino / Dave Bartholomew)
Fats Domino, "Ain't That a Shame"
The Beatles, "All You Need Is Love"
"La Marseillaise" (Claude Joseph Rouget de Lisle)
The Beatles, "She Loves You"

R

The Beatles, "Rain"
The Beatles, "Rock and Roll Music" (Chuck Berry)
Little Richard, "Rip It Up" (Robert Blackwell / John Marascalco)
The Beatles, "Rip It Up"
Little Richard, "Tutti Frutti" (Richard Penniman / Dorothy LaBostrie)
Little Richard, "Long Tall Sally"
Little Richard, "Good Golly Miss Molly" (John Marascalco / Robert Blackwell)
Little Richard, "Ready Teddy" (John Marascalco / Robert Blackwell)
Sam Cooke, "You Send Me" (Sam Cooke)
The Beatles, "Rocky Raccoon" (John Lennon / Paul McCartney)
The Beatles, "Run for Your Life" (John Lennon / Paul McCartney)
Elvis Presley, "Baby Let's Play House" (Arthur Gunter)
Wings, "Rock Show" (Paul McCartney / Linda McCartney)
Lee Dorsey, "Ride Your Pony" (Allen Toussaint)
Lee Dorsey, "Working in the Coal Mine" (Allen Toussaint)
George Harrison, "Ride Rajbun" (George Harrison / David English)
Paul McCartney, "A Room with a View" (Noël Coward)
Noël Coward, "A Room with a View"
Wings, "Richard Cory" (Paul Simon)
Simon & Garfunkel, "Richard Cory"
Paul and Linda McCartney, "Ram On" (Paul McCartney)
Paul and Linda McCartney, "Monkberry Moon Delight" (Paul McCartney / Linda McCartney)
The Searchers, "Love Potion Number 9" (Jerry Leiber / Mike Stoller)
The Clovers, "Love Potion Number 9"
The Beatles, "Revolution 1" (John Lennon / Paul McCartney)
The Beatles, "Revolution 9" (John Lennon / Paul McCartney)
The Beatles, "Revolution" (John Lennon / Paul McCartney)
The Beatles, "Hey Jude"

S

The Beatles, "Sexy Sadie" (John Lennon / Paul McCartney)
Ringo Starr, "She's About a Mover" (Doug Sahm)
Sir Douglas Quintet, "She's About a Mover"

Sir Douglas Quintet, "Mendocino" (Doug Sahm)

Marvin Gaye, "Can I Get a Witness" (Brian Holland / Lamont Dozier / Eddie Holland)

The Beatles, "She's a Woman" (John Lennon / Paul McCartney)

The Beatles, "Girl"

John Lennon, "Stand By Me" (Ben E. King / Jerry Leiber / Mike Stoller)

Ben E. King, "Stand By Me"

John Lennon, "Sweet Little Sixteen" (Chuck Berry)

Chuck Berry, "School Days" (Chuck Berry)

George Harrison, "So Sad" (George Harrison)

The Beatles, "Here Comes the Sun"

The Beatles, "Savoy Truffle" (George Harrison)

The Beatles, "Got to Get You into My Life"

Lou Reed, "Walk on the Wild Side" (Lou Reed)

The Beatles, "She Loves You"

The Beatles, "All My Loving"

The Beatles, "Till There Was You"

The Beatles, "I Saw Her Standing There"

The Beatles, "I Want to Hold Your Hand"

Bobby Rydell, "A World Without Love"

Peter & Gordon, "I Don't Want to See You Again" (John Lennon / Paul McCartney)

The Beatles, "Sgt. Pepper's Lonely Hearts Club Band"

The Beatles, "She's Leaving Home" (John Lennon / Paul McCartney)

Peter & Gordon, "Lady Godiva" (Mike Leander / Charlie Mills / Gordon Mills)

The Beatles, "Strawberry Fields Forever" (John Lennon / Paul McCartney)

The Beatles, "Penny Lane"

T

The Beatles, "Ticket to Ride"

The Beatles, "Taxman" (George Harrison)

The Beatles, "Tell Me Why" (John Lennon / Paul McCartney)

The Beatles, "And I Love Her"

The Beatles, "If I Fell"

"The Blue Danube" (Johann Strauss)

The Beatles, "She's Leaving Home"

The Beatles, "Baby's in Black"

The Beatles, "You've Got to Hide Your Love Away" (John Lennon / Paul McCartney)

The Beatles, "This Boy"

The Beatles, "Oh! Darling"

The Beatles, "Norwegian Wood (This Bird Has Flown)"

The Beatles, "A Taste of Honey" (Bobby Scott / Ric Marlow)

The Beatles, "Lucy in the Sky with Diamonds"

The Beatles, "Here Comes the Sun"

The Beatles, "Good Morning Good Morning"

The Beatles, "Happiness Is a Warm Gun" (John Lennon / Paul McCartney)

The Beatles, "All You Need Is Love"

The Beatles, "Penny Lane"

The Beatles, "Got to Get You into My Life"

The Beatles, "Martha My Dear"

The Beatles, "Within You Without You" (George Harrison)

Black Dyke Mills Band, "Thingumybob" (John Lennon / Paul McCartney)

Black Dyke Mills Band, "Yellow Submarine"

The Beatles, "Hey Jude"

Tommy Quickly, "Tip of My Tongue" (John Lennon / Paul McCartney)

The Beatles, "Tell Me What You See" (John Lennon / Paul McCartney)

The Beatles, "Things We Said Today" (John Lennon / Paul McCartney)

U

Paul and Linda McCartney, "Uncle Albert/Admiral Halsey" (Paul McCartney / Linda McCartney)

The Beatles, "You Can't Do That" (John Lennon / Paul McCartney)

Peter & Gordon, "I Go to Pieces" (Del Shannon)

Peter & Gordon, "A World Without Love"

The Rooftop Singers, "Walk Right In" (Erik Darling / Bill Svanoe)

The Beatles, "You Like Me Too Much" (George Harrison)

The Beatles, "Don't Bother Me"

The Beatles, "I Need You"

The Beatles, "You Never Give Me Your Money" (John Lennon / Paul McCartney)

Sarah Vaughan, "You Never Give Me Your Money"

George Harrison, "You" (George Harrison)

The Beatles, "The Continuing Story of Bungalow Bill"

The Beatles, "Hey Jude"

George Harrison, Ringo Starr, and Paul McCartney, "Ain't She Sweet"

George Harrison, Ringo Starr, and Paul McCartney, "Baby What You Want Me to Do" (Jimmy Reed)

Paul McCartney, "Something" from the "Concert for George"

The Beatles, "Michelle"

Wings, "Mull of Kintyre" (Paul McCartney / Denny Laine)

V

Paul McCartney, "Vintage Clothes" (Paul McCartney)

The Beatles, "Strawberry Fields Forever"

Steve Martin and the Steep Canyon Rangers, "Best Love" (Steve Martin)

Vera Lynn, "(There'll Be Bluebirds Over) The White Cliffs of Dover" (Walter Kent / Nat Burton)

Vera Lynn, "We'll Meet Again" (Ross Parker / Hughie Charles)

Vera Lynn, "The Fool on the Hill"

Wings, "Venus and Mars" (Paul McCartney / Linda McCartney)

Paul McCartney, "Valentine Day" (Paul McCartney)

Paul McCartney, "My Valentine" (Paul McCartney)

The Beatles, "Honey Pie" (John Lennon / Paul McCartney)

The Beatles, "Your Mother Should Know"

W

The Beatles, "When I'm Sixty-Four" (John Lennon / Paul McCartney)

Paul McCartney, "Dance Tonight" (Paul McCartney)

Keith Moon, "When I'm Sixty-Four"

The Beatles, "With a Little Help from My Friends"
James Taylor, "With a Little Help from My Friends"
James Taylor, "Handy Man"
James Taylor, "How Sweet It Is (To Be Loved by You)" (Brian Holland / Lamont Dozier / Eddie Holland)
James Taylor, "You've Got a Friend"
Joe Cocker, "With a Little Help from My Friends"
The Beatles, "While My Guitar Gently Weeps" (George Harrison)
George Harrison, "Wreck of the Hesperus" (George Harrison)
Ringo Starr, "When You Wish Upon a Star" (Leigh Harline / Ned Washington)
The Beatles, "We Can Work It Out"
The Beatles, "Day Tripper"
Paul McCartney and Wings, "Band on the Run" (Paul McCartney / Linda McCartney)

X

Paul McCartney, "Drive My Car" on *X Factor*
Paul McCartney, "Live and Let Die" on *X Factor*
The Beatles, "Penny Lane"
Ringo Starr, "Liverpool 8"
Pete Best Band, "Haymans Green" (Pete Best / Roag Best / Phil Melia / Paul Parry)
Paul McCartney, "Maybe I'm Amazed" (Paul McCartney)
John Lennon/Plastic Ono Band, "Love" (John Lennon)
Ringo Starr, "Wine, Women and Loud Happy Songs" (Larry Kingston)
George Harrison, "Give Me Love (Give Me Peace on Earth)" (George Harrison)
George Harrison, "My Sweet Lord"
The Beatles, "I'm Looking Through You" (John Lennon / Paul McCartney)
George Martin, "March of the Meanies" (George Martin)
The Beatles, "I Should Have Known Better" (John Lennon / Paul McCartney)
The Beatles, "You've Got to Hide Your Love Away"
The Beatles, "Yesterday"
The Beatles, "Blackbird"
The Beatles, "Norwegian Wood (This Bird Has Flown)"

Y

Ringo Starr, "Y Not" (Richard Starkey / Glen Ballard)
The Beatles, "Yes It Is" (John Lennon / Paul McCartney)
The Beatles, "Ticket to Ride"
The Beatles, "This Boy"
The Beatles, "I Need You"
The Coasters, "Young Blood" (Jerry Leiber / Mike Stoller / Doc Pomus)
The Beatles, "Young Blood," BBC Recording
The Coasters, "Searchin'" (Jerry Leiber / Mike Stoller)
The Beatles, "You're Going to Lose That Girl" (John Lennon / Paul McCartney)
The Beatles, "You've Got to Hide Your Love Away"
George Harrison, "Your Love Is Forever" (George Harrison)
The Traveling Wilburys, "You Took My Breath Away" (Traveling Wilburys)
Wings, "You Gave Me the Answer" (Paul McCartney / Linda McCartney)
The Beatles, "Yer Blues" (John Lennon / Paul McCartney)

The Beatles, "Let It Be"

James Taylor, "Steamroller" (James Taylor)

The Dirty Mac, "Yer Blues"

The Beatles, "You Know My Name (Look Up the Number)" (John Lennon / Paul McCartney)

The Beatles, "Yellow Submarine"

The Beatles, "Eleanor Rigby"

Zed

George Harrison, "When We Was Fab"

George Harrison, "Zig Zag" (George Harrison / Jeff Lynne)

Louis Armstrong, "St. James Infirmary" (Don Redman)

Monty Python, "Always Look on the Bright Side of Life" (Eric Idle)

Zoo Songs:

In the aviary, a blackbird: The Beatles, "Blackbird"

A bluebird: Paul McCartney and Wings, "Bluebird" (Paul McCartney / Linda McCartney)

A bird that can sing: The Beatles, "And Your Bird Can Sing" (John Lennon / Paul McCartney)

A bird that is spectacularly free: The Beatles, "Free as a Bird"

Beyond the aviary, a dog with a name: The Beatles, "Martha My Dear"

One dog of a specific breed: The Beatles, "Hey Bulldog"

There are also cats: The Beatles, "Three Cool Cats" (Jerry Leiber / Mike Stoller)

And a kitten: The Beatles, "Leave My Kitten Alone" (Little Willie John / Titus Turner / James McDougal)

A horse, with a name: The Beatles, "Being for the Benefit of Mr. Kite!"

Cows [till they come home]: The Beatles, "When I Get Home" (John Lennon / Paul McCartney)

A large and mysterious walrus: The Beatles, "I Am the Walrus" (John Lennon / Paul McCartney)

The Beatles, "A Day in the Life"

The Beatles, "All You Need Is Love"

The Beatles, "Two of Us" (John Lennon / Paul McCartney)

Acknowledgements

Above all, of course, thanks to the Beatles and to George Martin for the music that changed the world.

Thanks to Olivia and Dhani, to Yoko, to Ringo and Barbara, and to Paul; to Jeff Jones and Jonathan Clyde and all my friends at Apple for their encouragement and assistance; to Paul Golob at Henry Holt for this book idea and Fiora Elbers-Tibbitts for clearing all the photos; to Ken Follett for his advice on the book biz; to Lou Simon, Randy Dry, and Steve Leeds, and all my friends at SiriusXM; to Keith Putney for his help and guidance; to Jeff Alan Ross for helping me create the radio show in the first place; and to David Zonshine and David Mirkin for their assistance and encouragement.

Illustration Credits

Index

About the Author

Peter Asher is a singer, musician, record producer, broadcaster, and writer, and he is the winner of multiple Grammy Awards, including twice being named Producer of the Year. Born in London in 1944, he got his start as half of the duo Peter & Gordon and was the first head of A&R for Apple Records. As a producer he has worked with James Taylor, Linda Ronstadt, Neil Diamond, Robin Williams, Cher, and many other artists. He continues to perform regularly in addition to his ongoing music production for records and movies. He lives in Malibu, California, with his wife, Wendy.